Handbook of Home Remodeling and Improvement

LeROY O. ANDERSON

VNR **VAN NOSTRAND REINHOLD COMPANY**
NEW YORK   CINCINNATI   ATLANTA   DALLAS   SAN FRANCISCO
LONDON   TORONTO   MELBOURNE

Handbook of Home Remodeling and Improvement

LeRoy O. Anderson

VNR **VAN NOSTRAND REINHOLD COMPANY**

NEW YORK   CINCINNATI   ATLANTA   DALLAS   SAN FRANCISCO
LONDON   TORONTO   MELBOURNE

To My Wife

AMY

Van Nostrand Reinhold Company Regional Offices:
New York Cincinnati Atlanta Dallas San Francisco

Van Nostrand Reinhold Company International Offices:
London Toronto Melbourne

Copyright © 1978 by Litton Educational Publishing, Inc.

Library of Congress Catalog Card Number: 77-18219
ISBN: 0-442-20343-8

Manufactured in the United States of America

Published by Van Nostrand Reinhold Company
135 West 50th Street, New York, N.Y. 10020

Published simultaneously in Canada by Van Nostrand Reinhold Ltd.

15 14 13 12 11 10 9 8 7 6 5 4 3 2 1

Library of Congress Cataloging in Publication Data

Anderson, LeRoy Oscar, 1905–
    Handbook of home remodeling and improvement.

    Includes bibliographical references.
    1. Dwellings—Remodeling. 2. House construction.
I. Title.
TH4816.A52   643'.7   77-18219
ISBN 0-442-20343-8

Preface

The cost of building a large new house for a growing family is becoming an increasingly serious problem. The once satisfactory two-bedroom home is no longer adequate as the children grow older. Because the median price of a new house in 1977 was about $50,000 in many areas of the country, and because building costs are rising each year, the dream of having a new home often fades away for many families.

What are the alternatives? It would appear that the purchase of an old larger house would be one solution. Another more logical answer, perhaps, is to remodel the interior of your existing house or to build an addition to it. Such construction can include extra bedrooms and a bath, a large family room, or various other combinations.

The wood-frame house, in sound condition can be remodeled more economically than other types of houses. While the cost of all building products have increased, those required for a wood-frame house can still compete with most other building and remodeling materials. Furthermore, the construction of a wood-frame addition, for example, can be accomplished by the handyman with little (if any) help from a carpenter or a talented friend.

One factor which should be considered in providing additional space in your existing home is the advantage of staying in the "old" neighborhood. Close friends, convenient schools and shopping centers, and good transportation are benefits which cannot be questioned. It is sometimes possible to provide the needed extra bedrooms and bath with the addition of a dormer in the attic space. In other cases, the construction of an addition is necessary to provide this needed space.

This book provides basic details necessary for the improvement and rehabilitation of the older house as well as information required for the construction of an addition. It does not include data related to heating, plumbing, and wiring except those details concerned with the framing and finishing of the house. Much of the information is based on the results of many years of research on the wood-frame house, as a unit and of its separate components. The use of vapor barriers, the need for adequate ventilation with the attic insulation, the proper selection of materials, and many other details needed for construction of a wood-frame structure are included. Other details are based on standard methods commonly used in the construction of many wood-frame houses. This information, with or without a carpenter's assistance, should assure a properly rehabilitated house or a beautifully thought-out addition to your existing home or to a newly purchased older home.

Madison, Wisconsin   LeRoy O. Anderson

Contents

1

Design Considerations

WITHOUT EXTERIOR ADDITIONS

Minimum Expansion

Providing extra space within existing 1- or $1\frac{1}{2}$-story homes having stairs to the attic space can be quite easily accomplished. The roof slope must be sufficient to provide adequate head room, and the floor joists large enough to carry the loads. The roof

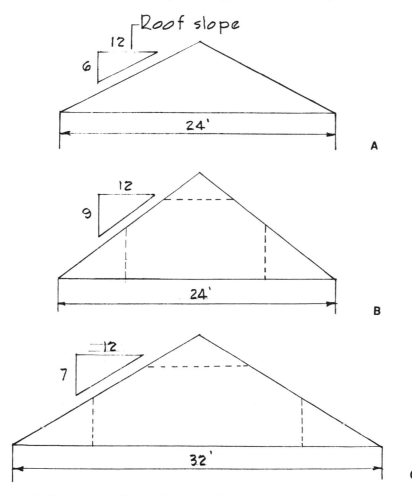

NOTE: Roof slope is the rise (vertical) over the run (horizontal). Thus a 6/12 roof slope is: for 12 feet (or other unit) of "run" there would be a "rise" of 6 feet.

Fig. 1. Roof slopes of existing houses.
A. No attic rooms for 6/12 slope.
B. Attic rooms ok for 9/12 slope.
C. Attic rooms ok for 7/12 slope.
(32 ft wide house).

slope should be a minimum of 9 in 12 ("rise-to-run") for a house width of 24 feet or greater, but it can be as low as 7 in 12 for a house width of 32 feet, Fig. 1. In other words, a 9/12 slope for a 24-foot wide house has approximately a 9 foot height at the ridge while a 6/12 slope has only a 6-foot height.

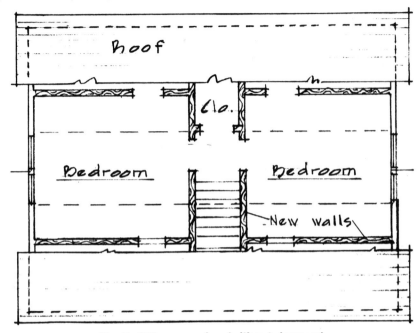

Fig. 2. Attic expansion (without dormers).

In second floor rooms, it is usually necessary to comply with building codes which normally state that one-half of the ceiling area of the future room have a minimum room height of $7\frac{1}{2}$ feet. Thus if your attic space has windows at the gable ends, sufficient head room, and proper size floor joists, the construction of one or more rooms is relatively simple. Thus there is no need for exterior remodeling, Fig. 2. Extension of existing heat and return air ducts or installation of an alternate heating system and proper wiring should result in a satisfactory expansion to your existing home at a minimum cost. Construction details for this and other related work are covered in the proceeding chapters.

Use of Dormers

To provide more floor space and wall space for new windows, dormers are normally recommended. Two types of dormers may be used: (1) The shed dormer, Fig. 3, and

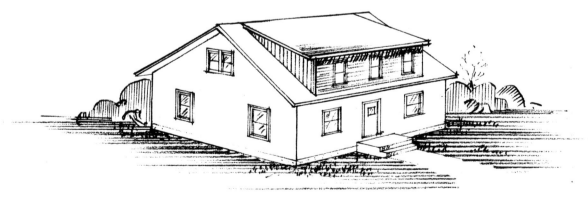

Fig. 3. One and one-half story house with shed dormer addition.

(2) the window dormer, Fig. 4. The shed dormer is perhaps the most practical because it adds a great deal of wall space and is relatively simple to construct. However, it is not as pleasant in appearance as the window dormer and therefore should be used at the rear of the house when possible. Early American homes were often constructed with a shed dormer in the rear and two or more window dormers at the front.

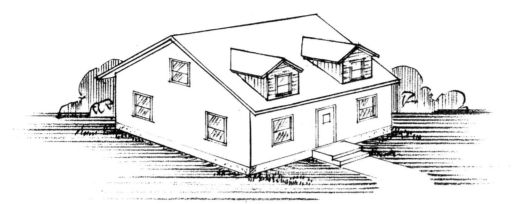

Fig. 4. One and one-half-story house with two window dormers.

The addition of dormers can often be accomplished without removing the entire roof of the existing structure. This might be done by establishing the rear and side walls by first removing only a portion of the shingles and sheathing. Suggestions will be outlined in further chapters of this manual.

WITH EXTERIOR ADDITIONS

In a one-story house with a low-pitched roof or in a two-story house where additional space is required, the construction of a new connecting unit to the rear or side of the house may be the best answer for more space. In such additions it is good practice to use a design in keeping with the architecture of the original house. This

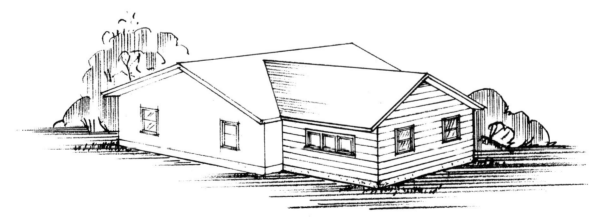

Fig. 5. Single story house with an addition to the rear.

may include roof slopes, window types, exterior finish, etc. One such addition to an existing one-story house is shown in Fig. 5. The roof slope of this new section should be the same as the original unit. If the width of the addition is the same as the existing house, the ridge heights of both units will be at the same level.

Figure 6 illustrates an original two-story house with a new one-story addition.

Fig. 6. Single story addition to a two-story house.

The roof slope in such construction can be the same or flatter (3/12 to 4/12) than the original house. This might be necessary to avoid the existing windows on the second floor. The difference in the roof slopes will not be objectionable from the appear-

Fig. 7. Family room and open porch over a double garage.

ance standpoint. Figure 7 shows a completed addition to a Cape Cod house on a sloping corner lot. The slope allows for a double basement-level garage and an enclosed family room off the living room plus an open porch, both at the first floor level.

4

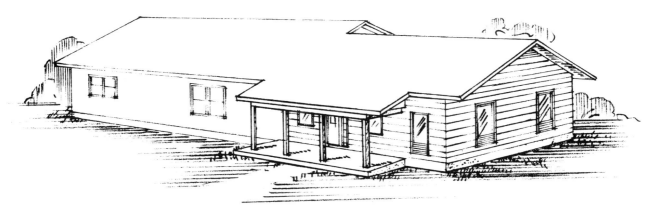

Fig. 8. Addition at side of small single story house.

The design in Fig. 8 consists of an addition to the length of an existing gable-roofed house. The roof slope should be the same as the older house. As shown, this addition can be quite extensive or might involve only a double garage or a simple porch.

A low slope or a flat roof on an addition to a house with a pitched roof should be studied carefully from the standpoint of appearance. However, it is usually satisfactory for a small addition such as a porch, Fig. 9. When a larger flat-roofed addition is used, the elevation might be enhanced by the use of a pleasing railing and baluster combination around the perimeter of the roof. Thus, with large combination rafter-joists for air spaces above the insulation, good overhang for soffit ventilators, and a slight slope for good roof drainage, a satisfactory addition should result.

Additions to houses with mansard and similar double-slope roof constructions should be in keeping with the original unit. It might be possible to use a low-pitch roof, but the design of an addition for such a house should also be studied carefully. Small-scale models made of stiff paper or cardboard or a detailed isometric drawing may be justified in such cases.

Fig. 9. Simple porch addition (with a low-slope roof).

PLANS AND LAYOUTS

With the addition of one or more dormers (depending on location of the stairway, the 1½-story house with sufficient head room can include a minimum of two bedrooms and a bath, Fig. 10. A shed dormer to the rear of the house with the side walls located at the second or third rafter from the end of the house (16 or 32 inches) will allow extra windows for the bedrooms and space for a full bathroom. In houses that are perhaps 38 to 40 feet in length, a third bedroom might even be added. The bathroom should be located so that the new plumbing wall is directly above the plumbing wall on the first floor so that water and waste connections can be more simply made.

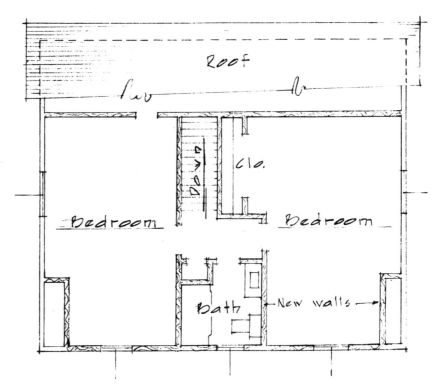

Fig. 10. Shed dormer allows the addition of two bedrooms and a bath.

This suggested design is merely one of a number which might be used with the addition of one or more dormers on the second floor. Your needs and the cost of the remodeling should govern the design.

A plan of a side extension to a one-story gable- or hip-roofed house is shown in Fig. 11. This can include two extra bedrooms, a study, a full bath, and a redesigned entryway. If desired, such an addition can be almost as large as the original house. These side extensions, of course, usually depend on the width of the lot.

Most of the previously suggested layouts can be adapted to the addition of a single or double garage along the side or to the rear of the house. A garage for two cars should ordinarily be a *minimum* of 20 feet deep by 22 feet in width and include a single 15- or 16-foot-wide overhead door or two 8- or 9-foot-wide doors. Perhaps a more desirable size for a double garage is 22 feet deep by 24 feet wide.

The construction of an open patio is sometimes desirable when it is adjacent to an existing living room or dining room. A window can be removed and a door substi-

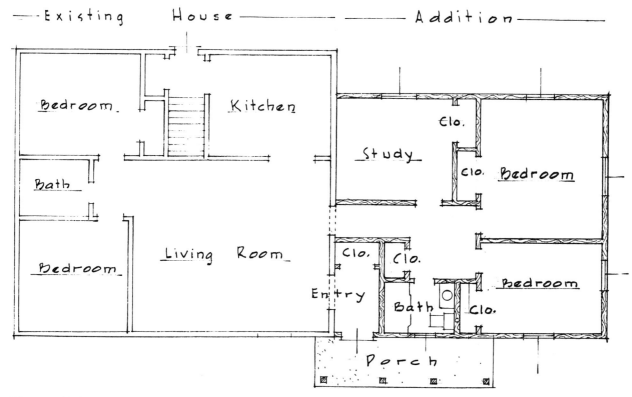

Bedroom

Kitchen

Bath

Living Room

Bedroom

Study

Clo.

Clo.

Bedroom

Clo.

Clo.

Entry

Bath

Bedroom

Clo.

Porch

Fig. 11. Addition at side of a small house provides a second bath, a new entry, and three spacious rooms.

tuted for easy access to such an addition. However, the use of a simple concrete slab or similar paved surface might not be practical because of a severe slope or uneven grade. This is especially true, for example, of homes in the hilly areas of Washington and Oregon. It is common practice under such conditions to construct a wood deck of decay-resistant or treated wood over a suitable floor framing system. Such a deck may be constructed adjacent to a living room as shown in Fig. 12.

Foundation Considerations

In planning additions, consideration should be given to the foundation, whether a full basement is desired or whether a crawl space is satisfactory. In most areas of the East, the North, and the Lake States, full basements are commonly a part of the original house. While the cost of a full basement is greater than a partial foundation wall, it does provide usable space and might be needed if the original house is small. However, in many cases, an addition with a crawl space could be adequate. Much depends on the slope of the lot. If the slope away from the house is quite steep, it may be necessary to have a full-height foundation wall. Under such conditions a full basement should be considered.

When the slope of the ground at the location of the new addition is level, a concrete slab might be one solution. One such design is the so-called "grade-beam" slab which is used when frost is a factor. Thus with adequate insulation and a good vapor barrier, such a design would be a satisfactory cost-saving solution and adequate for construction of a room or rooms above. In fact, in many areas of the country a concrete slab is a standard method for new house construction.

Fig. 12. Open wood deck easy access from living room.

Building Permit Requirements

In most urban and rural areas, a building permit is required before major additions to a house can be started. In order to obtain this permit certain construction details must be presented, usually in the form of drawings or sketches. Normally the following details must be shown, but first check with the building commission in your area before preparing them:

1. Plot Plan—This sketch should show the outline of your existing house and the location of the addition with any side yard measurements.
2. Plan—A scaled layout of the addition showing the overall size, location of windows and doors, etc.
3. Cross Section—This sketch should include: footing and foundation wall size; height of room; size, spacing, span, and size of floor and ceiling joists (and grade and species, if required); rafters and roof slope; interior and exterior finish; and other necessary details. An elevation is also sometimes needed.

Although this might seem somewhat detailed, all can be included on one or two letter-size sheets if the scale is correctly chosen. You might use 1 inch = 50 feet for the plot plan and $\frac{1}{8}$ inch = 1 foot for the other sketches. However, your local building requirements may govern the scale to be used.

2
Costs

Remodeling or constructing an addition to your house is, of course, a major investment. However, it can be the most profitable method of gaining living space when compared to the cost of a new house. The square-foot cost of constructing a new house (and this can vary considerably) is usually in the $20 to $40 and over range. The $20 figure is for a very spartan home and the $40 and over for a more luxurious home. These are merely estimates and can vary to a great extent in different parts of the country and on future costs. The square-foot cost of an addition to your existing home should be much less than a new house depending on what is involved. If a bath is not included, a 7 percent reduction can be assumed. If kitchen cabinets, etc., are not involved, another 7 percent can be subtracted. The structure itself including foundation, framing, covering materials, insulation, etc., is about 38 percent of the total cost. A further estimated breakdown of the other 48 percent of the total cost might be as follows:

	(%)
Heating	5
Electrical	5
Roofing	5
Windows and siding	15
Interior walls and floors	9
Doors and trim	4
Interior and exterior painting	5
	48

The material and labor cost percentage of new construction varies by components. Assembled kitchen cabinets may have a material cost of more than 90 percent and a labor installation cost of less than 10 percent. Painting, on the other hand, may be 10 to 15 percent for materials and the remainder for labor. Millwork, such as complete window units and prehung doors and frames, are primarily a material cost with perhaps only a 5 to 10 percent labor cost for installation. Thus with your share of work and perhaps help from a knowledgeable friend, it is possible to reduce the overall cost by as much as 30 to 35 percent. A 400- to 500-square-foot addition may mean a saving of up to $3000.

Remodeling the interior of a house, such as the addition of bedrooms in an existing attic space, will, of course, not be as expensive per square foot as the construction of a new addition. When dormers are used, there is the need for ceiling joists and rafters, exterior walls and finish, windows, roofing, and greater expenditures for interior coverings and finish. This may more than double the per square foot cost if dormers are not included. However, the extra floor area and exterior walls for the needed windows may make this remodeling well worthwhile. Judge such remodeling by your needs and your means.

Another factor which should be considered in your planned addition is the choice of foundations. The use of a concrete slab can result in a saving over the use of a crawl space, and a crawl space can and does cost less than a full basement. However, whichever method is used, each should be constructed properly to provide a good base for the new room or rooms above. Such construction will be covered in future chapters as well as the details for framing and finishing of the new addition.

3
Material Selection

Materials and construction details should generally conform to your existing house. This primarily concerns those materials used on the exterior, such as exterior covering, roofing, windows, and trim. This will aid in making the new addition appear as though it were a part of the original house.

WOOD

Framing materials for the floors, walls, and roof structure in most parts of the country are wood. Masonry walls with a plastered exterior and wood-furred interior walls are common in many areas of the South and Southwest. However, the interior wall framings and the roof systems utilize wood members in the majority of these houses.

Wood is used as a covering material for framed walls and roofs. It can be in the form of plywood or wood boards for sheathing and still other forms for finish siding and trim. On the interior it is used for floor coverings, as trim around doors and windows, and in other forms of millwork. Wood has the advantage of being easy to saw,

TABLE 1. Broad classification of woods according to characteristics and properties.[a]

Kind of Wood	Working and Behavior Properties							Strength Properties			Freedom from Pitch
	Hardness	Freedom from Warping	Ease of Working	Paint Holding	Nail Holding	Decay Resistance of Heartwood	Proportion of Heartwood	Bending Strength	Stiffness	Strength as a Post	
Ash	A	B	C	C	A	C	C	A	A	A	A
Western red cedar	C	A	A	A	C	A	A	C	C	B	A
Cypress	B	B	B	A	B	A	B	B	B	B	A
Douglas fir, larch	B	B	B–C	C	A	B	A	A	A	A	B
Gum	B	C	B	C	A	B	B	B	A	B	A
Hemlock, white fir[b]	B–C	B	B	C	C	C	C	B	A	B	A
Soft pines[c]	C	A	A	A	C	C	B	C	C	C	B
Southern pine	B	B	B	C	A	B	C	A	A	A	C
Poplar	C	A	B	A	B	C	B	B	B	B	A
Redwood	B	A	B	A	B	A	A	B	B	A	A
Spruce	C	A–B	B	B	B	C	C	B	B	B	A

[a] A—among the woods *relatively high* in the particular respect listed.
  B—among woods *intermediate* in that respect.
  C—among woods *relatively low* in that respect.
[b] West coast and eastern hemlocks.
[c] Includes western and northeastern pines.
Note: Data from U.S. Dept. of Agriculture Handbook No. 432.

nail, and fit even with hand tools. With proper use and protection provided by good construction details, a wood addition will give excellent service. For the best service and durability, it is normally recommended that dimension material (2 by 4's, 2 by 6's, etc.) have a moisture content no greater than 19 percent. Wood used as a finish on the interior should have a moisture content of not more than 10 percent.

Treated Posts and Timbers

Wood posts and timbers which are embedded in soil and used to support a wood deck or an enclosed addition to your house should be pressure-treated. The heart portion of decay-resistant species can also be used. Sizes of timbers for this purpose may be as small as 4- by 4-inch members for short unsupported heights up to 6- by 6-inch members for greater lengths. Pressure-treated round posts and poles with 6-inch or greater top diameters can also be used.

Preservative treatments commonly available are oil-type preservatives and leach-resistant waterborne salt preservatives. For squared timbers not in contact with the soil and with proper protection, most of the denser woods such as Douglas fir, southern pine, larch, and similar species are satisfactory. The woods with a natural resistance to decay are redwood, the cedars, and cypress as shown in Table 1. From this table you will be able to compare the various species of wood available in your area for each specific use.

Dimension Material

Surfaced dimension material (2 to 4 inch-thick) as received from the lumber company is not full-sized as ordered. For example, a nominal 2 by 4 usually has a finish size of $1\frac{1}{2}$ by $3\frac{1}{2}$ inches because this is the resultant size after surfacing and drying. Moisture content of dimension material conforming to the American Lumber Standards does not exceed 19 percent.

The following tabulation shows the surfaced lumber sizes as normally received from the lumberyard.

Nominal Size (in.)	Dry Size (19%) (in.)
1	$\frac{3}{4}$
2	$1\frac{1}{2}$
4	$3\frac{1}{2}$
6	$5\frac{1}{2}$
8	$7\frac{1}{4}$
10	$9\frac{1}{4}$
12	$11\frac{1}{4}$

The first wood materials used after the foundation is complete are the floor framing members including beams and joists. These members require adequate strength in bending and moderate stiffness. Species vary by these properties as outlined in Table 1.

Wall studs (the structural members making up the wall framing) are usually nominal 2 by 4's and are spaced 16 or 24 inches on center. Their strength and stiffness are not as important as for floor joists and species such as white fir, the spruces, and the softer pines are satisfactory as well as are the denser species.

Members for trusses, rafters, beams, and ceiling joists have about the same requirement as the floor joists. They should have adequate strength in bending and moderate stiffness. When members do not meet these properties it means that the allowable span is less for these species with their lower strengths. If ceiling joists of the first floor act as floor joists for the second floor, they should be designed as floor joists. Rafters resist not only snow loads but also wind loads and are designed with these factors in mind. In areas where snow loads need not be considered, the allowable spans, of course, can be greater.

Roof trusses are available in many lumberyards and can be used to advantage. They serve both as ceiling joists and rafters and have the advantage of providing a full-span open area below. Check your supplier if such components seem desirable.

COVERING MATERIALS

Floors

Floor sheathing (subfloor) normally consists of board lumber or plywood. The thickness of the subfloor depends on joist spacing and the type of finish flooring or other covering to be used over it. Tongued and grooved plywood in $\frac{5}{8}$- or $\frac{3}{4}$-inch thickness is sometimes used as a base for carpeting when joists are spaced no more than 16 inches on center. Douglas fir and southern pine plywoods are perhaps the most easily obtainable at lumberyards and are slightly greater in strength than the softer species. Plywoods are usually marked with an "Identification Index" which indicates the allowable floor joist spacing and rafter and roof truss spacing for each thickness of a standard grade suitable for this purpose. Plywood sheets which are suitable for underlayment are often marked with the proper edge and end spacing. When long exposure to weather is a factor, an exterior grade, or interior grade plywood with exterior glue, is recommended. When a single layer is used for subflooring, tongued and grooved plywood with exterior glue should be specified. Square-edged, ship-lapped, or tongued and grooved boards in nominal 1-inch thickness may be used as subfloor in most species. Some type of covering such as plywood, flakeboard, or hardboard is normally used over such subfloor.

Walls

The walls of a wood-frame house must have resistance to the racking forces of high winds. This can be provided by sheathing or by diagonal bracing. Wall sheathing, if used as a covering material, can consist of plywood, wood boards, structural insulating board, or gypsum board. Because of its insulating value, the use of a foam insulation in sheet form is gaining in popularity. However, when such material is used, some type of bracing must be provided. Some such materials are ordinarily resistant to the movement of water vapor and consequently the need for a superior vapor barrier on the interior of all exposed walls is evident. Plywood and structural fiberboard in 4- by 8- or 4- by 9-foot sheets applied vertically with perimeter nailing normally do not require corner bracing. A C-D exterior grade plywood is sometimes used for wall sheathing. Lumber sheathing when applied horizontally requires some type of corner bracing; however, if applied diagonally the need for bracing can be eliminated. It is often used in this manner in hurricane areas. If a rustic board and batten effect is desired, rough-sawn plywood with several patterns is available. This covering is applied vertically and often serves both as a sheathing and as an exterior finish. With perimeter nailing no other bracing is required. To resist air infiltration, a sheathing paper is first used over the studs.

Roofs

Roof sheathing, like the subfloor, most commonly consists of plywood or board lumber. Where exposed wood beams, spaced 4 or more feet apart, are used in low-pitched roofs, wood decking or fiberboard roof deck in 2- to 3-inch thicknesses are satisfactory. These materials serve as an interior finish, have some insulating properties, and also serve as a base for roofing if greater insulation in not required.

Exterior Trim

Some exterior trim, such as facia boards and other cornice and gable finishes, is placed before the roofing is applied. When a paint finish is planned, wood trim should be free of knots and other grain variations. Table 1 lists the species which are most desirable for a paint finish. Rough-sawn boards are most often used for a stain finish.

ROOFING

Asphalt shingles are one of the lower cost and universally used roofing materials. They can often be applied with or without underlayment when roofs are sheathed with plywood and have a slope greater than about 6/12. Your local building code will usually govern the proper combination. Lower pitch roofs normally require an underlayment (15- or 30-pound asphalt felt) and a further requirement of having self-sealing tabs. A minimum weight of 240 pounds per square (100 square feet) is a normal requirement for most 3-in-1 tab asphalt shingles.

Wood shingles or shakes are more costly than asphalt shingles, but for the sake of appearance and longer life might be used if the original house is roofed with them. There may be some restrictions in the use of such shingles in certain areas because of lower fire resistance. However, fire-resistant treatments are available.

Tile and similar heavier roofing materials are used in some areas but are perhaps not as easily applied as other roofing materials. However, building regulations in some areas require this type roofing.

WINDOW AND DOOR FRAMES

Double-hung, casement, or awning windows normally consist of prefitted weather-stripped sash in assembled frames ready for installation. A double-hung window is one in which the upper and lower sash slide vertically past each other. A pair of casement sash are hinged at the side or slide sideways in a double track. Awning windows are normally hinged at the top and swing outward. A fixed sash or window is one in which the unit is stationary and cannot be opened.

Doors normally consist of the flush or the panel types. Interior flush doors may be hollow-core in thickness of $1\frac{3}{8}$ inches and widths from 2 feet 0 inches or narrower to 3 feet 0 inches in width. Solid wood panel doors are also available in various widths. Exterior doors are usually $1\frac{3}{4}$ inches in thickness. Exterior flush doors should be solid core when used in colder climates to minimize bowing during the winter. Both windows and doors can normally be supplied with screen or storms or in combination units made of wood or metal.

EXTERIOR COVERINGS

Exterior coverings, such as horizontal wood or hardboard siding and vertical board combinations, require some type of backing in the form of sheathing or horizontal nailers (for vertical boards). Exterior plywood (grooved) siding has a lap joint and can be used without sheathing. It is applied vertically in 4- by 8- or 4- by 9-foot sheets. Good practice dictates the use of a sheathing paper under the plywood to minimize air infiltration.

Other nonwood materials such as vinyl or aluminum siding, brick, or plaster over masonry walls are materials which can be used to conform to your existing house.

INSULATION AND VAPOR BARRIERS

All houses should have some type of insulation to reduce heat loss in the winter and heat gain in the summer. This will be even more important as fuel costs increase. Perhaps the most common thermal insulations are the flexible (blanket and batt) and the fill types in rock wool, fiberglass, and similar materials. Another form of insulation is reflective insulation and consists of aluminum or aluminum-faced paper. Fiberboard, plywood, and foam insulation in sheet forms (such as polystyrene) which might be used as a wall sheathing, have varying insulating values. However, they are usually not sufficient alone and require additional insulation between the studs and other framing members.

It is good practice to use full-thick ($3\frac{1}{2}$ inches) blanket or batt insulation in the walls. Some of the wall-thick ($3\frac{1}{2}$ inches) insulation can be obtained without a covering (unfaced). Four batts, 15 by 23 inches, can be used between the floor plate and top plate of exterior walls.

Ceiling insulation should be no less than 8 inches in thickness and 10 to 12 inches is almost becoming standard when batt or fill type is used in the colder areas of the country. If an unheated crawl space is a part of your new addition, at least 6 inches should be placed between the floor joists.

Vapor barriers, usually a part of blanket or batt insulation, minimizes the movement of water vapor into the wall or attic spaces. This vapor can cause problems if it condenses on cold surfaces and is absorbed by sheathing or siding. Vapor barriers can consist of asphalt-coated paper, aluminum foil, and plastic sheet materials such as polyethylene. A very good practice consists of using a covering of polyethylene film over all exposed walls from floor to ceiling even though the insulation between the studs contains some type of vapor barrier. Friction-fit insulations, which fit tightly between framing members, are usually not provided with vapor barriers. In such cases a full covering with a vapor barrier is a must.

INTERIOR FINISH MATERIALS

Coverings

Perhaps the interior coverings most adaptable to self-installation are sheetrock, plywood, and hardboards in sheet form as well as wood and fiberboard paneling in various widths and patterns. Thicknesses of these materials vary from $\frac{1}{4}$ inch or less in the plywoods and hardboards to $\frac{3}{4}$ inch in wood and fiberboard paneling. Fiberboard in 12- by 12-inch or larger sizes can be used as a ceiling finish or perhaps above a wall wainscot of wood paneling. It can be applied to 1 by 2 or 1 by 3 nailers fastened across the ceiling joists. Suspended ceiling systems utilize tile sizes up to 2 by 4 feet. Plaster walls and ceilings normally require a rock lath base in $\frac{3}{8}$- or $\frac{1}{2}$-inch thickness.

Interior Finish and Millwork

Interior finish and millwork normally consists of the doors and door frames (previously mentioned), moldings for the base of walls, casing and other trim around windows and doors, flooring, kitchen and other cabinets, and shelving, fireplace mantels, and similar components. If the new addition is relatively simple, and does not include a kitchen or a masonry fireplace, many of these millwork items will not be needed and consequently will lower the total cost of materials.

A wood finish might be painted or have a natural or stained finish. Thus the type of finish often dictates the species of wood to be used. The species more adaptable to a natural or stained finish are the oaks, birch, and mahogany. The pines and similar species are usually painted. However, the oaks and birch are normally higher in cost than the other species. Remember, while the interior selection of millwork and wood species need not be exactly like your existing house, it should tie together in some manner. As a suggestion, a paneled or similar wall of your addition might have a sheetrock ceiling painted to conform to the ceiling of the adjoining room of your existing house.

FASTENINGS

Nails

In wood-frame construction, nailing is the most common method of fastening the various parts together. However, bolts and lag screws may also be used in the con-

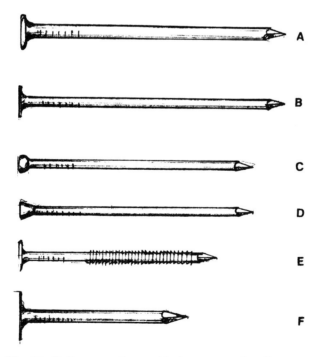

Fig. 13. Nails normally used in house construction.
- A. Common
- B. Box-type
- C. Finish
- D. Casing
- E. Ring-shank
- F. Roofing

TABLE 2. Nail sizes. (Normally obtainable in the sizes shown.)

Penny Size	Common Nails		Approximate Number/Lb	
	Length (in.)	Approx. no/lb	Casing Nails	Finishing Nails (Brad Head)
4^d	1$\frac{1}{2}$	315	470	584
5^d	1$\frac{3}{4}$	270		500
6^d	2	165	235	309
7^d	2$\frac{1}{4}$	150	210	
8^d	2$\frac{1}{2}$	105	145	189
9^d	2$\frac{3}{4}$	95		
10^d	3	70	94	121
12^d	3$\frac{1}{4}$	60		
16^d	3$\frac{1}{2}$	50	71	90
20^d	4	30		
^{a}30^d	4$\frac{1}{2}$	24	52	62
^{a}40^d	5	18		
^{a}50^d	5$\frac{1}{2}$	14		
^{a}60^d	6	11		

^{a}Usually classed as spikes.

Note: (1) Nails vary in diameter and gauge. For example, an 8^d common nail is 10$\frac{1}{4}$ gauge; a 8^d casing is 11$\frac{1}{2}$ gauge; and a 8^d finish is 12$\frac{1}{2}$ gauge.

(2) Siding nails are usually obtainable in 5^d, 6^d, 7^d, 8^d, 9^d, and 10^d (penny), and have the same diameter as the casing nail.

struction of exposed wood decks or in anchoring of sill plate to foundation walls. There are various types of nails used in the construction of a new addition. The common nail, in various sizes, is used in framing and also in application of covering materials. Some of the other nails most often used in construction are shown in Fig. 13. The box-type nail might be used, in a galvanized or cadmium plate finish, in the application of the exterior finish. It has a moderate size head and a thin shank. Siding nails have a moderate size head and a medium shank diameter. Finish and casing nails are used for nailing interior finishes and are set below the surface. The ring shank nail with its "Fetter" shank has great withdrawal resistance. They may be used in smaller sizes than smooth shank nails for the same purpose. Roofing nails with their large heads are used for roof coverings such as asphalt shingles. Table 2 lists various type nails showing their lengths, for various penny sizes, and the approximate number per pound.

Most of the nailing methods required in the construction of your addition or remodeling project will be covered in the following construction chapters. However, a general guide for good fastening practice is as follows.

Guide for Fastening Use

1. Use galvanized, cadmium plated, or stainless steel fastenings for exterior use.
2. Always fasten a thinner member to a thicker member.
3. Nail length should be at least three times the thickness of the thin member and usually penetrate not less than 1$\frac{1}{2}$ inches in the receiving member. For example,

a $\frac{3}{4}$-inch plus member fastened to a thick member requires a nail longer than $2\frac{1}{4}$ inches, i.e., a $2\frac{1}{2}$-inch or eightpenny nail.

4. To reduce splitting of boards (when necessary, especially for exterior siding or finish):
   a. Blunt nail point.
   b. Predrill ($\frac{3}{4}$ nail diameter) first member. This is especially true for the ends of siding or finish members.
   c. Use smaller diameter nails and a greater number.
   d. Place nails *no closer* to edge than one-half of the board thickness and *no closer* to the end than the board thickness.
5. Use a minimum of two nails per board, i.e., two nails for 3-, 4-, and 6-inch-wide boards and three nails for 8- and 10-inch widths.
6. Avoid end grain nailing when possible. If this is the only fastening at the joint, screws might be substituted.
7. Toenailing (angle nailing) should start on the first member about one-half the nail length above the receiving member ($1\frac{3}{8}$ inches for a 3-inch tenpenny nail). Start the nail at a 45° angle and finish driving at a 60° angle with the horizontal or direction of receiving member.

Many carpenters when framing and sheathing a wood-frame house use only eightpenny and sixteenpenny nails. The eightpenny nails are used for applying sheathing, subfloor, and for some toenailing. The sixteenpenny nails are used for nailing headers to floor joists, sole plates to floor framing, top wall plates to the first wall plate, rafters to ceiling joists, etc., as well as for nailing of ceiling joists and rafters to the top wall plates. However, unless the ceiling joists and rafters are white fir, spruce, or the softer pines, splitting often occurs. Many contractors prefer the use of tenpenny or twelvepenny nails for the toenailing of rafters and ceiling joists to the wall plates. This is a critical fastening area and when roofs do fail in areas where very high winds occur, the failure can usually be traced to inadequate fastening at this point. The twelvepenny nails provide more penetration than the eightpenny nails and are not as inclined to split the members as do the sixteenpenny nails.

Bolts and Lag Screws

Use a flat washer under the head and nut of a machine bolt and under the nut of a carriage bolt. Also use a flat washer under the head of a lag screw. Holes for bolts should be the exact diameter of the bolt. For lag screws, the hole in the first member should be the same diameter as the lag screw and about $\frac{2}{3}$ to $\frac{3}{4}$ the diameter in the receiving member.

Adhesives

Construction adhesives and similar types of materials are being used in some phases of house construction. Panel adhesives are used in laminated application of sheetrock to eliminate surface nails. The use of construction adhesive with a few nails (until the adhesive has set) might be applicable in some phases of house construction. Adhesives are also available for fastening furring strips or blocks to various surfaces.

PAINTING AND FINISHING

Exterior paints consist mainly of latex, lead-base, and alkyd-base combinations. Unlike some of the earlier paints, they are fast drying and have less resistance to the movement of water vapor from the interior of the walls eliminating the chance for blisters and other paint failures. Pigmented oil and latex base stains are easy to apply and are perhaps most adaptable to rough or sawn surfaced sidings. Paints are most adaptable for smooth surfaced siding material and for the exterior trim. Water-repellent preservatives provide a natural clear finish for wood surfaces but usually must be renewed more often than the pigmented stains or the paints.

Many interior paints are suitable for walls and ceilings, the latex and alkyds perhaps being the most popular. They can be obtained in flat, semigloss, or gloss finishes. Oil types are also suitable. Varnishes and similar clear finishes together with stains might be selected for interior woodwork. If an unfinished wood floor is involved, the regular floor sealers provide a satisfactory finish.

MISCELLANEOUS

The construction of chimneys and fireplaces may vary from the elaborate masonry designs to the more simple Franklin or similar open heating units. Installation of the latter are perhaps quite within the capacity of many handymen. They usually are supplied with a complete stovepipe kit and easily followed instructions. If such additions are planned, adjust your ceiling and roof framing to accommodate the stovepipe and exterior chimney. Check your local building codes for exact requirements.

Plumbing, heating, and wiring phases might be beyond the capacity of the owner's ability. Furthermore, the installation of such utilities normally require a professional. Most local building regulations have rigid requirements in regard to the installation of such materials. However, you can plan location of switches and convenience outlets as well as heat inlets and returns and sewer and water connections if these are a part of your addition. They should always be considered and provided for during construction.

4

Site Layout

The first detail in building an addition to your house is to establish the corners at the house and outside the house. The method used to locate the addition can be quite simple. If one wall of the addition is in line with a side of your existing house, extend this line for a distance of x, the length or width of the new section, Fig. 14. Mark the corner with a stake and a nail. Measure distance y along the house (width or length) and mark the siding or foundation wall. By swinging the tape the distance y from the new outside corner and the distance x from the house, the second outside corner is established, Fig. 14. Mark with a nail driven into a stake. Now to check if this layout is square, measure along one side a distance of exactly 12 feet

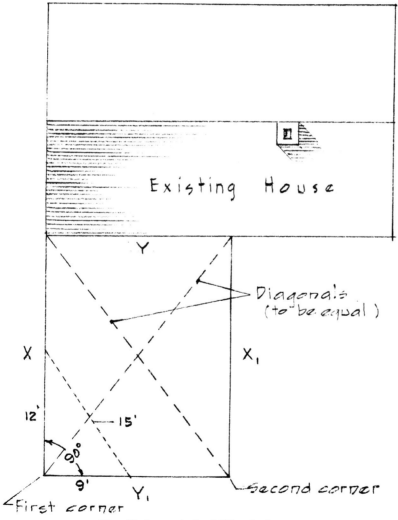

Fig. 14. Layout of addition to house.

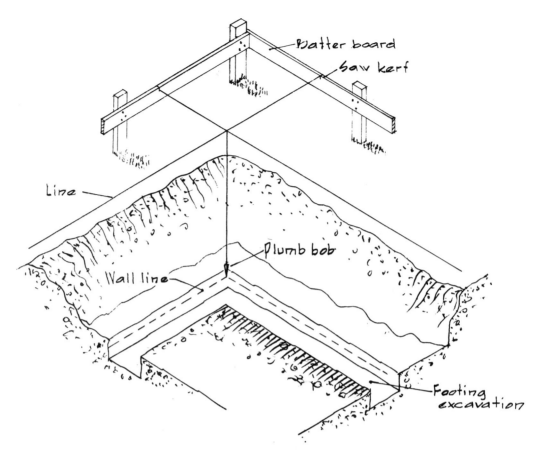

Fig. 15. Locating and sustaining corner of addition.

and 9 feet along the end. If the diagonal distance is exactly 15 feet, you have a square baseline; if not, make the necessary adjustments. Another method is to measure the two diagonal distances which should be equal. When the wall line of the new addition is not in line with the house, use the same extended baseline x. Now measure along the house the required distance (2 feet, 4 feet, or other amount) from the house corner and from the x-y_1 corner and continue the layout. Drive a stake at these corners and mark with a nail.

If excavation is required for the footings and foundation, it is necessary to establish the corners so that the soil can be removed. A nail or pencil mark can be used at the juncture with the house, Fig. 14, but the two outside corners must be established in a different manner. The use of batter boards is a common practice and consists of stakes and boards at each outside corner. Three stakes and two boards are set several feet outside the corners. With lines and a plumb bob, the corners can be established. A saw kerf is made at each board to establish the wall line of the addition. Set the batter boards far enough away so that the excavation does not disturb the stakes. Any time during or after the excavation corners can be found by use of stretched lines and a plumb bob lowered at their intersection, Fig. 15. A final check to determine if the building outline is on the square consists of again measuring the diagonal distances from the house to each outside corner. They should be exactly equal.

5
Footings and Foundations

The choice of footing and foundation types for your new addition were covered briefly in previous chapters. They can be (1) wood or masonry piers for an exposed wood deck or open foundation area for a porch or other addition, (2) concrete slab for a patio or combination grade beam and slab for a structure above, (3) a partial masonry wall for a crawl space area, or (4) a full masonry wall which will provide a full-height basement.

FOOTINGS FOR POSTS AND PIERS

Perhaps the simplest foundation for a wood structure consists of treated wood posts or timbers or of masonry piers. Embedded wood pilings have been used for many years in structures subjected to hurricanes and high tides. For wood structures in severely sloped back yards and for summer cabins, the use of such systems results in a more than adequate support for the wood floor framing. This can also result in substantial cost savings. However, such support systems result in an open crawl space area. If the ground is level, the open perimeter can be shielded by a simple skirt-board system, if desired. Posts, when spacing is 8 feet or greater, should normally be 4 by 6 or 6 by 6 inches in size. A better fastening area for the beams is thus provided. When treated round posts are used (embedded in the soil), they should have a top no less than 6 inches in diameter.

Figure 16A shows a treated wood post supported by well tamped soil or gravel. Embedment depth for this support is usually $4\frac{1}{2}$ to 5 feet or more. Soil should be added gradually and tamped well. If the post is long, it can be positioned by braces nailed to the pole and to adjacent stakes during erection. This type of foundation should usually be limited to round treated poles. In Fig. 16B a concrete pad is used as a base with tamped soil holding the pole or timber in place. The embedment depth can be less than when soil is used for full support but should be enough to provide adequate lateral resistance, usually $2\frac{1}{2}$ to 3 feet.

When frost is not a factor, a concrete footing and pedestal on the surface might be used for support of a wood post. In such designs, an anchor bolt is placed in the concrete as the pedestal is poured. The bolt is then used to anchor a metal stirrup, Fig. 16C. A variation of such a metal stirrup to anchor the post is shown in Fig. 16D. The important detail in such construction is to keep the end of an untreated post above the concrete surface to prevent moisture absorption.

A masonry pier made of an 8- by 8-inch concrete block also results in a satisfactory support, Fig. 16E. When blocks are hollow and the height of the pier is perhaps over 4 or 5 feet above grade, reinforcing rods should be installed and the hollow areas filled with concrete. A metal anchor for fastening the floor system should also be placed at this time. A heavy perforated galvanized strap can be used to anchor a beam to the masonry pier.

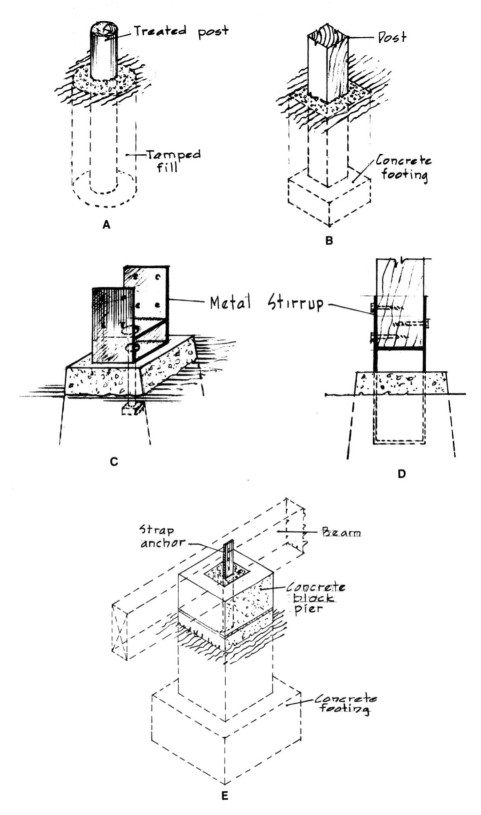

Fig. 16. Footings for posts and piers.

    A. Post with tamped fill.
    B. Post with concrete footing.
    C. Metal stirrup.
    D. Alternate stirrup design.
    E. Masonry pier.

22

FOOTINGS FOR MASONRY WALLS

Footings act as a continuous supporting base for masonry walls and must be wide and deep enough to transmit the load of the house to the soil. Usually the minimum size is 8 inches deep by 16 inches wide. For 10-inch walls the size might be 10 by 20 inches. Much depends on the type of soil under the footings. Here again, consult your local building codes for required sizes in your area.

A few rules that apply to footing design and construction are as follows:

1. If footing excavation is too deep, *never* fill with soil; fill with concrete during pouring operations.
2. If soil prevents sharply cut trenches, use form boards.
3. Footings must be below the frostline in cold climates.
4. Reinforce footings (lengthwise) with steel rods where they cross pipe trenches.
5. Use a key slot in the top for poured walls. This will result in better resistance to water entry into a basement area, Fig. 17A.

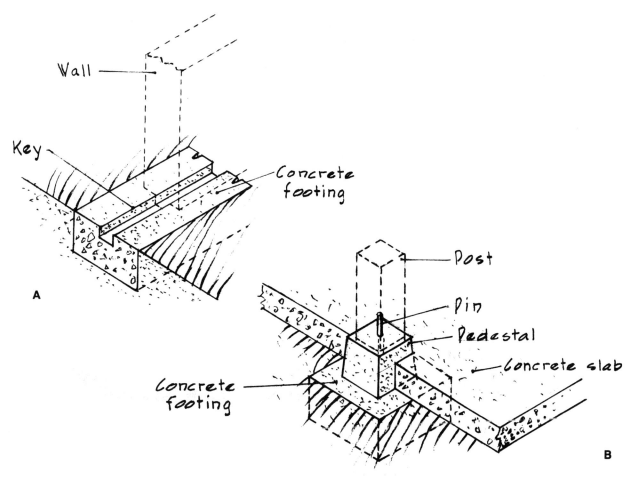

Fig. 17. Footings for masonry walls and interior posts.
A. Concrete footing for walls.
B. Post footing.

When footings for interior posts supporting load-carrying beams are required, a pedestal with an anchor bolt or pin is used, Fig. 17B. Footing sizes for such post supports are usually 20 by 20 inches in size or larger, and 10 to 12 inches in depth.

6
Concrete Slabs

Two types of concrete slabs are normally used and are classed as "floating" and "grade-beam". A "floating" slab is normally used where there is no frost to cause slab movement and possible failure. There should also be good drainage away from the edges.

FLOATING SLAB

A typical layout for a floating slab is shown in Fig. 18. This type might be used for an open patio, for example. Form boards are used around the perimeter and are held

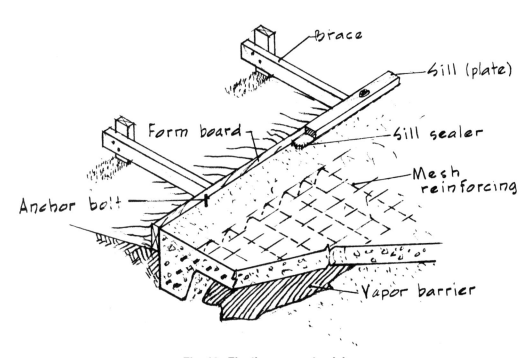

Fig. 18. Floating concrete slab.

in place during pouring of the concrete by braces nailed to the form board and to adjacent stakes. The use of a well tamped gravel base covered with a good vapor barrier such as 4- or 6-mil polyethylene is good practice. A 6- by 6-inch mesh reinforcing wire should be used throughout and carried into the outer edges. All water lines and other connections should be made before the slab is poured. In cold climates this type of slab should not be tied to the house foundation as it can move when frost leaves the ground.

GRADE-BEAM SLAB

In cold climates where deep frosts are encountered, a grade-beam design is often used for concrete slab construction. Another method consists of the construction of a masonry wall which supports the slab. Construction of a grade-beam slab is somewhat more involved than the floating slab, mainly because of the supporting piers and the insulation. However, this method can be accomplished in two stages. When the outline of the addition to your house is established, holes are dug around the perimeter for the piers. Spread them at the bottom for a greater area. The bottom of the excavation should be below the frostline. Holes can be 8 to 10 inches in diameter and spaced 6 to 8 feet apart. Pour the concrete to the bottom of the grade-beam elevation and insert four $\frac{1}{2}$-inch or larger reinforcing rods into the fresh pour, Fig. 19A. They should be long enough so that 2 feet are in the pier; and when bent to

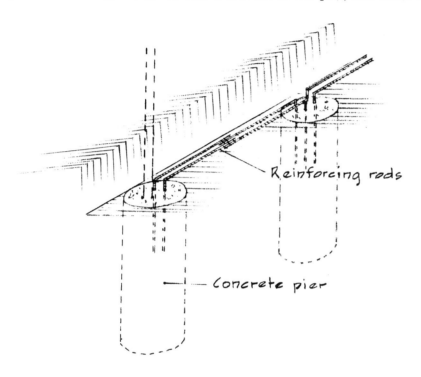

A

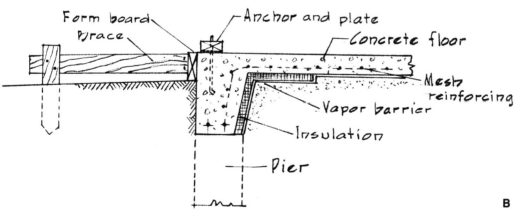

B

Fig. 19. Grade beam concrete slab.
A. Phase one.
B. Phase two.

form bottom reinforcing for the edge beam, they can be tied to the rods of the adjacent piers. For example, if the piers are 8 feet apart, the rods should be about $8\frac{1}{2}$ to 9 feet long which allows for the bend and will extend beyond the halfway distance of the next pier.

Form boards around the perimeter can now be set as for normal slab construction and the grade-beam area excavated. After the excavation has been completed, the rods can be bent and tied together with wire. The rods should be 2 to 3 inches above the bottom of the beam. One or two inches of rigid insulation should be used on the inside of the beam location *after* the vapor barrier has been placed, Fig. 19B. The following sequence is then the same as described for the simple or floating slab. When sole plates are required for walls of the addition, anchor bolts should be placed after the slab has been leveled off. You can use $\frac{3}{8}$ - by 8-inch machine or carriage bolts. Place them about $2\frac{1}{2}$ inches from the edge and 4 to 6 feet apart. They should extend about $2\frac{1}{2}$ inches above the surface.

Because the grade-beam slab is designed as a stable unit, it can be tied to the foundation wall of the existing house. This can be done by drilling holes into the house wall and fastening heavy punched strap to the wall with anchor bolts. The strap will extend into the beam section of the slab.

7
Masonry Walls

Two types of masonry wall are commonly used in the construction of houses, concrete block walls and poured concrete walls. The block wall is perhaps more adaptable to the skill of the average handyman and does not require forming and bracing as does the poured wall. The poured wall is usually 9 inches thick for one-story houses (or additions) while the block wall must usually be 10 inches thick. However, here again check your local building code. It is possible that thinner walls might be satisfactory in your area for small additions to your house. If you desire the finished floor of the addition to be the same level as the floor of the house, adjust the height of the masonry wall where necessary to accommodate the floor framing and the floor covering. Mark the floor level of the house on the siding in several places as a baseline. This can be done by measuring the height of a window stool above the house floor and transferring this distance to the exterior.

CONCRETE BLOCK WALL

Modular concrete blocks can be obtained in 6-, 8-, 10-, and 12-inch widths for walls requiring these thicknesses. The block length and height is actually $15\frac{5}{8}$ and $7\frac{5}{8}$ inches, respectively. Thus, with $\frac{3}{8}$-inch horizontal and vertical mortar joints, an 8- by 16-inch face module is obtained. Block courses of the wall start at the concrete footing over a mortar bed with $\frac{3}{8}$-inch-thick vertical and horizontal mortar joints, Fig. 20A.

Mortar ready for mixing, with only sand and water, can be obtained at your local lumber or brick yard. In preparing the mortar, mix it dry before adding water. Practice will educate you on the amount of water to be used—too much and a $\frac{3}{8}$-inch joint cannot be obtained as the block will settle. If the mortar is too stiff and dry, there is little or no adhesion. In hot dry weather when mortar sets up too fast, *light* sprinkling of the block before use will help. Joints should be struck (excess mortar removed with your trowel) and tooled to form a smooth, moisture-resistant joint. Full bedding of mortar should be used on all contact surfaces of the block (including the ends). Keep the courses level and plumb as you lay the block.

When walls are long, it is often necessary to use a pilaster of wider block. This extra projection should be placed on the interior of the wall. Your local building codes should spell out their spacing. Basement window and door frames are normally placed, plumbed, and braced while the block is being laid. They should be keyed into the block (whether of wood or metal) to form an airtight as well as watertight joint, Fig. 20B. A beam pocket should be provided at the top of the wall when a wide addition requires the use of a center beam.

Block walls should be capped with 4-inch solid concrete blocks or a capping of poured concrete. Use form boards on each side of the wall to provide a level surface. In addition, bolts or punched straps for sill plates or header joists are placed during

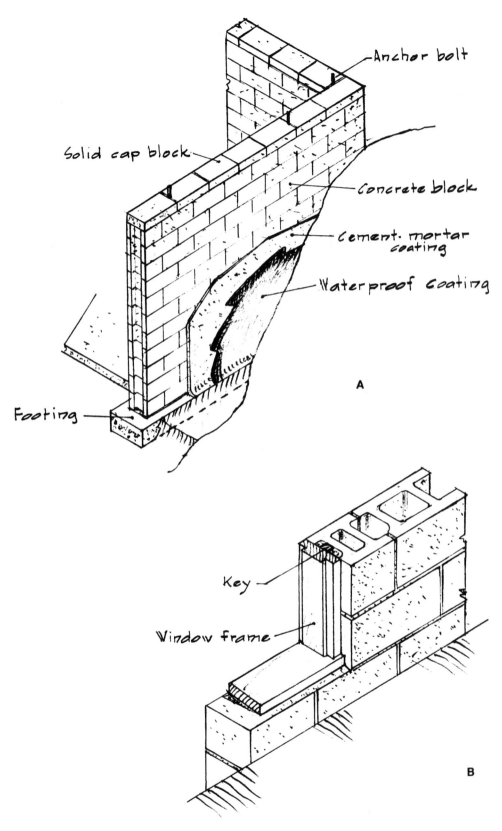

Fig. 20. Concrete block wall.
A. Common bond wall.
B. Window detail.

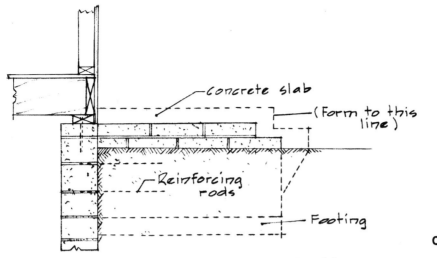

Fig. 20. Concrete block wall (*cont'd*).
C. Concrete stoop.

laying of the last two filled block courses, Fig. 20A, or when a poured cap is used.

It is good practice to tie the walls to the foundation of the existing house. This can be done by using anchor bolts to fasten metal ties which are located at every third or fourth mortar joint. A perforated strap is satisfactory and should be embedded in the mortar joints.

When moist soil conditions are present, it is often desirable to minimize moisture movement into a basement area by using a cement-mortar coating below grade. A cement cove can also be formed at the junction of the wall and footing, Fig. 20A. The waterproof coating of asphalt or similar material can then be applied over the cement.

Crawl space areas should be ventilated and should also have a ground cover to minimize vapor movement into the heated addition above. Ground covers can consist of 4- or 6-mil polyethylene held in place with partial bricks or pieces of concrete.

When a masonry stoop for an outside door is involved, provision should be made for the supporting walls. Pencil rods (small-diameter rods) or other reinforcing can be installed at each course where the walls of the stoop occur, Fig. 20C. Use a 6-inch block over a poured footing for each of the walls. After the backfill has settled: (1) fill the area between the walls with sand; (2) install forms for the top slab and the step; (3) install reinforcing wire; and (4) pour concrete between form walls, Fig. 20C.

POURED CONCRETE WALLS

If you desire a poured concrete wall, you can have it contracted for or rent or make forms and do it yourself (with some expert help). Forms are placed on the footings and tied and braced somewhat as shown in Fig. 21. Metal spacer ties are used to keep walls at a constant thickness.

Frames for windows and doors are fastened to the forms and blocked out the full thickness of the wall. As with the concrete block walls, anchor bolts or punched strapping for sills or joists are placed as pouring is being completed. The poured walls can be tied to the existing walls of your house by fastening ties to the wall before the pouring operation.

A coating of asphalt or tar on the exterior below the finish grade can be used if drainage is poor or soil contains a great deal of moisture.

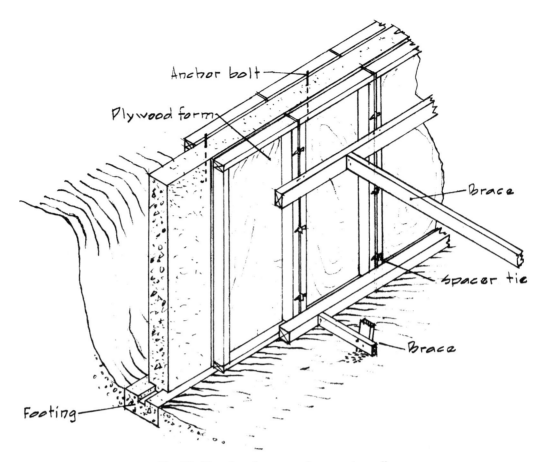

Anchor bolt

Plywood form

Brace

Spacer tie

Brace

Footing

Fig. 21. Forming for poured concrete wall.

A concrete stoop can be constructed in the same manner as described for the concrete block wall. Use $\frac{5}{8}$- or $\frac{3}{4}$-inch deformed reinforcing rods for the walls of the stoop. The inner ends should be bent to provide good anchorage when the concrete of the main wall of the addition is poured.

8
Floor Framing

The bearing members of a wood floor system are the floor joists usually terminated at the outside ends with "header" joists. The edge parallel joist is usually called the "stringer" or "band" joist. Joists are supported and nailed to anchored wood sills, 2 by 6's or 2 by 8's, and to a center beam (when spans are long enough to require two lengths of joists). When a wood sill is not used, strap anchors together with a concrete beam fill provides a firm anchorage to the foundation wall. Floor systems for open decks usually consist of beams, joists, and deck boards.

FLOOR FRAMING FOR EXPOSED WOOD DECKS

Framing for an exposed deck can consist of all or part of the following, depending on the design: (1) Posts—anchored to a pier or embedded in the ground, (2) beams or double joists bolted or lag screwed to the posts, (3) floor joists resting on and fastened to the beams, (4) deck boards, and (5) the railing and balusters (if desired). One such combination which might be used is shown in Fig. 22A. The beam can consist of a solid 4- by 6-, 4- by 8-, or 4- by 10-inch timber (depending on the span) bolted to the post. The bolts as well as all fasteners should be galvanized or have other rustproof finishes, If required, the posts can be temporarily braced in a true vertical position before the beams are fastened to them. The beam may also be fastened to the top of the post at this or other locations when the post does not act as part of the railing. Such a fastener might consist of a galvanized stirrup such as shown in Fig. 22B. Heavy galvanized nails or lag screws can be used for fasteners.

Post Braces

If posts are quite long because of a steep slope and are not embedded in the soil, it is usually necessary to provide some type of bracing. Bracing is placed between the posts and beams to provide a lateral or racking resistance. When posts are 8 feet and more in unsupported height, a single direction brace system might be used, Fig. 22C. The members should be 2 by 6 or 2 by 8 inches. Galvanized lag screws (with washers) should be used for fastening. Shorter posts (6 to 8 feet) can be braced with the partial brace system, Fig. 22D.

Beams

The size of the beams used to support the floor joists depends not only on the spacing between the beams but also on the span of the beams (distance between posts or other supports). Table 3 can be used as a guide in determining the size of the beam under various conditions. Three general species groups of wood are listed.

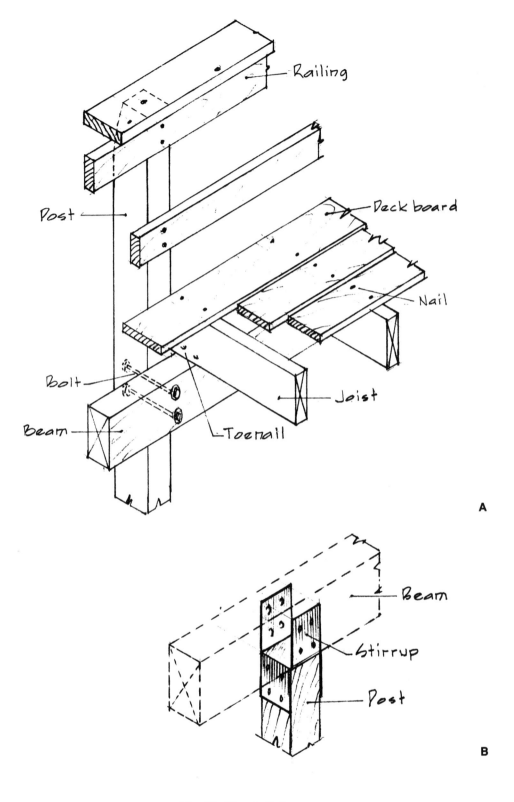

Fig. 22. Wood deck.
A. Typical member arrangement.
B. Post-beam connection.

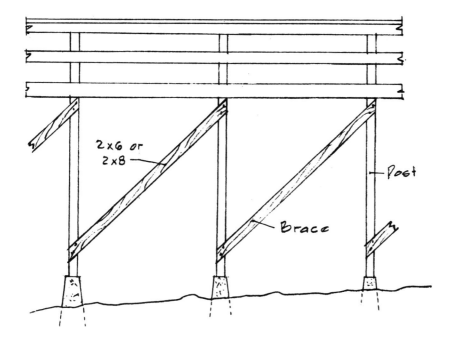

C

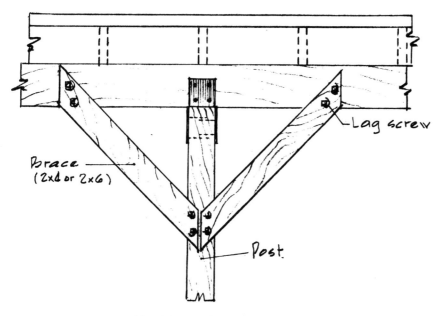

D

Fig. 22. Wood deck (cont'd).
C. Single brace.
D. Partial brace.

Posts

The size of the posts depends on the deck areas they support as well as their height. Table 4 lists the recommended sizes of posts under variations in area, height, and species.

TABLE 3. Guide in selecting beams. (Minimum beam size and span.)

Species	Beam size (in.)	Spacing Between Beams (Ft)[b]		
		6	8	10
Douglas fir,	4 × 6	Up to 6′ span →	—	—
Larch, and	4 × 8	Up to 8′ ——→	Up to 7′ ——→	Up to 6′ ——→
Southern pine	4 × 10	Up to 10′ ——→	Up to 9′ ——→	Up to 8′ ——→
Hemlock (east and	4 × 6	—	—	—
west coast), White	4 × 8	Up to 7′ span →	Up to 6′ ——→	—
fir, and similar	4 × 10	Up to 9′ ——→	Up to 8′ ——→	Up to 7′ ——→
species				
Western and	4 × 6	—	—	—
Eastern pines,	4 × 8	Up to 6′ span →	—	—
Cedars, Spruces,	4 × 10	Up to 8′ ——→	Up to 7′ ——→	Up to 6′ ——→
and Redwood				

[a]Beams are on edge. *Spans* are center to center distances between *posts* or supports. (Based on 40 lb/sq ft deck live load plus 10 lb/sq ft dead load material weight.) Grade is No. 2 or better; No. 2 medium grain southern pine.

[b]Example: If the beams are 9′-8″ apart and the species are Hemlock, etc., use the 10 ft column (third column): A 4 by 10 in. beam up to a 7-ft span would be satisfactory.

Note: Data from U.S. Dept. of Agriculture Handbook No. 432.

TABLE 4. Minimum post sizes. (allowable height)
(Wood beam supports.[a])

Species	Post Size (In.)	Load Area[b] In Sq Ft (Beam Spacing Times Post Spacing)		
		Up to 60 (6′ × 10′ area)	60 to 96 (8′ × 12′ area)	96 to 120 (10′ × 12′ area)
Douglas fir,	4 × 4	to 12 ft height	to 10 ft height	to 8 ft height
Southern	4 × 6	← —————— to 12 ft height —————— →		
pine,				
or equal				
Redwood,	4 × 4	to 10 ft height	to 8 ft height	to 6 ft height
Cedars,	4 × 6	to 12 ft height	to 10 ft height	to 8 ft height
Spruces				

Note: For heights greater than 12 ft use 6 by 6 in. posts.

[a]Based on 40 lb/sq ft live load plus 10 lb/sq ft dead load (material weight). Standard and better grade for 4 by 4 in. posts and No. 1 and better for 4 by 6 in. posts.

[b]Example: if beam supports are spaced 8 ft apart and posts are spaced 10 ft apart (80 sq ft), use: (second column) 4 by 4 Douglas fir, southern pine etc., for 10 ft heights, 4 by 6 for 12 ft heights etc.

Data developed from U.S. Dept. of Agriculture Handbook No. 432.

Joists

Joist sizes vary with their spacing, span, and wood species. Table 5 may be used as a guide in selecting the correct size for your deck. The grades listed are commonly

TABLE 5. Guide for selecting floor joists for exposed wood decks.[a]
(Maximum allowable span.[b])

Species	Nominal Size (in.)	Floor Joist Spacing (in.)		
		12	16	24
Douglas fir, Larch,	2 × 6	10'-8"	9'-9"	7'-11"
and Southern pine	2 × 8	14'-6"	12'-10"	10'-6"
	2 × 10	17'-10"	16'-5"	13'-4"
Hemlock fir, and	2 × 6	9'-8"	8'-7"	7'-0"
Douglas fir (south)	2 × 8	13'-0"	11'-4"	9'-3"
	2 × 10	16'-2"	14'-6"	11'-10"
Western pines and	2 × 6	8'-8"	7'-9"	6'-2"
Cedars, Redwood,	2 × 8	11'-8"	10'-2"	8'-1"
and Spruces	2 × 10	14'-8"	13'-0"	10'-4"

[a]Based on a similar table contained in U.S. Dept. of Agriculture Handbook No. 432.

[b]Based on 40 lb/sq ft live load plus 10 lb/sq ft dead load (material weight). Grade is No. 2 or better; No. 2 Medium grain southern pine.

TABLE 6. Guide for selecting deck boards for exposed wood decks.[a]
(Maximum allowable span for spaced deck boards.)

Species	Maximum Allowable Span (In.)[b]			
	Laid Flat		Laid on Edge	
	1 × 4	2 × 3, 2 × 4, 2 × 6	2 × 3	2 × 4
Douglas fir, Larch, and Southern pine	16	60	90	144
Hemlock (east and west coast) White fir and similar species	14	48	78	120
Western and eastern pines, Cedars, Spruces and Redwood	12	42	66	108

[a]These spans are based on the assumption that more than one floor board carries the normal load. If concentrated loads are a rule, spans should be reduced accordingly.

[b]Based on construction grade or better (select structural, Appearance No. 1 or No. 2).

Note: This table developed based on a similar table in U.S. Dept of Agriculture Handbook No. 432.

classed as No. 2 or better and No. 2 medium grain southern pine at your lumberyard. However, they may be classed differently in your area. The grade and species used should have good strength and stiffness properties commonly required for joists and beams. Check your local building codes so that the correct species and size are selected.

When the joists cross the supporting beams, they should be fastened by toenailing into the beam with tenpenny galvanized nails. The thickness of the deck boards is controlled by the spacing of these joists.

Deck Boards

Deck boards can consist of nominal 1- or 2-inch material depending on the joist spacing. Table 6 lists the allowable spans for a number of species. Two nails should be used in each deck board 3 or more inches in width. Avoid deck boards over 6 inches in width.

For best results use eightpenny galvanized ring shank nails for 1-inch boards and sixteenpenny galvanized ring shank nails for 2-inch-thick deck boards. The ring shank nail minimizes nail movement which can result in the nailhead showing above the surface after many wetting and drying cycles. When necessary, splitting can be eliminated at board ends by predrilling. Space deck boards about $\frac{1}{8}$ inch apart, and allow space at the ends so they can dry out after rains.

A Typical Deck

Another system of deck construction (other than that shown in Fig. 22A), which is

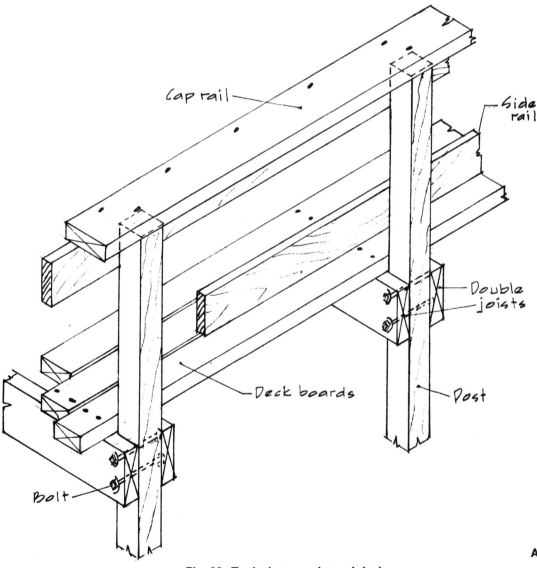

Fig. 23. Typical exposed wood deck.
A. Post and joist arrangement.

36

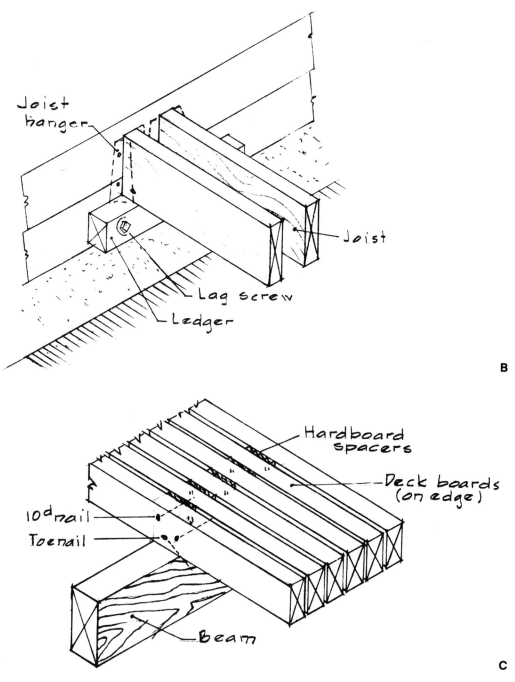

Joist hanger

Joist

Lag screw

Ledger

B

Hardboard spacers

Deck boards (on edge)

10^d nail

Toenail

Beam

C

Fig. 23. Typical exposed wood deck (*cont'd*).
B. Ledger support at house wall
C. Long-span deck boards.

quite simple, is shown in Fig. 23A. In this type of arrangement, the beams, as such, are not required as the joists act as the beams and also serve as the support for the deck boards. Joists are doubled and bolted to each side of the posts which are supported by a pier, Fig. 16C, or are embedded in the soil over a concrete pad, Fig. 16B. As an example, let us assume a typical deck with a 10-foot depth by a 16-foot or greater length consisting of the following.

Post of 4- by 4- or 4- by 6-inch sizes are normally used for supports. In checking joist sizes in Table 5, we find that a 2- by 8-inch joist (Douglas fir, larch, or southern pine) with 24-inch spacing is satisfactory for a span of 10 feet 6 inches. Thus a double joist is okay for 48-inch spacing if the deck boards can span this distance. Table 6 lists several species which might be used as deck boards for a 48-inch span in 2- by 3-, 2- by 4-, or 2- by 6-inch sizes. Because the posts extend above the deck, they are used to fasten the railings as shown in Fig. 23A. The opposite ends of the joists against the house are supported by a 3- by 3- or 3- by 4-inch ledger lag screwed to the house framing, Fig. 23B. If the ledger must be located below the floor framing of the house, anchor bolts should be used in the foundation wall. Joist ends are sometimes supported by joist hangers.

Because the 4- by 4-inch posts extend above the floor, they are used as the vertical members to support the railing components. A 2- by 6-inch cap rail and 1- by 6- or 1- by 8-inch siderails are used between the posts, Fig. 23A. When end joints of horizontal members occur at a post or at a double joist, a $\frac{1}{8}$-inch space should be allowed so that a moisture trap is not formed. Seats can be constructed with a 2- by 4-inch horizontal seat support bolted to each post and to a 2- by 4-inch vertical support member resting on the deck proper.

This example is only one of the many variables possible in constructing a wood deck. Railing design, deck size, and other details can be varied to suit the site.

Long-Span Deck Boards

As shown in Table 6, nominal 2-inch members used on edge have greater allowable spans than when used flatwise. Such a system can be used when long spans are desirable to decrease the number of posts and beams. When deck boards consist of 2 by 3's or 2 by 4's on edge, use $\frac{1}{8}$-inch-thick hardboard spacers at about 4-foot intervals. Nail through the spacers into the rear edge floor board with two tenpenny galvanized nails, Fig. 23C. At beam crossings, toenail into the beam with tenpenny or twelvepenny nails. Keep spacers in line for best appearance. For example, if beams are spaced 7 feet apart, use spacers at the beams and at half points. Spacers and nailing at these points prevents the edge flooring members from tipping under loads.

FLOOR FRAMING FOR ENCLOSED ADDITIONS

Beams

In general, floor framing for an enclosed addition is about the same as has been outlined for an exposed wood deck. Joists must have some type of bearing at or near each end (a wall or a beam). When the width of the addition is quite great, a center beam or other means of support is required.

If the width (length of joists) of your addition is about 16 to 18 feet or greater, a center beam is normally used to support the interior ends of the joists. The center beam can consist of laminated (nailed together) 2-inch wood members, a solid wood member, or a steel beam. One type of arrangement for a laminated beam is shown in Fig 24A. The joists rest directly over the center beam and on the masonry foundation. The same arrangement can be used for a solid beam.

A laminated beam of three or more members is assembled by face nailing at each side with twentypenny nails spaced about 32 inches on center in a staggered pattern. End joints should always occur over a supporting post. Wood beams are fastened to a wood post by toenailing and by the use of angle irons, Fig. 24A. The base of the

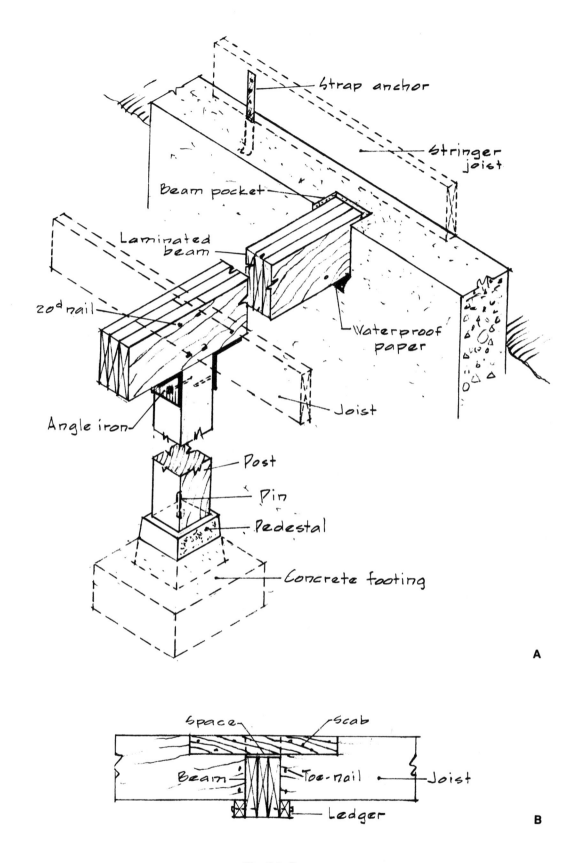

Fig. 24. Beams.
A. Laminated beam (direct support of joists).
B. Ledger support.

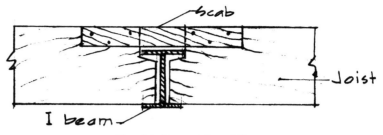

Fig. 24. Beams (cont'd).
C. I beam.

post rests on a concrete pedestal held in place by a steel pin. A steel post with top and bottom plates can also be used to support solid or laminated wood beams. The top plate is lag screwed to the post and to the underside of the beam. The bottom plate rests on a concrete footing. Lateral resistance is provided when the concrete floor is poured. Joists are toenailed with tenpenny or twelvepenny nails to the top of wood beams they cross.

Joists may also be supported by a ledger lag screwed or well nailed to the beam, Fig. 24B. A 2- by 3-inch scab is spiked to each opposing pair of joists. Allow a space above the beam for shrinkage of the joists, Fig. 24B and 24C. In such an arrangement the beam pockets in the masonry wall can be much shallower than shown in Fig. 24A. A clearance of $\frac{1}{2}$ inch at each side and end of the beam should be allowed to prevent moisture absorption at the masonry wall. In addition, use a pad of roll roofing where the beam bears on the masonry.

A wide flange steel beam can be used in a similar manner, Fig. 24C. Notch the floor joists and let them bear on the lower flange. A 2- by 3-inch scab is used to tie opposing joists together.

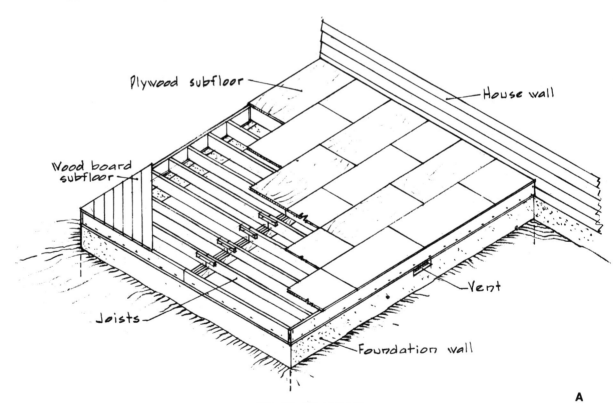

Fig. 25. Floor joists.
A. Typical arrangement.

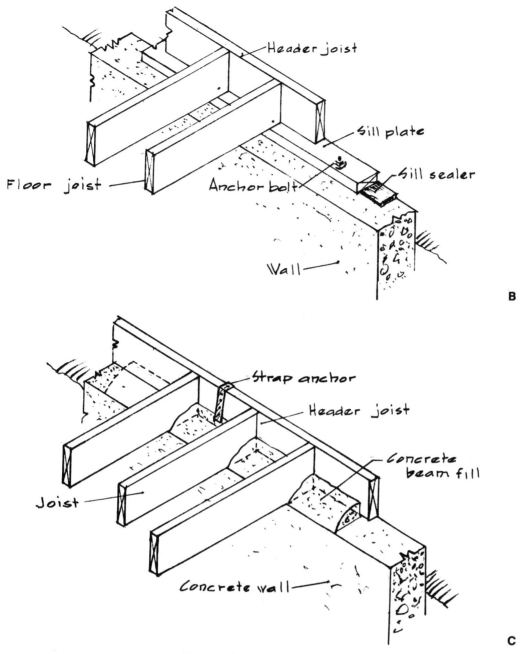

Header joist

Sill plate

Sill sealer

Floor joist

Anchor bolt

Wall

B

Strap anchor

Header joist

Concrete beam fill

Joist

Concrete wall

C

Fig. 25. Floor joists (cont'd).
B. With sill plate at wall.
C. Without sill plate at wall.

Floor Joists

Floor joists for your enclosed addition can be arranged as shown in Fig. 25A. They are normally spaced 16 inches on center. The size of joists required for various spans can be determined from the span guides listed in Table 7. These sizes are based on spans, species, and grades of materials as well as the spacing. Check your local building regulations for final selection.

When sill plates (perimeter members upon which the joists rest) are a part of your design, they should be bolted to the top of the foundation, Fig. 25B. The sill plate is usually placed inside the edge of the masonry wall the thickness of the sheathing

TABLE 7. Guide for selecting floor joist sizes[a]
(Maximum allowable span based on 40 lb/sq ft live load.)

Species and Grade	Nominal size (in.)	Floor Joist Spacing (in.)		
		12	16	24
Southern pine,	2 × 6	10'-9"	9'-9"	8'-4"
No. 2 grade	2 × 8	14'-2"	12'-10"	11'-0"
(or equal)	2 × 10	18'-0"	16'-5"	14'-0"
	2 × 12	21'-11"	19'-11"	17'-1"

[a] From Southern Pine Technical Bulletin of Span tables.
[b] Equivalent grades in Douglas fir, larch, etc.

when siding is used as an exterior finish. When a single covering is used, such a vertical plywood siding, the sill may be placed flush with the outside edge of the wall. Use a sill sealer (usually a fiberglass or similar pad) under the sill plate.

When a sill plate is not used, the header and stringer joists are anchored to the masonry wall with perforated metal straps, Fig. 25C. A concrete beam fill serves to further anchor the floor system to the masonry wall.

When assembling the floor system, header joists may be marked for joist locations which can also serve as a guide for nailing. The following nailing schedule should generally be followed in fabrication of the floor framing.

1. Header to joist—end nail with three sixteenpenny nails.
2. End of joist to wood sill—toenail with one tenpenny nail on each side.
3. Header and stringer joists to wood sill—toenail with tenpenny nails spaced 16 inches on center.
4. Joist to wood center beam—toenail with one tenpenny nail on each side.

Floor Openings

When framing for medium to large openings, such as stairways or fireplace locations, the joists and headers around the opening should be doubled, Fig. 26A. The first joists (trimmer joists) are nailed to the first and second headers before the second trimmers are placed. The first headers are nailed to the tail beams before the second headers are located, Fig. 26A. Toenailing of headers and tail beams is also good practice. An opening length of about $9\frac{1}{2}$ to 10 feet is usually required to provide head room for the descending stairs.

Wall Projections

It may be desirable, such as in the design of a special window, to project the house wall beyond the foundation wall line. The simplest method is to extend the joists beyond the wall. Edge joists are doubled as shown in Fig. 26B. Nail the header to the ends of the extended joists and the second joist to the header with three sixteenpenny nails. A 16- to 24-inch overhang is usually considered normal because it should not extend beyond the roof overhang unless the roof is also extended.

Wall projections which are at right angles to the joist direction are more complicated as they require a doubled joist (usually the third from the edge) and cantilevered members. Doubled edge stringers for the extension are fastened by toenailing (and

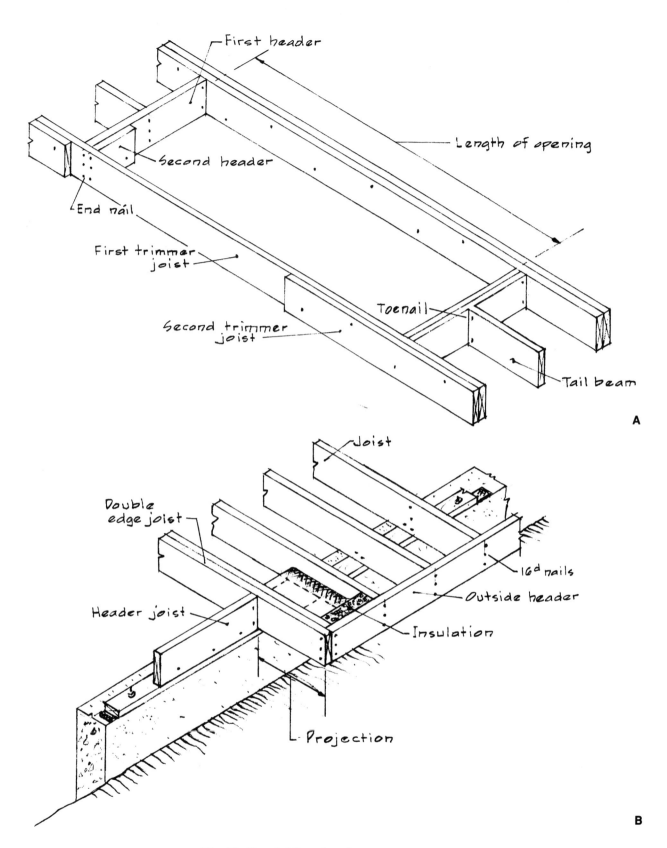

Fig. 26. Special floor framing.
A. Stair opening.
B. Wall projection (joist extension).

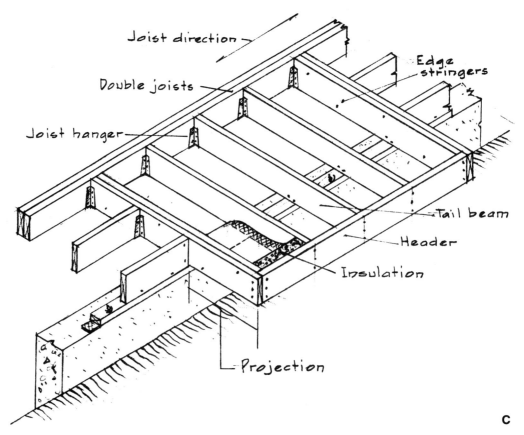

Joist direction

Double joists

Joist hanger

Edge stringers

Tail beam

Header

Insulation

Projection

C

Fig. 26. Special floor framing (cont'd).
C. Wall projection at right angle to joist direction.

by the use of joist hangers) to the interior doubled joists, Fig. 26C. Tail beams and an outside header are also required. Plan to insulate these overhangs.

Subfloor

As previously described under the Chapter "Materials," subfloor normally consists of 1-inch wood boards or of plywood. Wood boards may be laid diagonally (for great racking resistance), Fig. 25A, or at right angles to the joists. When a wood board subfloor is used, wood strip flooring or an underlayment of some type is normally placed over the wood boards.

Plywood subfloors should be installed with the grain direction of the outer plies at right angles to the joists, Fig. 25A. (Thickness and species for various joist spacings were covered in the Chapter "Materials.") Use two eightpenny nails for 4- and 6-inch-wide wood boards and three nails for 8- and 10-inch-wide boards. Plywood should be nailed to the joists and other bearing members on 6- to 7-inch centers. Use seven-penny nails for $\frac{1}{2}$-inch plywood and eightpenny or ninepenny nails for $\frac{5}{8}$- and $\frac{3}{4}$-inch plywood. Plywood should not be laid with tight joints. Use $\frac{1}{32}$-inch end and $\frac{1}{16}$-inch side spacings.

Bridging

Bridging, either solid (2-inch members) or 1- by 3-inch cross-bridging, is placed in the center of long spans to minimize tipping of the floor joists, Fig. 27A. They can be

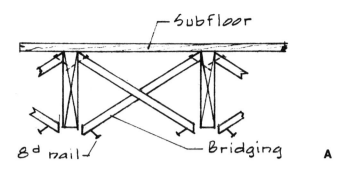

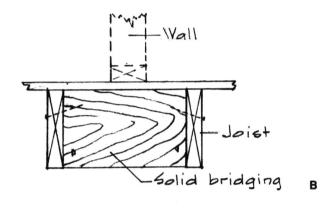

Fig. 27. Bridging.
A. Cross-bridging.
B. Solid-bridging.

used when spans are 10 feet or longer. Bridging has some value when single flooring is used. However, solid bridging should mainly be used between joists when parallel partitions are not located directly over the joists, Fig. 27B. Space these members about 24 inches on center. The cross-bridging should be nailed to the top of the joists with two eightpenny nails. The bottom of the bridging is not nailed until the joists are well dried out.

Second Floor Joists

Existing floor joists in attic spaces should be large enough to support normal loads (design load of 40 pounds per square foot) when the attic is remodeled for living space. Usually, if there are attic stairs, the floor joists are likely to be large enough. If covered, the joist size may be determined as follows: If the downstairs ceiling height is 8 feet 0 inches and the floor-to-floor height (first to second) is about 8 feet to 9 feet 10 inches, the joists are likely to be 2 by 8's. The allowable span for 2 by 8 joists is usually about 11 feet if they are a species such as southern pine or equal in a good grade and spaced 16 inches or less, Table 7.

As important as strength is the deflection of the joists under design load when the ceiling of the first floor is plastered. Excessive deflection can cause plaster cracks. Check Table 7 for the sizes normally used to support such a floor system. Also consult your local building regulations.

9

Wall Framing

The floor system, with its subfloor covering, is now complete and provides a convenient working platform for fabrication of the wall framing. A concrete slab, if this has been your choice of construction, is also a good area for fabrication of the walls. Wall framing normally consists of studs (vertical members), a horizontal sole plate (bottom), and two top plates in nominal 2- by 4-inch sizes. These members can be a second grade material in most of the wood species available in a lumberyard and are normally used for studs. Headers, which carry loads over door and window openings, should be of first grade quality in species similar to those of the floor joists.

Headers over windows and doors are always doubled and may be nailed together before assembly of the wall. Use three $\frac{1}{2}$-inch-thick spacers between the 2-inch members to produce a $3\frac{1}{2}$-inch final thickness. Use two twelvepenny nails at each spacer. To provide a header which has better insulation, use $\frac{1}{2}$-inch styrofoam, or other foam insulation, between the wood header members instead of the three spacers. The foam (sheet) insulation should be the same size as the wood members.

If your dimension materials are not $1\frac{1}{2}$ inches thick (a 2- by 4-inch member $1\frac{1}{2}$ by $3\frac{1}{2}$ inch), the opening widths, stud lengths, etc., listed in the following sections should be adjusted accordingly.

The following sizes may be used as a guide in selecting your headers over windows and doors.

Maximum Span (ft)	Header Size (Nominal in.)	
$3\frac{1}{2}$	2	2 × 6
5	2	2 × 8
$6\frac{1}{2}$	2	2 × 10
8	2	2 × 12

In estimating the number of studs and plates needed (sole plate and two top plates), many contractors order one stud for each lineal foot of wall. This should take care of doubled corners and the extra framing around window and door openings with studs spaced 16 inches on center. For each foot of wall, plan on 3 lineal feet of 2 by 4's for the plates. If the addition to your home is 16 by 24 feet, for example (16-foot side against the house), with a 16-foot-long interior wall plan on six 16-foot lengths (or equal) and twelve 12-foot lengths or equal. There are 80 lineal feet of walls in this example and therefore 240 lineal feet of 2 by 4's are required for the plates. Splices of the two top plates should not be made above one another.

A logical procedure in laying out the stud location on the sole and top plates, is to select the longest wall and cut the sole plate and first top plate to the length of this wall. Mark the location of each stud (16 inches on center) on the edge of the plates. Plate splices, when required, should be made at the center of a stud location, Fig. 28A.

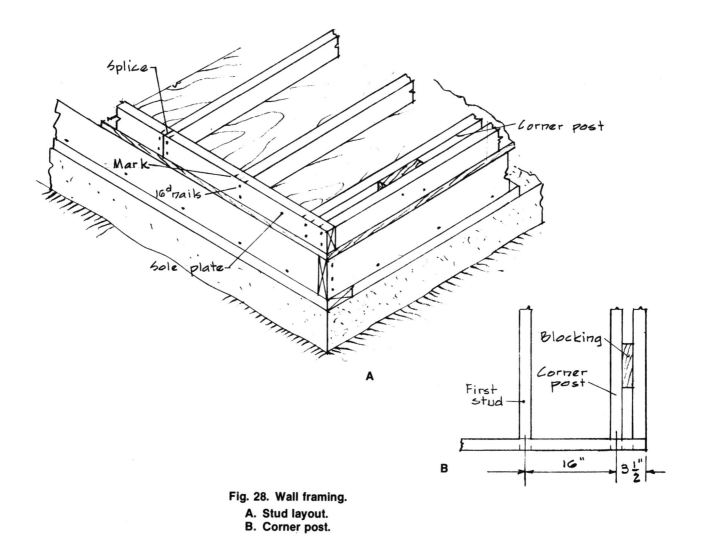

Fig. 28. Wall framing.
A. Stud layout.
B. Corner post.

The corner studs are doubled with several 2- by 4-inch spacer blocks between them. This will provide a nailing surface for the interior finish. The corner posts (as were the headers) can be assembled before erection of the wall and located as shown in Fig. 28B.

Studs are normally cut to a length of about 93 inches when the sole plate and two top plates are $1\frac{1}{2}$ inches thick and when a plastered ceiling and a $\frac{25}{32}$-inch finish floor are planned. Stud length should be about $92\frac{1}{2}$ inches when a $\frac{1}{2}$-inch dry wall ceiling is used and the subfloor is single (consisting of tongued and grooved plywood) without an underlayment for carpeting. This allows the use of full 8-foot lengths of dry wall, or other wall coverings which might be used, without the need for cutting. Similar adjustments should be made for other combinations. Assembly procedure consists of nailing the sole plate and the first top plate to each stud with two sixteen-penny nails, Fig. 28A.

During the marking and layout of the sole and top plates for the studs, windows and doors can also be located. The rough openings (inside stud-to-stud measurement) for windows are normally listed in lumber company catalogs for window and door frames. For example, a double-hung window of 24- by 24-inch glass size (both upper and lower sash have a glass size of 24 in. in width and height) has a rough frame opening width of 2 feet 6 inches and a height of 4 feet $9\frac{3}{4}$ inches. Your building

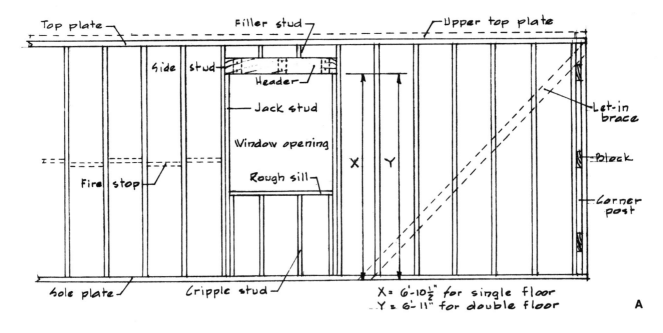

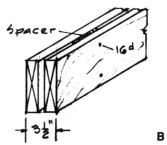

Fig. 29. Wall Layout.
A. Typical wall framing.
B. Window-door header.

supply catalog lists other sizes and normally includes information for all types of windows from casement units to gliding windows. The arrangement of the studs and a header for a window opening is shown in Fig. 29A. The preassembled headers should be 3 inches longer than the width of the rough opening to accommodate the $1\frac{1}{2}$-inch jack studs, Figs. 29A and B. The jack studs are the supporting members for the headers.

Rough opening widths for exterior and interior doors normally comply with the following:

Door Width			Rough Opening Width	
(ft)	(in.)		(ft)	(in.)
2	8	exterior	2	$10\frac{1}{2}$
3	0	exterior	3	$2\frac{1}{2}$
2	6	interior	2	$8\frac{1}{2}$
2	8	interior	2	$10\frac{1}{2}$

This allows sufficient clearance at the sides for leveling and plumbing of the frames.

Note: When wall sheathing or siding does not supply racking resistance, let-in or similar wall bracing is required, Fig. 29A.

Assembly of the framing members around a window opening can proceed as follows after the side studs have been nailed to the plates, Fig. 29A.

1. Nail side studs to header with two sixteenpenny nails (each member). The bottom of the header is located 6 feet 10½ inches or 6 feet 11 inches above the subfloor depending on the type of finish floor, Fig. 29A.
2. Nail through top plate into short filler studs (above header) when used, and toenail edges into header.
3. Cut and nail jack studs to each side stud with tenpenny or twelvepenny nails (space 16 inch on center and stagger).
4. Cut rough window sill to width of opening and cripple studs (studs under sill) to required length.
5. Side nail edge cripple studs to jack studs and toenail intermediate cripples to sole plate while nailing rough sill into top end of each cripple stud.

Procedures 3., 4., and 5. can be done after the wall is erected.

Note: Some codes require the use of fire stops. They normally consist of 2- by 4-inch blocking nailed between studs at midheight, Fig. 29A.

After assembly of the wall framing, the next procedure is to tilt the completed frame in a vertical position, plumb, and brace it with 1 by 6's nailed to a stud and to a 2 by 4 block fastened to the subfloor. While doing this, nail the sole plate into the

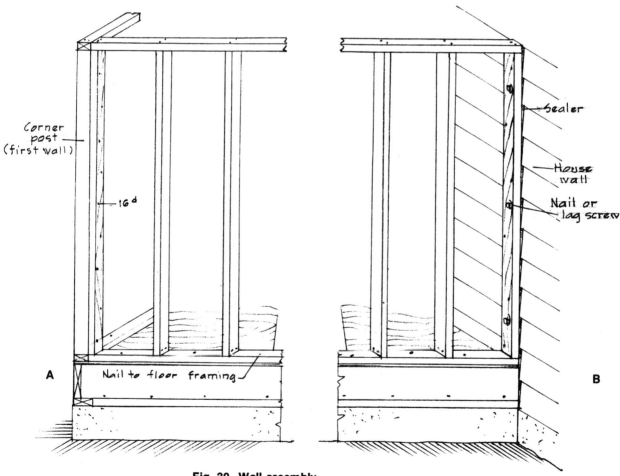

Fig. 30. Wall assembly.
A. To corner post.
B. To house wall.

edge floor member (header, joist, or stringer joist) with sixteenpenny nails spaced 16 inches on center; stagger. When the floor is a concrete slab with anchor bolts around the edge, predrill the sole plate and use a sill sealer between the plate and the concrete, Fig. 18. Under moist conditions, it is good practice to use a treated member for the plate when it is in contact with a concrete slab.

The remaining wall (or walls) can be assembled in the same manner as the first wall. The edge stud for the outside corner and the one against the existing house can be single. The length of this wall is the remaining distance between the house and the inside edge of the raised wall. After completion, this wall can be raised in place and the sole plate nailed to the floor framing as previously described. The edge studs of the joining walls can now be nailed to the corner post of the outside wall, Fig. 30A, and to the house (at an existing stud) with sixteenpenny nails spaced 16 inches apart, Fig. 30B. If there is no stud in the house at the wall location, use lag screws or toggle bolts. The joint against the house should be sealed with a calking or a "sill sealer" pad. An extra stud might be required inside the end stud if a corner board is used for the siding. This stud can be added anytime up to the application of the insulation, Fig. 31A.

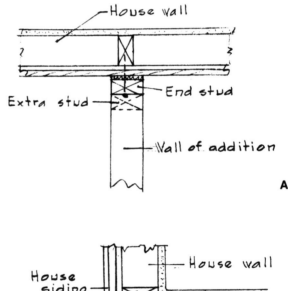

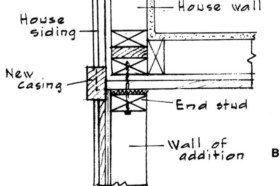

Fig. 31. Plan view of end studs of new addition walls.
A. At house wall.
B. At corner of house.

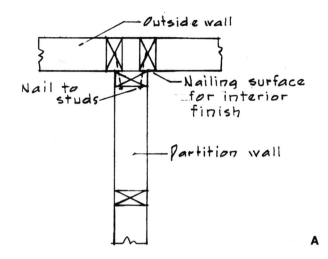

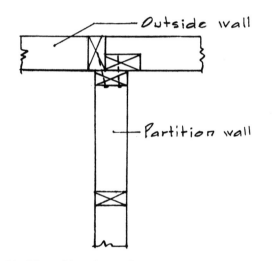

Fig. 32. Plan of interior wall connection to exterior wall.
A. Two edge studs.
B. One edge and one flat stud.

A nailing surface and a termination for the ends of the siding should be made where the new addition joins the outside corner of the existing house. This can be provided by an outside casing. If there are metal corners or nails along the corner of the siding, remove them. Then, with an electric saw and guide, cut vertically only deep enough to remove the siding. Thus after the wall sheathing has been applied to the addition, a casing of 6/4 by 4 inches can be installed, Fig. 31B. The casing serves as a termination for the ends of siding on the house as well as for the siding of the new addition.

If a plumbing wall for a bath is a part of your new addition, 2- by 6-inch studs are normally used to provide space for a cast iron soil vent stack. Some building codes allow the use of 3-inch plastic vent pipe so 2- by 4-inch studs may be satisfactory if the bath is on the first floor. Check your local code or the new houses in your neighborhood.

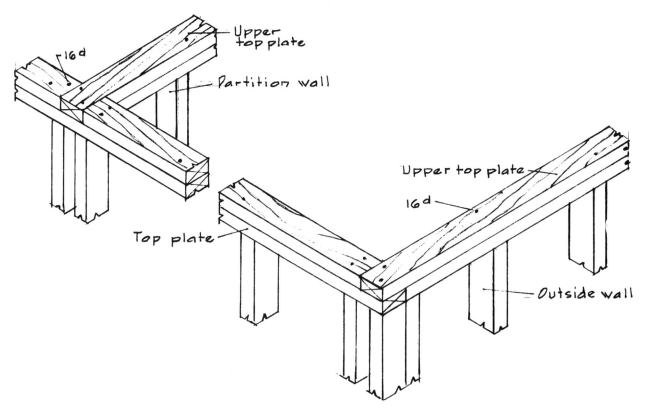

Fig. 33. Installing upper top plates of walls.

Interior partitions can be assembled in the same manner as the outside walls. The edge studs of these walls are nailed to studs of the exterior wall with sixteenpenny nails spaced 16 inches apart. Studs on the outside wall may be arranged as shown in Fig. 32A or 32B. They will also provide nailing surfaces for your interior wall coverings.

The upper top plates can now be cut and nailed to the top plates of the raised walls. These upper 2- by 4-inch plates should cross and be fastened to the adjoining walls at the corners and at the intersections as shown in Fig. 33. Stagger sixteenpenny nails, two at the ends of the plate and one above each stud along the wall. Two may be used at each stud or one extra between if the plate is a little warped. If all details were followed, your new addition should have a strong, plumb, and level wall system. The walls are now ready for the installation of the ceiling joists and rafters.

As a reminder, in assembly and erection of the walls consideration should always be made for heating and other utilities that might affect location of the studs in relation to the joists. For example, if a heat supply duct or a cold air return duct is involved, it is usually more convenient to locate the stud directly above the floor joists or to block around the opening. This is especially true when a cold air register is located on the wall and the space between the joists is used as a return duct, Fig. 34. The plate and subfloor can be cut later for installation of these ducts.

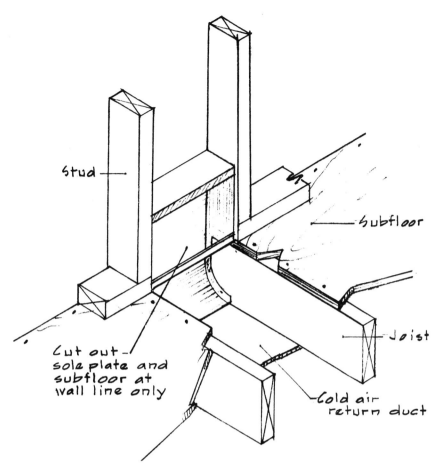

Stud

Subfloor

Joist

Cut out sole plate and subfloor at wall line only

Cold air return duct

Fig. 34. Framing for cold air return duct.

WALL FRAMING IN ATTIC

When expansion is planned for the attic space, assuming the floor joists are adequate and there is sufficient head room, the first requirement is a good subfloor. If there is no subfloor, use $\frac{1}{2}$-inch or thicker plywood or 1-inch boards for 16-inch joist spacing when some type of underlayment might be used over the subfloor. If carpeting or a resilient floor tile is planned, use $\frac{5}{8}$- or $\frac{3}{4}$-inch tongued and grooved plywood over the entire area.

Knee wall heights might be as low as 4 feet for steeply pitched roofs but a 5-foot minimum is more often used. A 2- by 6-inch or 1- by 6-inch member should be used as a top plate against the rafters. Rip one edge to the slope of the roof and nail to each rafter, Fig. 35. Establish the sole plate (use a hand level and board guide from the top plate) and nail the plate to each floor joist below with sixteenpenny nails. Cut the studs to length and toenail to the sole and top plate with eightpenny or ten-

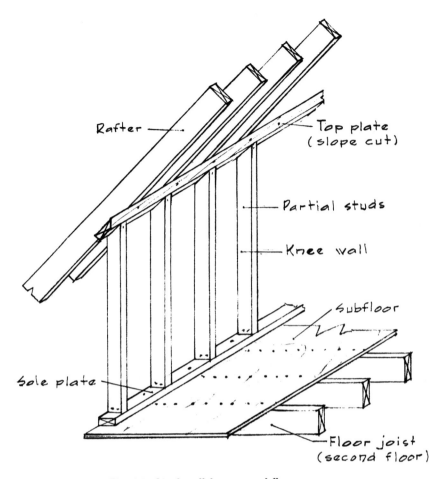

Fig. 35. Stud wall for second floor rooms.

penny nails. Space the studs 16 inches apart under each rafter (assuming the rafters are 16 inches on center).

10
Ceiling and Roof Framing

Under some conditions, there are certain advantages in applying the wall sheathing before ceiling joists and rafters are installed. One instance might be when a single covering of vertical plywood is used. This will serve both as a sheathing and a finish covering material. Wall sheathings, in general, will be covered in the following chapter. Normally, after walls have been erected, plumbed, and braced, the next step is the installation of ceiling joists and rafters (or roof trusses which serve both purposes).

CEILING JOISTS

Ceiling joists, when no rooms or storage are involved in the attic or space above, serve to tie the walls together and to provide nailing surfaces for the ceiling covering material. When serving as floor joists for rooms above, they must also carry the floor loads and are designed as floor joists rather than ceiling joists.

TABLE 8. Guide for selecting ceiling joist sizes[a]
(With *no* attic storage, 10 lb/sq ft total load.)

Species and Grade	Nominal Size (in.)	Ceiling Joist Spacing (in.)		
		12	16	24
Southern pine,	2 × 4	10'-10"	9'-10"	8'-7"
No. 2 grade	2 × 6	17'-0"	15'-6"	13'-6"
(or equal)[b]	2 × 8	22'-5"	20'-5"	17'-10"

[a] From Southern Pine Technical Bulletin of span tables.
[b] Equivalent grades in Douglas fir, larch, etc.

Table 8 can be used as a guide in selecting the size of your ceiling joists under a variety of spans and spacings. These allowable spans for the various sizes are based on *no* attic storage under average conditions. Again, check your local building requirements. If storage is contemplated for the area above, larger sizes should be used. Normally, provision should be made for access to the attic by means of a scuttle or an attic folding stair. Rough opening for an attic folding stair is about 26 by 54 inches.

Ceiling joists are toenailed to the top plates of exterior and interior walls with tenpenny or twelvepenny nails, Fig. 36. However, if splitting occurs, use two eightpenny nails at each side. Joists may be lapped or butt joined at center portions, Fig. 36. When butt joined, use a 1- by 4-inch scab well nailed to each joist with tenpenny nails. When joists are lapped, they should be nailed to the plates and to each other

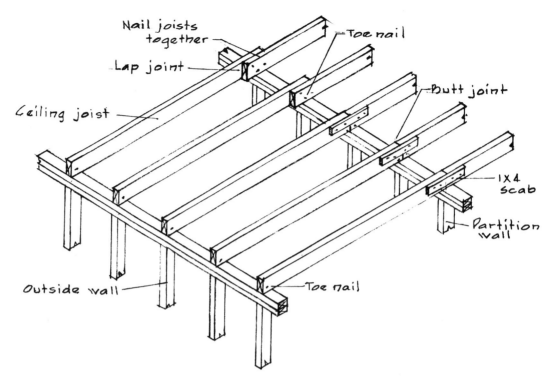

Fig. 36. Ceiling joist installation.

with a minimum of four twelvepenny nails (two on each side). This fastening is important because the ceiling joists serve as continuous ties between opposite walls. The joists along the existing house should also be nailed to the house wall where house studs (or top plates) occur. The ceiling joist along an outer wall should be located on the inner edge of the wall plate to provide a nailing surface for the ceiling covering material. Joists along a parallel wall should also be located to provide for such nailing, Fig. 37A.

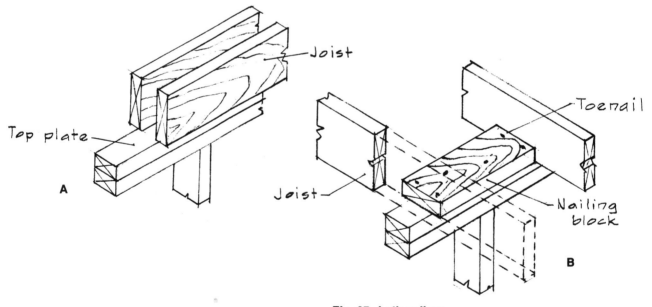

Fig. 37. Lath nailers.
A. Joists at wall plate.
B. Blocking.

Lath Nailers

So-called "lath nailers" or "lath catchers" are members (sometimes the joists themselves) which provide nailing surfaces for the ceiling finish. They can consist of an extra joist, Fig. 37A, or blocking between the joists, Fig. 37B. When blocking is used, it should be well toenailed to the plate and joists to prevent loosening when the inside finish is being applied.

Flush Ceiling Framing

It might be desirable in your design, when the width of your addition is greater than 15 to 16 feet or consists of several rooms, to have a flush ceiling over a portion of the area. Wood trusses span the entire width of an area allowing the use of nonload-bearing walls at any location. However, if a conventional joist and rafter system is used, wood joist hangers can be fastened to a beam by several methods. One such method is shown in Fig. 38. A beam, solid or laminated, of proper size is toenailed to the top plates of two load-bearing walls. Table 3 can be used as a guide for a beam size, but would be somewhat overdesigned. Joists are cut to the proper length and toenailed to the beam with eightpenny or tenpenny nails. Now nail a perforated strap across the top of each joist to provide a continuous tie to outside walls, Fig. 38.

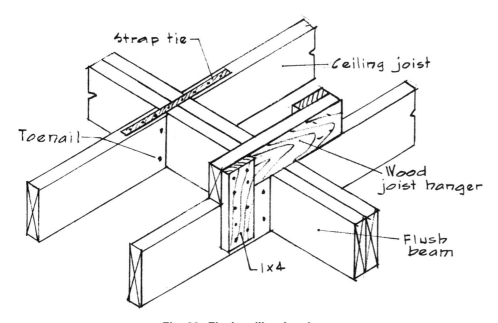

Fig. 38. Flush ceiling framing.

Supporting hangers (previously nailed together) made of a 2- by 4-inch horizontal member and two 1- by 4-inch upright members, is used at each joist location, Fig. 38. Nail the 1 by 4's to the joists with four to six eightpenny nails. Spans of the beams for such construction is usually no more than 8 to 10 feet.

Ceiling Joists for Attic Bedrooms

Remodeling of existing attic spaces for bedrooms may be such that only one-half of the area above the floor requires ceiling joists. In such cases, the sloped rafters of the roof serve as nailing surfaces for ceiling and wall finishes. For moderate spans, 2- by 4-inch ceiling joists may be large enough as shown in Table 8. Longer spans normally require 2- by 6-inch members or closer spacing.

Ceiling joists should be nailed to the rafters with two or three twelvepenny nails at each end. In order to have a level ceiling, it is often convenient to use a 2- by 4-inch upright with a "T" top to support and level the ceiling joists while nailing, Fig.

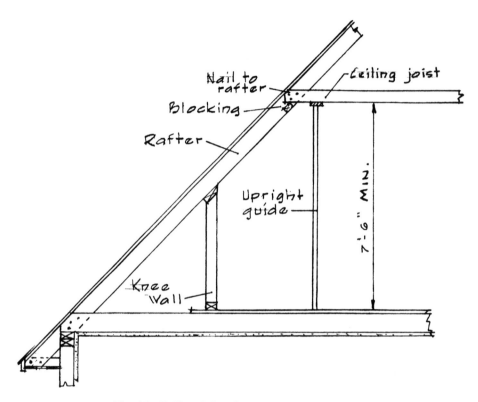

Fig. 39. Ceiling joists for second floor rooms.

39. To provide a nailing edge for the finish covering material at the top of the sloped wall, 2- by 4-inch blocking should be cut between and toenailed to the rafters, Fig. 39. Blocking may also be used between the ceiling joists if necessary.

TABLE 9. Guide for selecting rafter sizes[a]
(High slope rafters, over 3 in 12, with 30 lb/sq ft of light roofing.)

Species and Grade	Nominal Size (in.)	Rafter Spacing (in.)		
		12	16	24
Southern pine,	2 X 4	9'-5"	8'-2"	6'-8"
No. 2 grade	2 X 6	13'-9"	11'-11"	9'-8"
(or equal)[b]	2 X 8	18'-1"	15'-8"	12'-9"

[a] From Southern Pine Technical Bulletin of span tables.
[b] Equivalent grades in Douglas fir, larch, etc.
Note: For areas of very high snow loads, reduce allowable spans accordingly.

RAFTER FRAMING

Rafters for your additions are normally spaced the same as the ceiling joists as they are nailed to these members as well as to the wall plates. The required size, as were the floor and ceiling joists, is based on the species, span, and spacing. In areas where no snow loads need to be considered, the sizes are usually less than those used in the snow belt areas. Table 9 shows allowable spans which can be used as a guide in selecting your rafter sizes. Here again, check your local building regulations. The sizes are based on the clear horizontal distance (span) from the wall to the ridge board; normally one-half the width of the house.

Rafter Marking and Cutting

Rafters should be joined at the ridge with a ridge board (ridge pole) for a better fastening area and a level ridge line. The ridge board is usually 2 inches wider than the rafters for sloped roofs, i.e., 8 inches for 2- by 6-inch rafters. Ridge boards can be nominal 1-inch- or 2-inch-thick members.

One method for marking the rafter cuts at the ridge and at the outside wall is shown in Fig. 40. The floor can be used as a layout "table." Place the rafter flat to

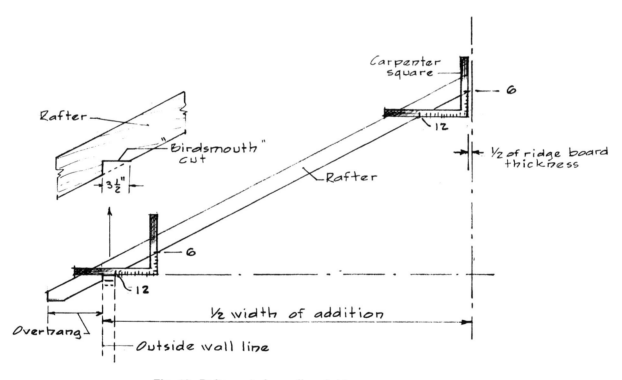

Fig. 40. Rafter cuts for wall and ridge.

equal the roof slope; i.e., 6-foot rise for a 6/12 slope and a 24-foot-wide addition. A carpenter square is used for marking cuts; they usually have a 16-inch-long leg and a 24-inch leg. If the slope of the roof is 6/12, for example, place the bottom edge of the square at 6 (inch markings) and at 12 and mark as shown in Fig. 40. The marking for the cut (birdsmouth) over the outside wall is made in the same manner as shown. The horizontal distance for this "birdsmouth" cut should usually be the width of the studs and top plates, normally $3\frac{1}{2}$ inches. Thus the clear horizontal distance (span) is the distance from the inner wall to the center of the building less one-half the ridge board thickness. The overhang can be any amount, usually up to 24 or 30 inches, depending on the type of soffit planned.

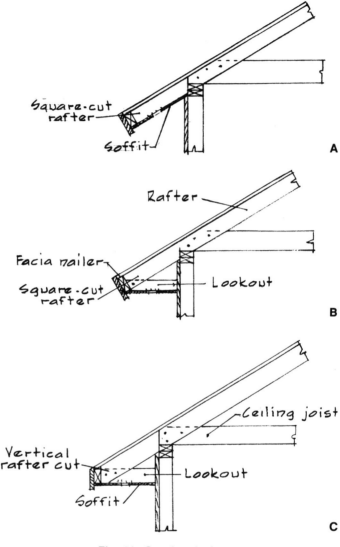

Fig. 41. Cornice designs.
A. Without lookout.
B. Square-cut rafter end.
C. Vertical rafter end cut.

The ends of the rafters may be cut and finished as shown in Fig. 41A, B, and C. In Fig. 41A the rafters are square cut and the soffit finish (when used) is nailed to the underside of the rafters. Figures 41B and C show horizontal blocking (lookouts) from the rafter to the wall which provides nailing areas for the soffit finish. Cornices with the horizontal lookouts are normally used on hip roofed houses. The ends of the rafters are terminated with a 2- by 4-inch facia-nailer nailed to the end of each rafter with two sixteenpenny nails unless the facia itself is $1\frac{1}{8}$ inches or more in thickness. This usually eliminates the need for a nailing backer.

Nailing of Rafters

Erection and nailing of rafters *can* be accomplished by one person *if* the ridge board is placed and braced beforehand. It is much more practical, however, to assemble these members with two workers. When a nominal 1-inch-thick ridge board is used, nail the ridge board to the top end of the rafter with two or three tenpenny or twelvepenny nails. When a 2-inch ridge board is used, nail with two or three sixteenpenny nails, Fig. 42A. The opposite rafter should then be toenailed to the ridge board and

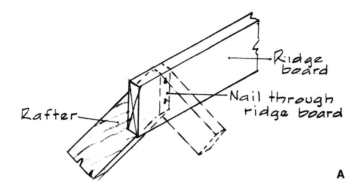

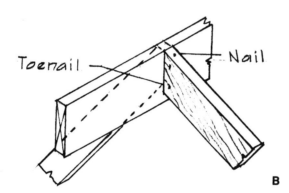

Fig. 42. Rafter nailing at ridge board.
A. First rafter.
B. Second rafter.

the first rafter with two tenpenny or twelvepenny nails on each side. A sixteenpenny nail can also be used at the top edge of the joist, Fig. 42B. Now toenail the bottom of the rafter into the top plate of the wall with two tenpenny nails, Fig. 43. This is usually done by the second worker while the first nails the rafters at the ridge. Be sure that the rafter notch is tight against the outside of the wall and the rafter is snug against the ceiling joist. Next nail the rafter to the ceiling joist with two or three twelvepenny nails on each side. The number used depends on the amount of nailing area. Low slopes present a greater nailing area and also require better nailing. Remember, in toenailing don't split the member. Either use shorter nails or start the nail slightly higher up from the bottom.

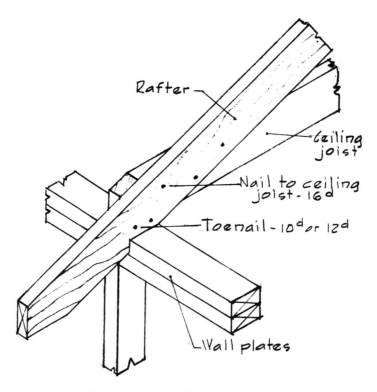

Fig. 43. Rafter nailing at outside wall.

Rafters to Wall (of Existing House)

Before the near rafters (that pair next to the house wall) are fastened in place, a strip of the siding can be removed along the slope of the new roof line, Fig. 44. This will provide an area for placement of the flashing when the shingles are installed. The following sequence can be used:

1. Level across from the adjacent rafters for the cutting lines.
2. Use a guide board for your portable electric saw.
3. Remove any siding nails which might be in the way.
4. Cut only through the siding.

A clearance of $1\frac{1}{2}$ to $1\frac{3}{4}$ inches above the top of the rafter is desirable.

This removal of the siding can be eliminated by using large size flashings (under the siding edges) which serve several shingle courses rather than the 5- by 7-inch standard shingle flashing.

The rafters can be fastened to the house wall with 5-inch (fortypenny) spikes nailing only into the studs of the house, Fig. 44. A lag screw might be used in place of a spike.

Collar Beams

Collar beams are used to provide ties between opposing rafters, Fig. 45. They are most often used for low roof slopes when the rafter spans are long. Use a 1- by 6-inch member and nail to the rafter with two to four eightpenny or tenpenny nails.

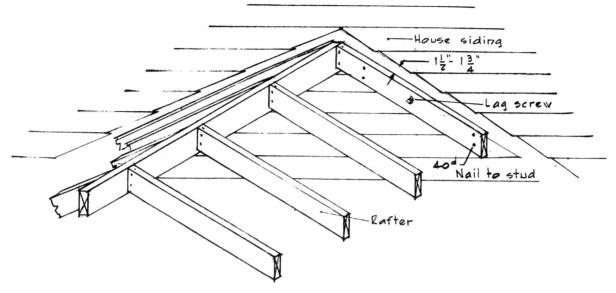

Fig. 44. Fastening rafter to house wall.

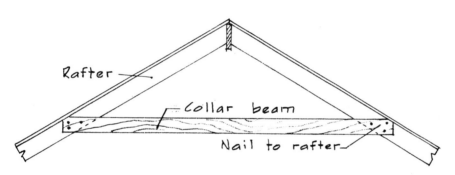

Fig. 45. Collar beam-nailing to rafters.

Collar beams are usually placed on every second or third pair of rafters. In steep roofs when rooms are planned, use 2 by 4's at every rafter. They thus serve as ceiling joists.

Valleys (Connection to Roof of House)

The roof line of the new addition, in many designs, intersects the roof of the existing house forming valleys such as shown in Fig. 5. In such cases, the end of the ridge board is cut at a slope and extends to the roof line of the house. A 1- by 8-inch valley board can be nailed to the roof (at rafters) along the roof slope at the valley, Fig. 46A. This valley board also provides good nailing for the short rafters as it is nailed securely to the rafters of the house. The valley board might be eliminated if roof boards are 1 inch thick. These short rafters, which extend from the ridge board to the roof line, are called jack rafters. They should be cut to fit the ridge board of the addition (at the top) with a double slope cut at the bottom, Fig. 46B and C. Toenail the jack rafters to the ridge board with two eightpenny or tenpenny nails on each side. The bottom of the jack rafters should be toenailed to the valley board and roof boards with tenpenny or twelvepenny nails. Later, when applying the shingles to the new roof, a strip of shingles along the valley can be cut and removed to make room for the valley flashing, Fig. 46A.

Hip Rafters

If a hip roof is part of the design in your new addition, the last full set of rafters should end at a point one-half of the width of the addition from the end, Fig. 47A. Hip rafters are cut and nailed to the ridge-rafter connection and to the top plates at the corner, Fig. 47B. Jack rafters are toenailed to the hip rafters at the top and at the bottom to the top plate of the wall. Use tenpenny or twelvepenny nails. Jack rafters are also nailed to the adjoining ceiling joists where they occur as shown in Fig. 43.

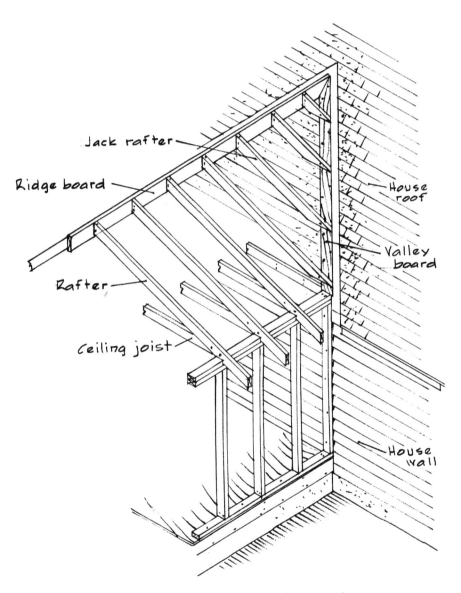

Fig. 46. Rafter connection to house roof.
A. Overall view.

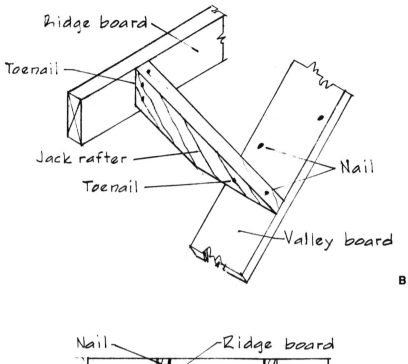

B

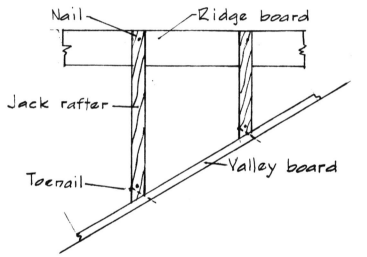

C

Fig. 46. Rafter connection to house roof (*cont'd*).
B. Isometric view.
C. Front view.

GABLE END STUDS

The gable end walls of your addition can be fabricated in two general ways. If a short (about 8 to 12 inches) roof overhang is planned, the extension of the roof sheathing provides ample strength to support the framing and trim. When a wider extension (ladder framing) is desired, 2 by 4's are used from the first inside rafter to beyond the end wall. They bear on a flat top plate.

Normal Framing

After the end pair of rafters are installed at the end wall plate, Fig. 48, end wall studs are cut. End studs, spaced 16 inches on center, are now toenailed to the plate

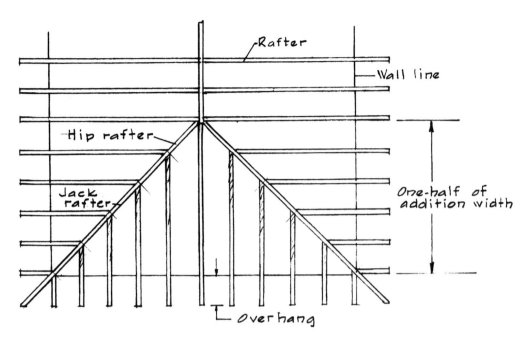

A

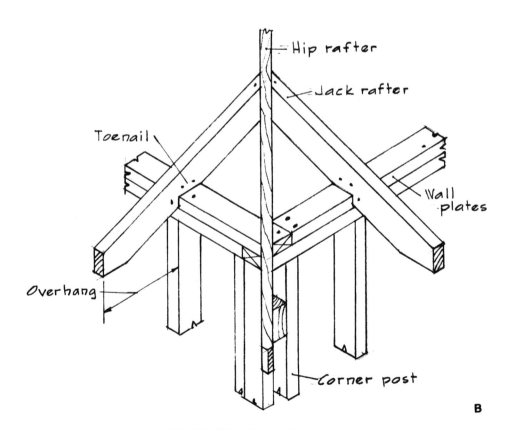

B

Fig. 47. Hip rafter roof.
A. Plan layout.
B. Detail at corner.

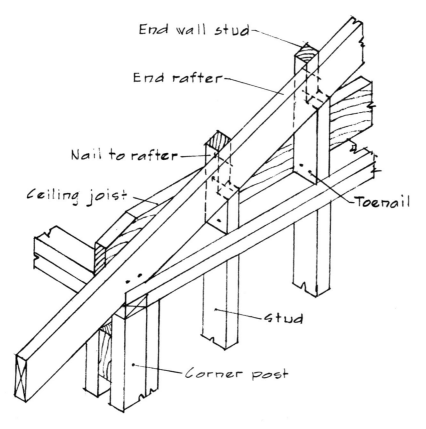

Fig. 48. End wall studs.

with eightpenny or tenpenny nails and face-nailed at the top to the rafter with twelvepenny nails.

Ladder Framing

"Ladder" framing is normally used for wide gable extensions. The end wall is constructed with a single flat top plate as shown in Fig. 49. The top of this plate should be lower than the top of the adjacent rafters a distance equal to the depth of a 2 by 4, usually $3\frac{1}{2}$ inches. The 2- by 4-inch members for the end overhang are toenailed to the 2- by 6-inch rafter and to the top wall plate, Fig. 49. Nail a 2- by 4-inch fly rafter (a backup nailer) at the outside ends of extended 2 by 4's with sixteenpenny nails. The fly rafter and the facia-nailer of the cornice should be nailed to each other, Fig. 49. As an alternate, a diagonal member from the rafter to the wall plate and to the junction of the backup nailers can be used, Fig. 49.

DORMER FRAMING

Shed Dormer

The construction of a dormer in the attic space of your house may be a part of your remodeling plan. This will not only provide more usable floor space, but also more wall space for additional windows. As previously outlined, the greatest increase in floor and window space is provided by the shed dormer. However, because of its undesirable appearance, it is best that it be located to the rear of the house. When a

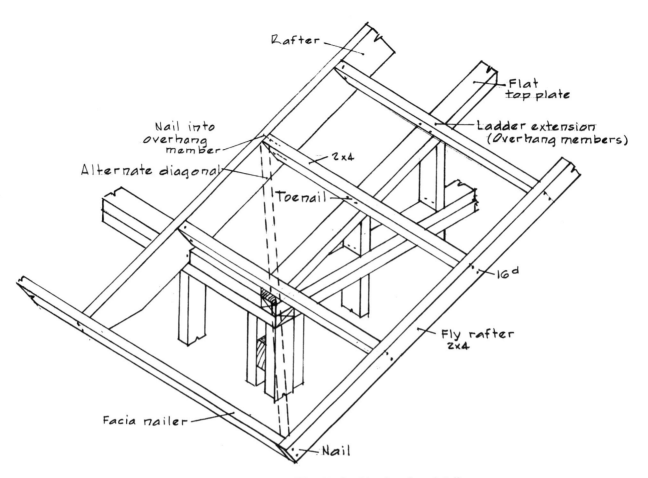

Rafter

Flat top plate

Ladder extension (Overhang members)

Nail into overhang member

2 x 4

Alternate diagonal

Toenail

16 d

Fly rafter 2 x 4

Facia nailer

Nail

Fig. 49. Ladder framing detail.

shed dormer is selected, a portion of the original slope of the roof should be retained. This means that the short side walls of the dormer be at the second or third rafter location, Fig. 50A. This will retain a portion of the roof at its original slope. However, if the sides of the dormer wall do coincide with the end wall of the house, the original gable molding at least should be retained for a somewhat better appearance.

Perhaps the simplest method of adding a shed dormer is to first erect a long end wall parallel to the length of the house. This will serve as a bearing wall for the new low slope rafters. Remove the roofing and sheathing under the proposed dormer. Add subfloor, if not present, to serve as a base for the sole plate. Remove enough existing rafters for fabrication of the wall. It is good practice to brace the ridge with extra members while this wall is being erected. Studs of the long wall can also be nailed to the ends of the existing rafters at the bottom of the wall after erection and before trimming the ends, Fig. 50B.

The slope of the new roof is normally governed by the needed head room at the outside wall and the height of the ridge. The top of this outside wall, however, should be high enough to allow a window rough framing height of about 6 feet 7 inches. This may mean a top plate height of about 7 feet 0 inch above the subfloor. You should strive for a shed dormer roof slope of *not less* than 2 to $2\frac{1}{2}$ in 12. This will allow the use of conventional asphalt shingles with doubled asphalt felt underlayment.

The short (side) walls can be erected over a sole plate in the same manner as the outside wall of the addition. Place the studs alongside a rafter, Fig. 50B. Studs can also be placed on a doubled rafter at each side wall of the dormer. In any case, *never*

68

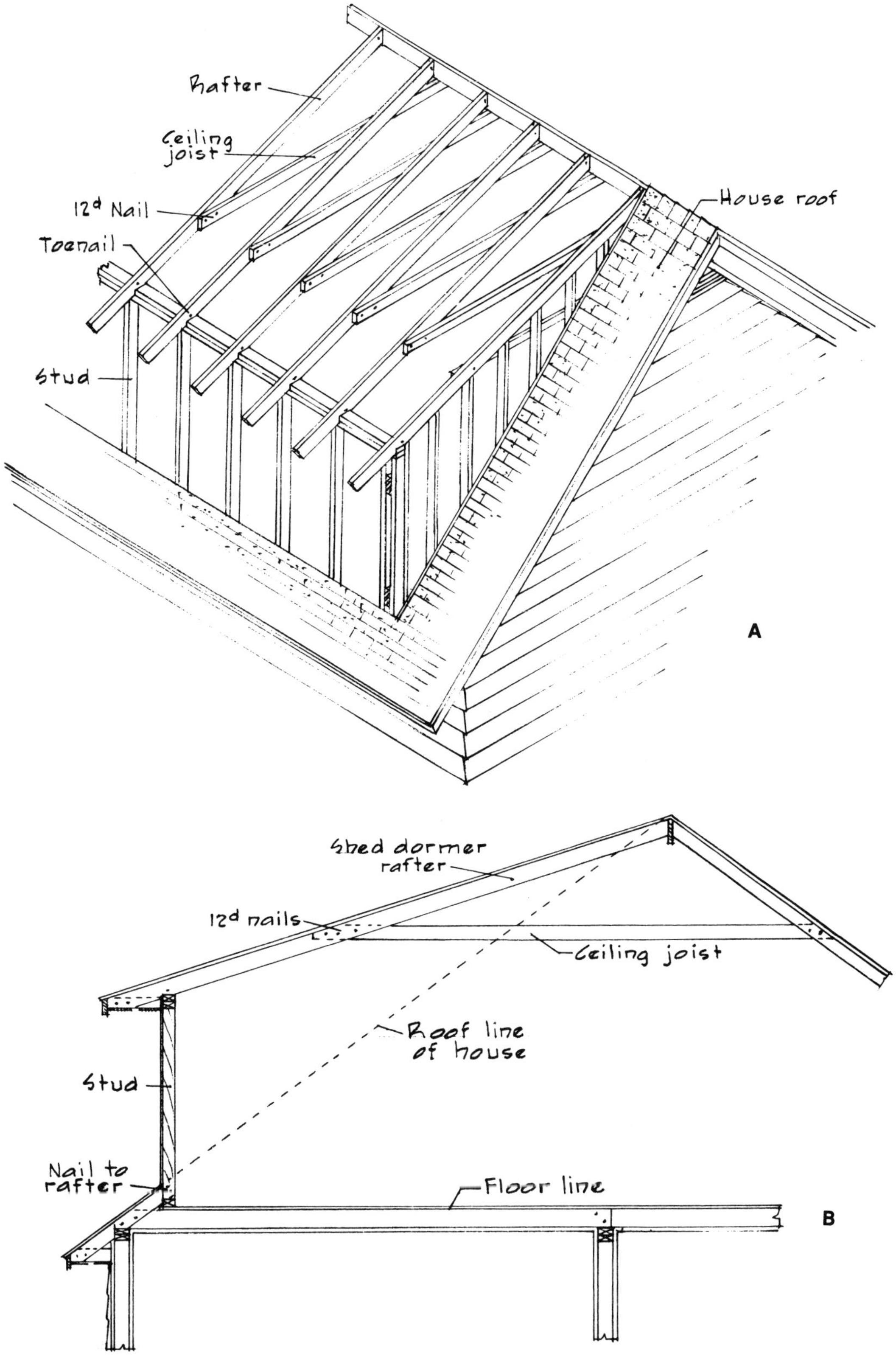
Rafter
Ceiling joist
12d Nail
Toenail
Stud
House roof
A
Shed dormer rafter
12d nails
Ceiling joist
Roof line of house
Stud
Nail to rafter
Floor line
B

Fig. 50. Shed roof addition.

A. Overall view.
B. Section detail.

remove all the existing rafters until the new roof framing is completed. The one exception would be the erection of a well braced temporary wall supporting the ridge and the rafters of the opposite side of the house.

Ceiling joists should be not less than 7 feet 6 inches above the floor to comply with most building codes. They are nailed to each rafter of the new dormer and its opposing rafter of the opposite slope with sixteenpenny nails, Fig. 50B. Windows are framed in the same manner as described in the Chapter "Wall Framing." Any remodeling of this type, of course, will likely require some type of covering for protection in inclement weather.

Window Dormers

Window dormers are small gabled extensions on moderate to steeply sloped roofs which provide a window area. They may have a simple shed roof or a gabled roof. If such dormers are added to your existing house, they should be located to provide a pleasing appearance. This can be done when two are used by placing them at equal distance from each end, Fig. 4. This placement depends, of course, to a great extent on the type and size of the rooms planned for the attic space.

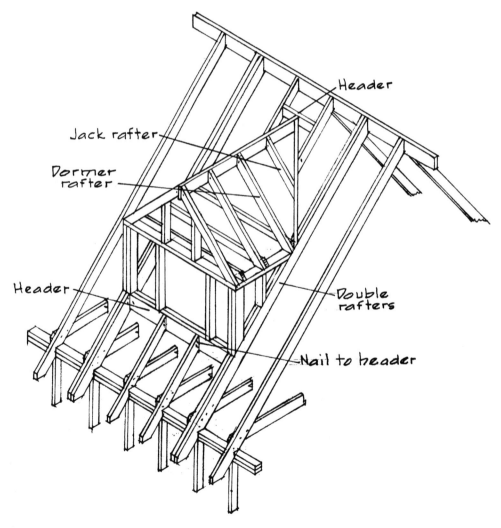

Fig. 51. Window dormer framing.

Window dormers can be constructed in a manner similar to the shed dormer with studs extending down to a plate on the subfloor, Fig. 50A and B. Side and end wall studs are thus nailed to an adjoining rafter at the side walls and to the lower ends of the rafters at the end (window) wall. The window dormer can also be constructed as follows:

1. Studs on the window wall can bear on a header fastened between doubled side rafters, Fig. 51.
2. Studs on the side can bear on the doubled rafters.
3. After installing top plates on the dormer, ceiling joists and rafters can be installed, Fig. 51. If the span is not too great, ceiling joists can be used from the opposite rafters to the top plate of the window wall.

For each of the two systems, use a small header fastened between two rafters of the existing house to serve as a fastening member for the ridge pole and the short jack rafters, Fig. 51. Toenail them in place with tenpenny or twelvepenny nails. For best appearance, the ceiling joists of the room proper should be the same elevation as the ceiling joists of the small dormers. This will result in a level ceiling for an easily applied finish whether dry wall or other material is used.

LIGHTWEIGHT WOOD ROOF TRUSSES

The simple wood truss or trussed rafter is a framework of wood members which serve as ceiling joists and rafters. One of the more common types is the "W" truss,

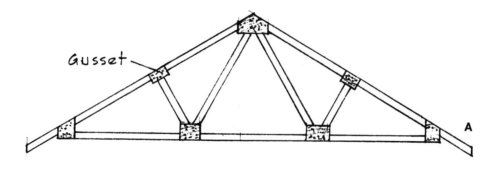

Fig. 52. Wood roof trusses (trussed rafters).
A. "W" truss.
B. "Scissor" truss.

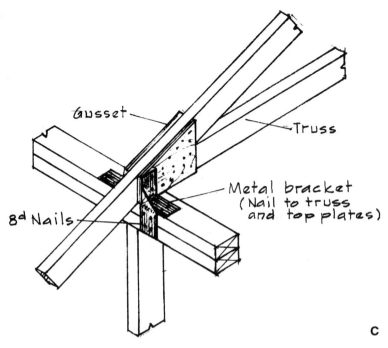

Fig. 52. Wood roof truss *(cont'd)*.
C. Fastening at wall.

Fig. 52A. Another type which is often used for a "cathedral ceiling" atmosphere is the "Scissor" truss, Fig. 52B. Trusses of these types, normally designed for spans of 20 to 32 feet, are made of 2 by 4's in the higher grades and species similar to those used for rafters. Trusses are normally spaced 24 inches on center and provide a clear span across the width of the house without the need for center supports. They can be obtained at most of the larger lumber companies and their use might be considered for your addition.

The majority of these trusses are fabricated with pronged metal plates used on each side of each joint. They can also be made with plywood gusset plates which are fabricated with adhesives. Nails are used to fasten the plywood at each joint.

The fastening of the truss to the outside walls is important to resist wind and snow loads. Toenailing the truss to the top plate is usually not enough for a rigid joint. The metal plate or the plywood gusset usually does not supply enough nailing area for this toenailing. Thus some type of extra fastening is desirable. One fastener which provides this feature is a metal bracket, Fig. 52C. This provides fastening to the truss, the side of the plate, and the top of the top plates. After erection, trusses are kept in alignment by temporary roof boards nailed across them with proper spacing (24 inches on center). These boards are removed as the roof sheathing is nailed in place.

POST AND BEAM CONSTRUCTION

Post and beam construction in its simplest form consists of spaced beams supported by posts. It is often used in contemporary designs usually with flat or low-slope roofs. Posts can be fastened to the floor plate and to the beam with metal angles or clips, Fig. 53A. Roof coverings can consist of 2- by 6-inch or 3- by 6-inch V-beaded wood decking which spans between the beams. The decking also serves as a ceiling finish. Conventional ceiling joists can also be used between beams. In post and beam

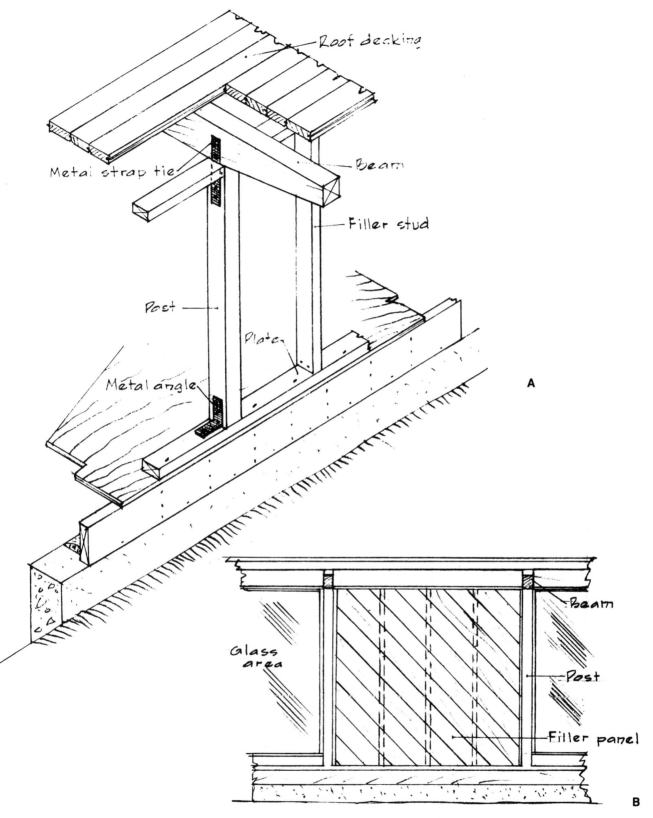

Fig. 53. Post and beam construction.
A. Post and beam connections.
B. Filler panel with large glass areas.

construction, wall spaces between posts can consist of large glass areas in combination with conventional wall sections, Fig. 53B. These sheathed sections provide racking resistance required for this type construction.

WOOD DECK ROOF DESIGNS

Other roof designs using wood decking for flat to low-slope roofs involve the use of a heavy ridge beam or a full-height center wall. This can consist of a large solid or

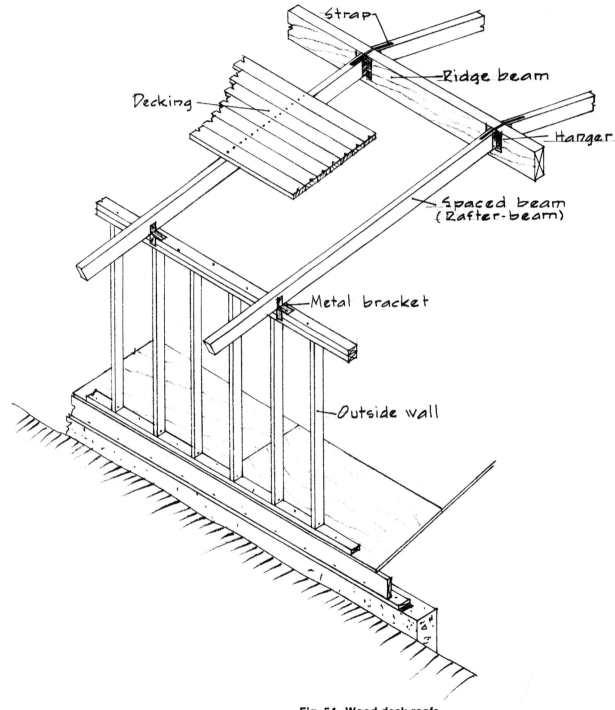

Fig. 54. Wood deck roofs.
A. Rafter-beam.

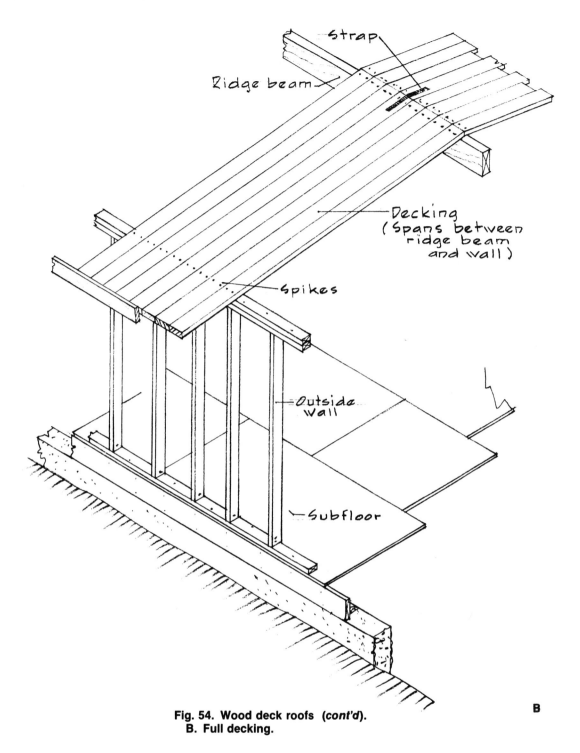

Fig. 54. Wood deck roofs (cont'd).
B. Full decking.

laminated ridge beam with spaced beams spanning between the ridge beam and the exterior wall, Fig. 54A. Depending on the spacing of these "rafter-beams," roof sheathing may consist of:

1. Nominal 1-inch tongued and grooved V-beaded boards for close beam spacing, and
2. 2- by 6- or 3- by 6-inch wood decking, or built-up insulated sheathing for wider spacings.

Another system of construction consists of a center ridge beam or a center partition wall which, with the outside wall, provides bearing for wood decking, Fig. 54B. For normal spans, 3- by 6-inch wood decking is ordinarily used and extends between the ridge beam and outer walls.

Fastenings

The rafter-beams should be fastened to the ridge beam with heavy double joist hangers or angle iron and to the outside wall with metal clips in addition to nailing, Fig. 54A. When wood decking is used from the ridge beam to the outside wall, fasten the decking with fortypenny or fiftypenny spikes. Use two spikes for each member at the wall and the ridge. A metal strap across the rafter-beams and on opposing wood deck boards will provide excellent ties between opposite walls, Figs. 54A and B.

11
Wall Sheathing

Wall sheathing is the outside covering used over the wall studs. It can also serve as a means of providing great rigidity to the walls when the material and application are so designed. When panel plywood siding is used and applied vertically in 4- by 8-foot or longer sheets, there is normally no need for sheathing as it serves both as sheathing and siding. In some area of the South, horizontal or similar siding is applied to the studs over a waterproof paper underlay. In such cases, let-in braces must be used to provide rigidity for the walls. These 1- by 4-inch members are applied diagonally to notches cut into the studs, Fig. 29A.

LUMBER SHEATHING

Wood sheathing consisting of nominal 1-inch boards of various widths is not often used in most areas of the country because of the ease of application of several types of sheet materials. Wood boards applied horizontally require let-in or similar braces to provide rigidity. Diagonally applied boards provide great strength and racking resistance but are more difficult to apply. When nailing, use two eightpenny nails at each stud for widths to 6 inches and three nails for 8-inch and wider boards.

PLYWOOD SHEATHING

Plywood sheathing in 4- by 8-foot and longer sheets should be applied vertically, Fig. 55A. Use sixpenny or sevenpenny nails spaced 6 inches apart along the edges and 12 inches apart at interior studs for $\frac{3}{8}$-inch plywood. When studs are spaced more than 16 inches on center, $\frac{1}{2}$-inch plywood is normally used. Use eightpenny nails for $\frac{1}{2}$-inch and thicker plywood with the same nail spacing. A C-D exterior grade or any interior grade with exterior glue is commonly used. Depending on the location of the sole plate with respect to edge of the floor framing, the plywood starts at the subfloor, Fig. 55B, or at the top of the foundation wall, Fig. 55C. Plywood or other sheathing carried from the bottom of the floor framing to the top plates provides a very rigid tie. This may be desirable in areas of high winds. However, longer sheets of plywood are required for this method, slightly increasing material costs. Vertical joints should always be made at the center of a stud. Space nails 6 inches apart around all window and door openings.

STRUCTURAL INSULATING BOARD

Vertical application of structural insulating board in 4 by 8 foot or longer sheets is usually recommended by the manufacturer because perimeter nailing is possible. Depending on local building regulations, spacing nails 3 inches on edges and 6 inches at

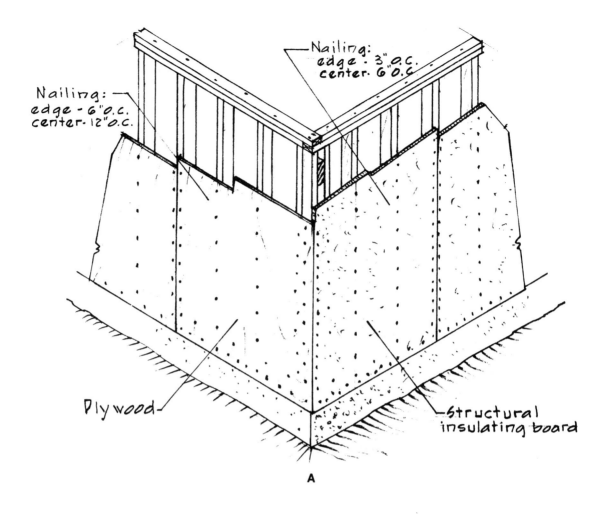

Nailing:
edge - 6" o.c.
center - 12" o.c.

Nailing:
edge - 3" o.c.
center - 6" o.c.

Plywood

Structural insulating board

A

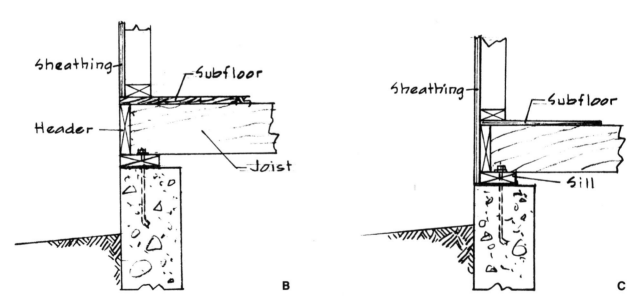

Sheathing

Subfloor

Header

Joist

B

Sheathing

Subfloor

Sill

C

Fig. 55. Wall sheathing.

A. Sheathing types commonly used.
B. Sheathing to subfloor.
C. Sheathing to foundation.

intermediate studs usually eliminates the need for corner bracing, Fig. 55A. This applies to $\frac{25}{32}$-inch structural insulating board sheathing or $\frac{1}{2}$-inch medium density structural insulating board. Use $1\frac{1}{2}$-inch roofing nails for the $\frac{1}{2}$-inch board and $1\frac{3}{4}$-inch roofing nails for the $\frac{25}{32}$-inch board.

MISCELLANEOUS SHEATHINGS

Gypsum sheathing in 4- by 8- and 4- by 9-foot sheets is also used for sheathing. It can be obtained in $\frac{1}{2}$-inch and $\frac{25}{32}$-inch thickness. Some building codes may allow the use of $\frac{25}{32}$-inch-thick sheets applied vertically without bracing at the corners. Check the regulation in your area if this material suits your needs. Use roofing nails for nailing these materials.

Gypsum sheathing and also insulating board can be obtained in 2- by 8-foot sheets. It is normally applied horizontally and thus would require some type of corner bracing.

Styrofoam and similar sheet foam insulating materials are being used for sheathing in many areas because of their good insulating properties. They can be obtained in $\frac{1}{2}$ and 1-inch thicknesses in 4- by 8-foot sheets. However, as previously indicated, many such materials are resistant to the movement of water vapor (closed cells). Thus, when such materials are used it is wise to use a very good vapor barrier on the inner face of all exposed walls. The barrier should be applied properly covering all inner surfaces. Corner bracing is mandatory when styrofoam and similar materials are used. While these materials have good insulating qualities, they do not eliminate the use of flexible insulation between the studs!

SHEATHING PAPER

Sheathing paper should normally be used over wood board sheathing and is also recommended when plywood panel siding is used without sheathing. Sheathing paper should be water resistant but not vapor resistant. Materials such as 15-pound asphalt felt or similar papers are normally used. Sheathing paper not only provides resistance to moisture entry but also reduces air infiltration, preventing drafts. Apply it horizontally with "shingle style" lap joints.

12

Roof Sheathing

Roof sheathing is normally applied after the wall sheathing has been installed. In sloped roofs where roof coverings consist of asphalt or wood shingles or shakes, the sheathing should be thick enough to hold the shingle nails or roofing nails. One-inch wood boards provide this thickness. In many areas $\frac{3}{8}$-inch-thick plywood is allowed for 16-inch spaced rafters. However, $\frac{1}{2}$-inch plywood provides better holding power for the nails. When $\frac{3}{8}$-inch plywood is used it is advisable to use ring-shank nails for the roofing.

LUMBER SHEATHING

Lumber sheathing of nominal 1-inch thickness (square edge, tongued and grooved or shiplapped) is usually adequate for rafter spacing of 16 to 24 inches. Use two eight-penny nails for 6-inch and narrower boards and three for 8-inch boards at each rafter. Boards wider than 8 inches can shrink and cause a rippled appearance when asphalt shingles are used. Boards are normally nailed with tight joints, Fig. 56. How-

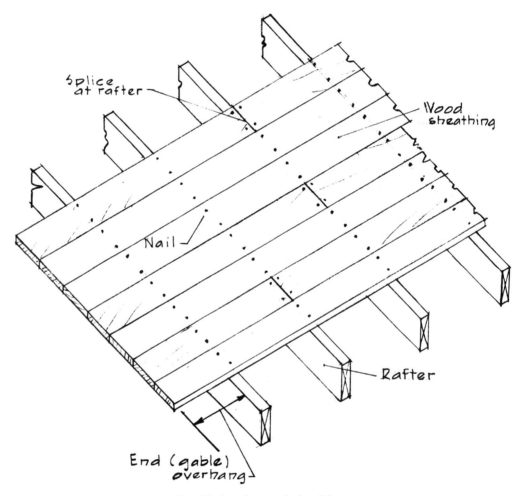

Fig. 56. Lumber roof sheathing.

ever, in damp climates they are often spaced for better ventilation. This usually applies to wood shingles or shakes. For example, if shingles are laid with a 5-inch exposure, 1- by 3- or 1- by 4-inch boards are spaced 5 inches on center so that nails occur at the center of these spaced boards. End joints should be made at the center of a rafter. Lumber sheathing can usually project 12 to 16 inches beyond the end walls without framing to provide a wide gable end overhang. Wide overhangs protect the end walls from the weather and furthermore have a better appearance for most house designs. Some contemporary designs use little or no rake projection. It is good practice to have the gable design of your addition conform to those on the existing house.

PLYWOOD SHEATHING

Plywood in 4- by 8-foot or longer sheets is laid with the face grain perpendicular to the rafters. A C-D exterior grade or interior grade with exterior glue can be used for roof sheathing and provides resistance to wetting without delamination. A sixpenny common nail is used for $\frac{3}{8}$-inch-thick plywood and an eightpenny common nail is normally used for $\frac{1}{2}$-inch and thicker plywood. All joints should be made over a rafter, Fig. 57. Space nails 6 inches apart along all edges and 12 inches at intermediate rafters. Plywood may be projected beyond the end walls of the house. Limit this projection to 6 to 8 inches for $\frac{3}{8}$-inch plywood and 8 to 12 inches for $\frac{1}{2}$-inch and thicker plywood if no support framing is used. Allow about $\frac{1}{8}$-inch edge spacing and $\frac{1}{16}$-inch edge spacing when laying the plywood.

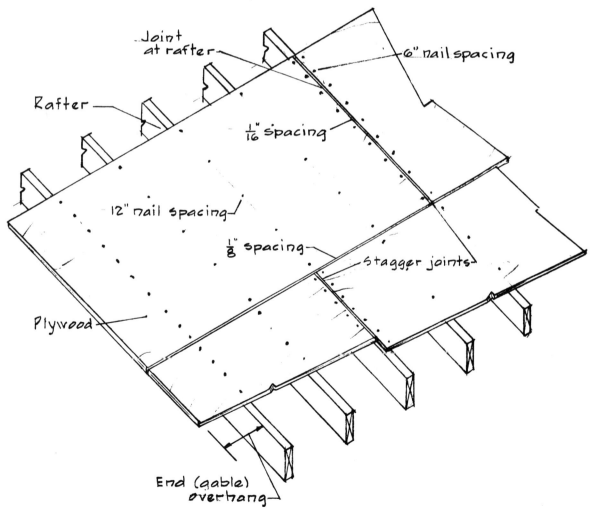

Fig. 57. Plywood roof sheathing.

13

Exterior Trim
(Cornice and Rake)

It is desirable to apply the roofing as soon as possible after the roof sheathing has been installed. You will often notice that the day after a contractor has installed the roof sheathing, shingles are in place. Before the shingles are applied, however, cornice and gable framing should be completed and the trim in place. Three types of cornices may be used to finish the rafter overhang at the side walls: (1) The close cornice (no rafter projection) which provides very little weather protection: (2) the boxed cornice with lookouts which is also adaptable to the hip-roofed house; and (3) the boxed cornice without lookouts.

CLOSE CORNICE
A close cornice is one in which the rafters are cut flush with the outside wall fram-

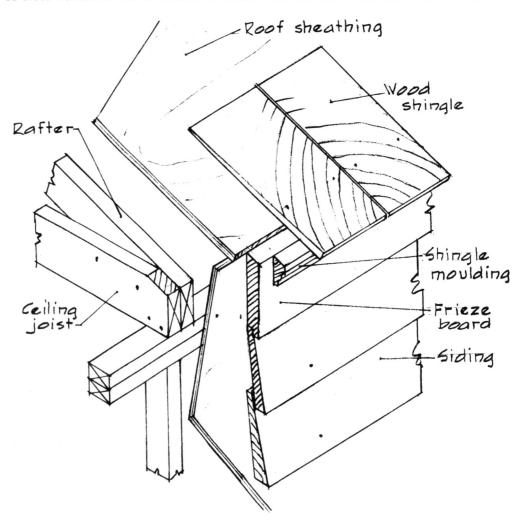

Fig. 58. Close cornice.

ing, Fig. 58. Wall sheathing can be carried to the junction of the rafter ends. Thus the roof sheathing will be flush with and terminate at the top of the wall sheathing. Some overhang is desirable in a close cornice from the standpoint of appearance and to provide a drip edge for gutters. This is accomplished by the use of a frieze board (siding termination) and a shingle molding, Fig. 58. In addition, a course of wood shingles or a metal overhang drip edge should be used. Use rust-resistant nails in applying the frieze board and shingle molding. Nail the frieze board to the top plate and rafter or ceiling joist ends with ninepenny or tenpenny nails. Galvanized nails in eightpenny size spaced 16 inches apart should be adequate for the shingle molding.

BOXED CORNICE (WITH LOOKOUTS)

A boxed cornice with lookouts is one in which the rafter extends beyond the wall and can be used for either a gable or hip roof. This provides good weather protection for the side walls, Fig. 59. Framing members (lookouts), usually 2 by 4's, are face nailed to the ends of the rafters and toenailed to the wall. The lookouts provide a nailing surface for the soffit. Soffit material can consist of plywood or a material such as primed hardboard, Fig. 59. The junction of the lookout with the wall should

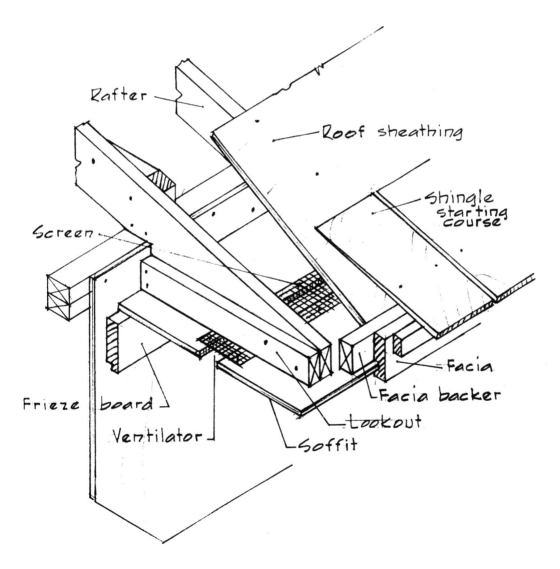

Fig. 59. Boxed Cornice (with lookouts).

be above the line of the window or door trim (top casing and drip cap). The slope of the roof usually determines the amount of this overhang; the lower the angle of the slope the greater the roof extension can be. Usually the overhang varies from 12 to 30 inches.

A 2- by 4- or 2- by 6-inch nailing header (facia backer) is nailed to the ends of the rafters with sixteenpenny nails. This is often eliminated if the facia is of $1\frac{1}{4}$- or $1\frac{1}{2}$-inch material. The important part of this portion of the roof line is to have rafter ends all in line. If they are not, use a snap chalk line and trim those extending beyond the line. The soffit can be nailed to the lookouts with sixpenny or sevenpenny galvanized nails depending on its thickness. Most wood facia boards are supplied with a sloped cut (to match the roof slope) and a rabbeted edge for $\frac{1}{4}$- or $\frac{3}{8}$-inch-thick soffit, Fig. 59. Nailing of the trim members and moldings is basically the same as described for the close cornice.

Many lumber companies supply complete prepainted nonwood soffit systems which might be used to advantage in your addition.

It is important, if there is an open space above the rooms of your addition, to provide adequate attic ventilation. This will be covered under the Chapter "Ventilation." The soffit serves as a perfect area for inlet ventilators which can be installed before the soffit is nailed in place.

BOXED CORNICE (WITHOUT LOOKOUTS)
A wide boxed cornice, without lookouts, provides a sloped soffit and is sometimes

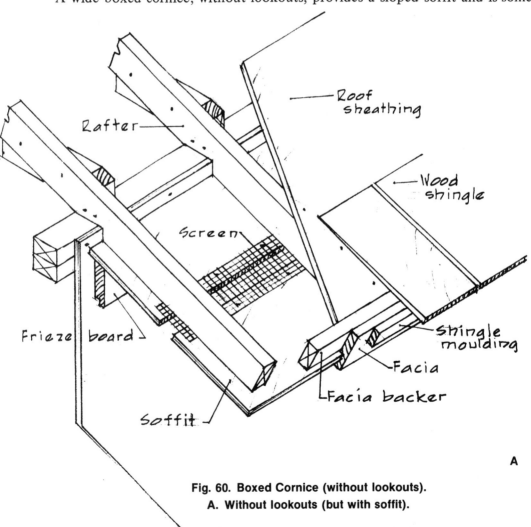

Fig. 60. Boxed Cornice (without lookouts).
A. Without lookouts (but with soffit).

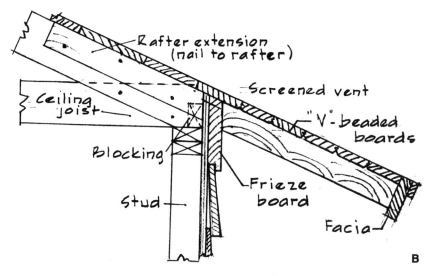

Fig. 60. Boxed Cornice (*cont'd*).
B. Without soffit (open cornice).

used for additions when a wide overhang is desired, Fig. 60A. This design is used most often for a gable roof. Soffit material is nailed directly to the rafters. Nailing headers, facia, and shingle molding is applied as shown in Fig. 60A. (Include ventilators in the soffit.) A continuous screened ventilator slot is sometimes used in this type of cornice.

Another method of treating the cornice finish is by the "rustic ranch" open cornice as shown in Fig. 60B. Rafter extensions consisting of 3- by 4-inch rough-sawn members are nailed to the rafters which end at the wall line. The extensions can be spaced 32 inches on center (on every other rafter). A single 2- by 6-inch facia can be used to finish the ends of the rafter extensions. It may be desirable to use 1- by 6- or 1- by 8-inch (or thicker) V-beaded boards or rough-sawn boards for roof sheathing over this extension, Fig. 60B. A wide frieze board is used as a termination for the top of the siding. Notch the frieze board for the 3- by 4-inch rafters. If vertical boards and battens are used, the frieze board could be eliminated, if so desired.

An open cornice, which might be used in the construction of a garage, is produced by eliminating the soffit. In such construction the frieze board, or siding, is notched to fit between the rafters.

GABLE END

The gable end (rake section) of a house can be close (without frame member extension) or extended beyond the end wall. The extension, when not too great, can be supported by the roof sheathing as previously brought out. When the extension is more than about 12 inches for $\frac{1}{2}$-inch plywood (and 16 inches for 1-inch lumber sheathing), 2- by 4-inch members fastened to an inside rafter support the overhang, Fig. 49.

Close Rake

When a close rake at the gable end is constructed, roof sheathing is cut flush with the wall sheathing, Fig. 61A. A facia nailer, which might be a 2- by 3- or 2- by 4-inch member, is then nailed to the edge rafter. A barge board (facia), 1 by 4 or 1 by 6 inches in size, is nailed to the 2-inch backer. A metal roof edge (drip edge) is commonly used along the facia to provide some extra overhang and strength along the slope. A facia molding or a simple 1- by 2-inch member can be used in place of the metal edging at the roof edge.

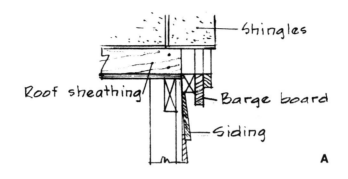

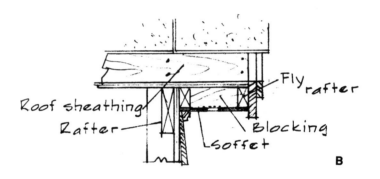

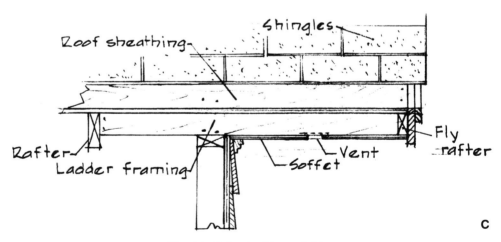

Fig. 61. Rake (gable end) trim.
A. Close.
B. Narrow.
C. Wide.

Narrow Boxed Overhang

As previously outlined, support for a narrow gable end extension can be supplied by the roof sheathing without special framing. In this type construction, a 2 by 3 fly rafter (or nailer for the barge board) is fastened by nailing into it through the sheathing, Fig. 61B. A soffit nailer, also a 2- by 3-inch member, is then nailed to the wall. Soffit, barge board, and other trim is then applied as previously described and illustrated. It is often a good policy in a boxed rake section to provide some ventilation. A small ventilator such as a screened 3- or 4-inch-diameter hole at the top and bottom is usually sufficient to provide adequate ventilation.

Wide Boxed Overhang

The framing for a wide boxed overhang is illustrated in Fig. 49. It consists of 2- by 4-inch or larger members (ladder framing) toenailed to the second rafter and to the top plate of the gable end wall. The ladder members are usually spaced no further apart than 24 inches. A 2- by 4-inch (or larger) fly rafter (or header member) is nailed to the ends of the extended framing and to the facia nailer of the cornice. This supports and provides a nailing surface for the facia (barge) and for the roof sheathing, Fig. 61C. The soffit, barge board, and other trim is applied in the normal manner. The soffit in this type of detail is often used to install attic ventilation. A narrow continuous screened slot can accomplish this.

14

Roof Coverings

Materials commonly used for coverings on pitched roofs may be asphalt, wood (shingles or shakes), tile, and similar materials. The most common and likely the lowest cost of these is the asphalt shingle. The wood shingle is often used in the eastern and northwestern areas of the country. Tile and similar roofing materials may be more common in the South and Southwest. It might be wise to roof your addition with the same type (and color) shingle that is on the original house.

A roof underlay material usually consisting of 15- or 30-pound asphalt felt should be used in moderate to low slope roofs covered with asphalt shingles or with tile and slate coverings. In fact, some buildings codes require a double coverage for low roof slopes of about 2 in 12 when asphalt shingles are used. In addition, a seal-tab shingle (adhesive under the tabs) is required.

Built-up roofs consisting of layers of asphalt roofing felt laminated with hot tar are used for flat or very low-sloped roofs. Such roofs are usually applied by professional roofers and are commonly known as a 15-year, 20-year, etc., roof. This means that the company warranties such roofs for those periods of time.

NUMBER OF NAILS

The number of fasteners required for asphalt shingles and for wood shingles is sometimes a problem when ordering your roofing nails. The following guides may be used.

Asphalt Shingles

The 1-inch galvanized roofing nail is commonly used for asphalt shingles on new roofs. When four nails are used for each 12- by 36-inch shingle strip (providing seal-tab shingles are used), plan to use about 1 pound for each square (100 square feet). Order more if you are using $1\frac{1}{4}$-inch nails when reroofing. When six nails are used for each shingle strip, plan on $1\frac{1}{2}$ pounds for each square. It is good practice, when roofing sheathing is of minimum thickness, to use a ring shank nail for both asphalt and wood shingles.

Wood Shingles

Galvanized shingle nails for wood shingles can sometimes be obtained in two classes: (1) The American Red Cedar type and (2) the regular zinc-coated nail. The American Red Cedar nails have a smaller diameter than the regular shingle nails and thus there are more in each pound. For the $1\frac{1}{4}$-inch length, which is standard for new roofs, you will require about $2\frac{1}{2}$ pounds of regular shingle nails for each square (100 square feet) of wood shingles based on a 5-inch exposure. This will cover some loss during the shingling process. Because longer nails are required for wood shakes, perhaps 4 to 5 pounds will be required in sevenpenny to ninepenny size.

ASPHALT SHINGLES

Asphalt shingles (3-in-1 tab shingles, 12 by 36 inches) are normally available in a 240-pound class. (They weigh 240 pounds per square or 100 square feet of coverage

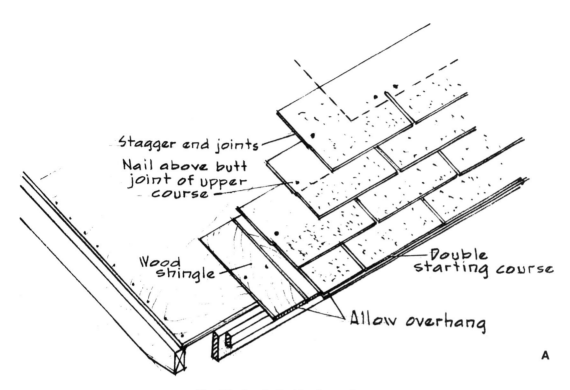

Fig. 62. Asphalt shingle roof.
A. Shingle application.

based on 5-inch exposure.) There are three bundles per square. A lock-tab shingle (250-pound per square) is also available as are special thick tab shingles treated to look like wood shingles.

To give stability to the edge of the roof, a metal drip edge or a row of wood shingles is applied over the asphalt felt, Fig. 62A. These should extend beyond the facia board molding of the cornice about $\frac{3}{4}$ inch. The first row of asphalt shingles are doubled or a starter strip can be used as the initial shingle course. The asphalt shingles should extend about $\frac{1}{2}$ inch beyond the wood shingles or metal edging. This will allow rain to run off without the chance of backing up under the roof proper. Use one roofing nail at each end and one above each notch for seal-tab shingles. A 1-inch roofing nail should be long enough for most roof sheathings. (Use ring shank nails for thin roof sheating.) Because the shingles have a 5-inch exposure, the nails should be placed about 6 inches *above* the shingle butt. In many areas where high winds are a factor or where nonseal-tab shingles are selected, it is necessary to use six nails per 12- by 36-inch shingle; one at each end and one beside and above each notch, Fig. 62A.

To provide a solid edge and protection for the asphalt shingles, a metal drip edge is often used along the gable edge, Fig. 62B. It can be nailed in place with $1\frac{1}{2}$-inch shingle nails. The asphalt shingles should extend beyond the drip edge about $\frac{1}{2}$ inch.

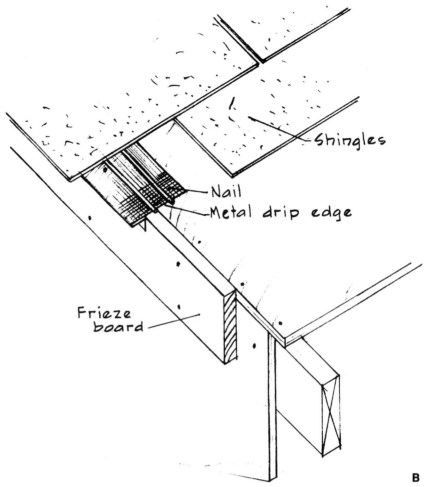

Fig. 62. Asphalt shingle roof *(cont'd).*
B. Rake detail.

The usual requirements for underlayment for asphalt shingles under various conditions are shown in the following tabulation and can be used as a guide for your roof:

| | Minimum Roof Slope | |
Underlayment[a] (36-in.-Wide Rolls)	(5-in. Shingle Exposure)	(4-in. Shingle Exposure)
Not Required	7 in 12	4 in 12
Single (34 in. exposed)	4 in 12	3 in 12
Double (17 in. exposed)	2 in 12	2 in 12

[a] 15-lb or heavier asphalt felt.

It might be helpful for the amateur in providing good alignment to use snap chalk lines vertically and horizontally as guides in laying the shingles. Flashing along the junction of the house siding and in valleys is part of the roofing. These details are covered in another section in this chapter. End joints should be staggered.

WOOD SHINGLES

The wood shingle most commonly found in lumberyards is of western red cedar or redwood. The usual length is 16 inches and, based on a 5-inch average exposure, four bundles will cover 100 square feet. Wood shingles cost almost three times as much as the standard asphalt shingle but usually will outlast them by many years.

The grade of wood shingle used for house roofs should be the No. 1 grade, which are all heartwood, all edge grain, and tapered. Second grade shingles might be used

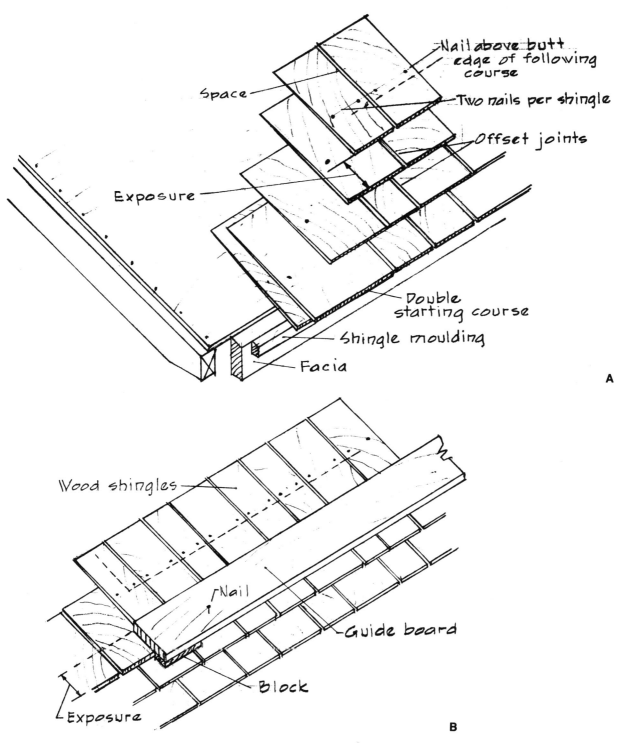

Fig. 63. Wood shingles.
A. Shingle application.
B. Guide board.

for secondary buildings and make excellent side walls for your house if chosen as a siding material.

Fig. 63A illustrates an approved method of applying wood shingles on a moderate to high pitched roof. Underlayment is usually not required when wood shingles are used except along the cornice for protection from ice dams. When the roof slope is 4 in 12, use about a $3\frac{1}{2}$- to 4-inch exposure for 16-inch shingles. When the slope is 5 in 12 and over, use a 5-inch exposure. Wood shingles are not usually recommended for slopes less than 4 in 12 without some underlay protection.

A guide can be used to aid in laying wood shingles. It can consist of a straight 1- by 8- by 12-foot piece of lumber with a butt section of shingle nailed to each end, Fig. 63B. The guide is held in place by lightly nailing through the board.

The following general rules can be used in applying wood shingles:

1. Use a double starting course at the eave line. The top shingles should overlap the bottom course about $\frac{1}{4}$ inch. The joints between these, and all shingles in courses above, should be offset at least $1\frac{1}{2}$ inches. Space shingles from $\frac{1}{8}$ to $\frac{1}{4}$ inch apart to allow for expansion when wet.

2. Shingles should extend $1\frac{1}{4}$ to $1\frac{1}{2}$ inches beyond the eave line and $\frac{3}{4}$ inch beyond the rake line (gable).

3. Use two threepenny or fourpenny galvanized or zinc-coated shingle nails in each shingle. Space them about $\frac{3}{4}$ to 1 inch from the edge of the shingle and $1\frac{1}{2}$ inches above the butt line of the following course, i.e., $6\frac{1}{2}$ inches above the bottom edge when exposure is 5 inches. A ring shank nail should be used when plywood roof sheathing is $\frac{3}{8}$ inch in thickness.

4. When a valley is involved, shingle *away* from the valley. Select and pre-cut (angle) from your widest shingles for this procedure.

Wood shakes are applied in much the same manner as wood shingles. Becasue they are longer and thicker than shingles, use long galvanized nails. Shakes for roofs are usually classed as "split-and-resawn." The resawn face is the under side in laying the shakes. Exposures for moderate and steep roof slopes are usually $7\frac{1}{2}$ inches for 18-inch-long shakes and 10 inches for 24-inch-long shakes. Before applying the shakes, underlayment of 30-pound asphalt felt should be laid across the roof in shingle fashion. The amount of exposure must be equal to the exposed face of the shakes ($7\frac{1}{2}$ or 10 inches). This will minimize wind-driven rain or snow from penetrating to the roof sheathing. This precaution is necessary because the split face does not allow a flat joint.

RIDGE AND HIP FINISH

The ridge can have added protection by using an 18-inch strip of 15-pound asphalt felt over the ridge before shingles reach this point. In laying asphalt shingles, the last shingle strip should be laid over the ridge and fastened at each side. Trim if necessary. A Boston ridge finish is normally used to finish the ridge. A 12- by 36-inch shingle strip is cut in three equal pieces at the slot, and the pieces laid across the ridge, Fig. 64A. Each shingle is lapped 5 to 6 inches to obtain double coverage. The ridge shingle covers the nails of the preceding shingle.

The Boston ridge for wood shingles consists of equal width shingles (5 or 6 inches) laid with alternating laps, Fig. 64B. For extra protection, a metal flashing strip can be used over the ridge before the shingles are applied. This will prevent wind-driven rain from penetrating under the shingles.

The termination of the shingles at a hip is finished in the same manner as at the ridge. Some tapering of wood shingle edges is usually necessary for a good fit.

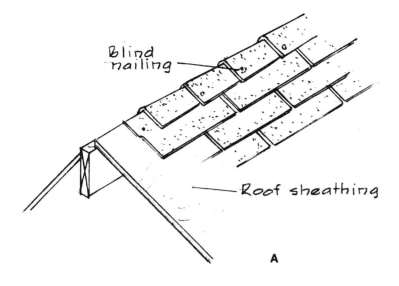

A

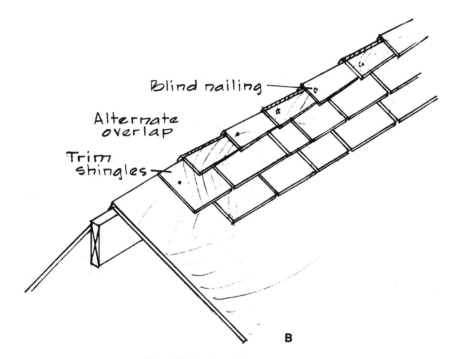

B

Fig. 64. Boston ridge.
A. Asphalt shingles.
B. Wood shingles.

FLASHING FOR SHINGLES

The roof line of your addition can meet the wall line, the chimney, or the roof line of the house. It is important that this juncture be watertight. This is accomplished by shingle flashing when the roof meets the wall line of the house. When two roof lines meet, a metal valley flashing is commonly used. Other areas also require flashing such as at material changes along a wall. Metal used for flashing may be aluminum, galvanized metal, or painted tin plate. Valley flashing can be obtained in 14-, 20-, and 28-inch widths.

At Wall Lines

The junction of the roof line with the house siding can be flashed with "tin shingles" which are 5 by 7 inches in size. They may be larger but this is a standard size used by roofers. As previously outlined, a strip of siding has been, or should be, removed to allow for about 1-inch clearance above the roof sheathing line, Figs. 44 and 65A. Bend the shingle flashings at a 90° angle over a board or other sharp edge. Bend them the long way so there is a 2½-inch leg on each side. Use one bent flashing under

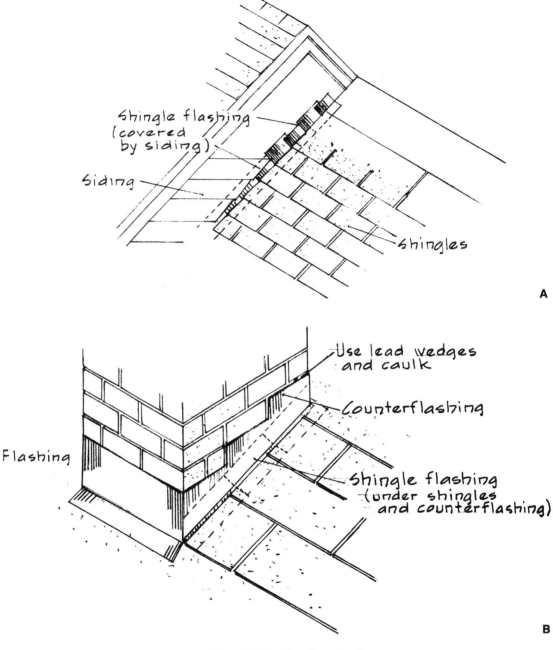

Fig. 65. Flashing for shingles.
A. At wall.
B. At chimney.

94

each shingle at the junction of the siding. The vertical leg of the flashing is placed *under* the siding. The roofing nail on the shingle course will hold it in place. With a 5-inch shingle exposure there will be a 2-inch lap for each flashing tin, Fig. 65A.

At Chimneys

The flashing around a chimney requires not only the shingle flashing but a counterflashing fastened in raked joints of the brick, Fig. 65B. Use shingle flashing in the normal manner under the shingles and up the face of the brick. Now insert prefitted counterflashing into the raked joint of the chimney. It is fastened with lead wedges and the joints calked. Asphalt shingle on the low side of the chimney can be carried up the bricks several inches, Fig. 65B, before the counterflashing is installed.

Valley Flashing

As previously outlined in the Chapter "Rafter Framing," a strip of shingles on the house proper should be removed along the valley. This can be about 4 inches at the

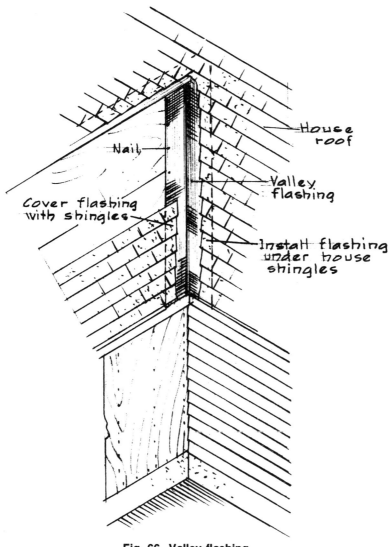

Fig. 66. Valley flashing.

top and slightly wider at the bottom. Place the prebent valley flashing, in 14- or 20-inch widths, under the house shingles and apply the shingles of the new addition over it, Fig. 66. Be sure the roofing nails are removed on the house roof so the flashing slides in place. The shingles along this area can then be renailed. At the ridge line of the valley, bend and overlap the valley flashing at each side to provide a water-tight lap. Do *not* face nail the flashing or shingles unless they are protected by a shingle overlap!

Ice Dam Protection

If you live in a snow belt area, you may have seen the piling up of snow at cornices with the typical icicles along the eave line. These are caused by poor attic insulation allowing the escape of heat from the heated rooms below and, in addition, inadequate ventilation. Together they allow attic temperatures to rise above the freezing point causing melted snow to follow the roof line and freeze at the cornice. This can result in the forming of ice dams and water pockets at the cornice and the entry of water into the wall or rooms below.

To prevent or minimize the formation of these ice dams, the following precautions should be followed: (1) provide good attic insulation (as much as 8 to 12 inches); (2) provide good ventilation at the soffit and at the gable ends or ridge line; and (3) use a 36-inch strip of heavy asphalt felt or roll roofing under the shingles at the cornice, Fig. 67. This will minimize moisture entry into the attic or wall if ice dams do form.

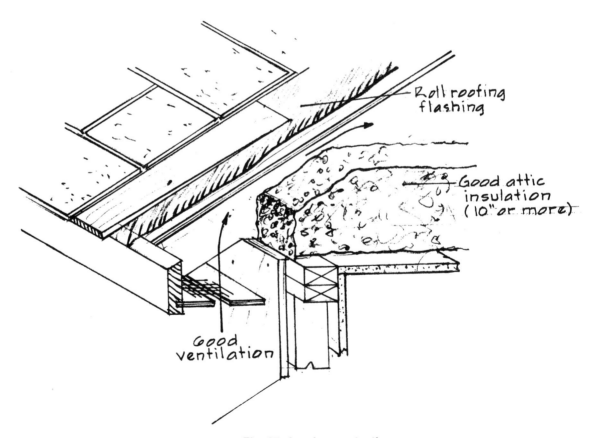

Fig. 67. Ice dam protection.

15
Exterior Frames (Windows and Doors)

Exterior window frame units consist of fitted sash, balances, weatherstrip, and the window frame proper. They are a millwork item usually assembled at the factory. Outside casing and top drip cap are included. In other words, they need only to be placed in the prepared rough opening over the sheathing, leveled, and nailed in place. Exterior door frames are also preassembled but the door is not normally prefitted because of the variation in hardware (locksets, hinges, etc.) that the customer might choose. However, most large lumberyards will fit and hang the door in the frame for a modest additional cost. Routing for three 4- by 4-inch hinges and fitting a heavy $1\frac{3}{4}$-inch-thick exterior door is a rather difficult job. However, it can be done with a little assistance.

All wood exterior door and window frame parts are normally treated at the factory with a water-repellent preservative which provides protection and serves as an excellent base for paint or other finish. Screens, storm sash, or combination units are available for most types of windows and exterior doors.

Under many building codes the glass area in habitable rooms is required to be at least 10 percent of the floor area. Natural ventilation, the amount the window can be opened, should not be less than 4 percent. However, this does not necessarily apply to completely air-conditioned houses. Check your local building codes for the specific requirements in your area when planning the number of windows each room requires.

TYPES OF WINDOWS

Windows are available in many types and those selected for your addition might generally conform to those in the house itself. The principal types are as follows: (1) The double-hung, (2) the outswinging casement, (3) the horizontal sliding casement, (4) the awning (hopper), and (5) the stationary or fixed window. They are made of wood or metal or a combination of the two materials. A wood frame, wood sash, and metal combination storm and screen inserts is a satisfactory combination. All-metal sash or frames are usually not suitable in cold climates because of the frost which can form and later melt on interior surfaces. Some metal frames are provided with a nonmetal gasket which reduces this problem somewhat. The wood contained in frames and sash are made from clear, kiln-dried stock. Species commonly used are ponderosa and similar pines, redwood, the cedars, and other suitable species.

Double-Hung Windows

A double-hung window is one with a lower and upper sash which slide vertically past one another, Fig. 68A. Storm and screen inserts are located on the outside of the sash for easy adjustment. A typical sill design is shown in Fig. 68B.

The glass area proper of both upper and lower sash can be obtained with a full glass pane or in divided patterns. The dividers (muntins) are also available in a snap-in form which simplifies painting of the wood sash. The double-hung window can be ordered as a single unit, as a double unit, or in various other combinations.

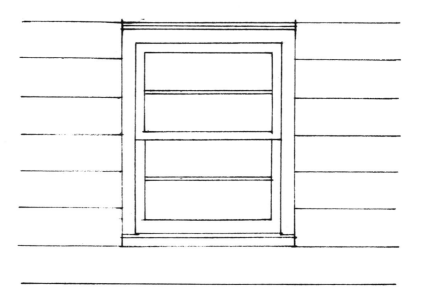

A

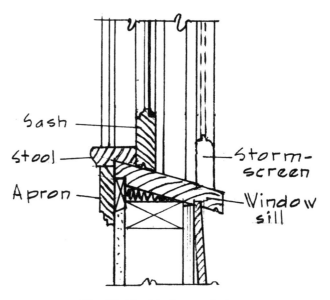

B

Fig. 68. Double-hung window.
A. Exterior view.
B. Section through sill.

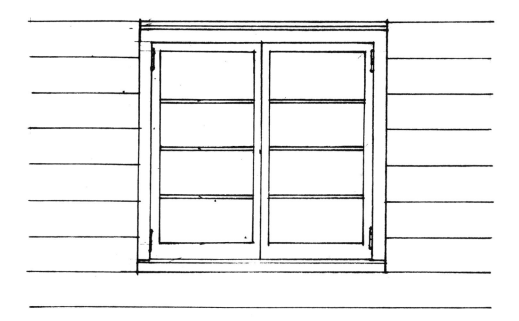

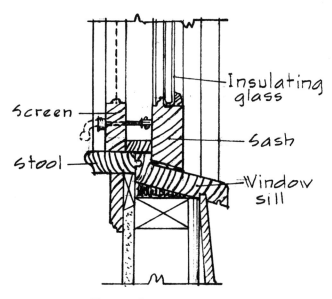

Fig. 69. Casement window.
A. Exterior view.
B. Section through sill.

Casement Windows

The outswinging casement window is supplied in single or multiple pairs, each sash hinged at the outside edges, Fig. 69A. It is designed to swing out because it is more easily weather stripped for resistance to rains and drafts than one which swings in. The sash is usually supplied with insulated glass which eliminates the need for a storm sash. The screen insert is located on the room side of the frame. A typical sill design is shown in Fig. 69B.

A sliding casement is often available at the larger lumber companies. This is one in which each casement sash slides horizontally in metal or plastic runners located at the sill and at the head (top) jamb.

Awning Window

The awning or hopper window is one in which the sash is hinged at the top and opens outward, Fig. 70. It can be ordered in a number of alternative combinations. As in the casement sash, the operating devise (usually a crank) which swings out the sash and the sash lock are located on the interior. Such sash are also furnished with insulated glass. Screens, when supplied, are located on the room side of the frame. The sill of the frame is similar to the one used for the casement sash, Fig. 69B.

Fixed Sash

A fixed sash is one which serves only to supply light and cannot be opened. It is commonly used in a large framed unit with a double-hung, awning, or single casement window at each side. These sash are also normally glazed with insulated glass.

Other Window Units

A number of special window designs may be available at your building supply company. One such unit is the "bow" unit which is a pressembled "bay" type of window. It commonly consists of four or five casement sash forming an outward bow. It may be about 6 to 10 feet wide and has an extension of up to 18 inches beyond the inside wall line. Determine the rough opening required when framing your walls if the design is to be part of your addition.

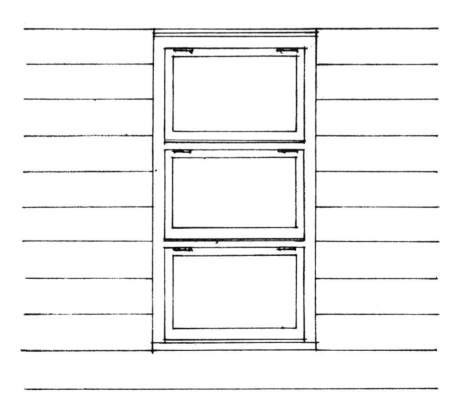

Fig. 70. Awning window unit.

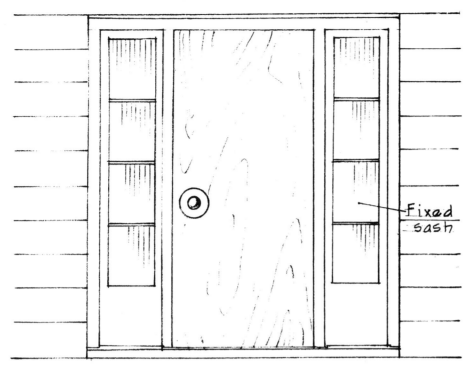

Fig. 71. Exterior door unit with fixed side sash.

EXTERIOR DOOR FRAMES

An exterior door frame is made up of heavy side and head jambs ($1\frac{3}{8}$ inches thick) and an oak sill. Side and head jambs are rabbeted on the inner edge for a $1\frac{3}{4}$-inch-thick door. Exterior casing supplies the framing and stops for screen or combination doors which are usually $1\frac{1}{8}$ inches thick. These frames can be obtained as a single unit only for the door or an entrance frame with one or two fixed side lights, Fig. 71.

Exterior doors are $1\frac{3}{4}$ inches thick and may be obtained in flush or panel designs. A solid-core flush door is preferred over a hollow-core flush door for exterior use because there is more resistance to bowing during the winter months. So if you live in a cold climate, select the solid-core design.

INSTALLING WINDOW FRAMES

It is good practice, no matter what type sheathing is used, to frame the window opening with strips of 15-pound asphalt felt or similar paper. This not only resists moisture entry but also minimizes air infiltration. Use 12-inch-wide strips of paper around each opening, Fig. 72A. Allow them to extend 3 to 4 inches into the opening—top, sides, and bottom.

The window frame is placed in the opening and fastened by nailing from the casings into the side studs and the header of the opening, Fig. 72B. Use a carpenter's level on the sill and on a side jamb to be sure the frame is plumb before nailing. Temporary blocking may be used at the sill to hold it in place. Use twelvepenny galvanized or cadmium-plated nails spaced about 12 inches apart at side and head jambs. To protect the side jamb from hammer marks, it is usually a good idea to drive the last $\frac{1}{8}$ inch with a heavy nail set. The nail should be flush with the surface. Do not nail the sill into the rough 2- by 4-inch sill below.

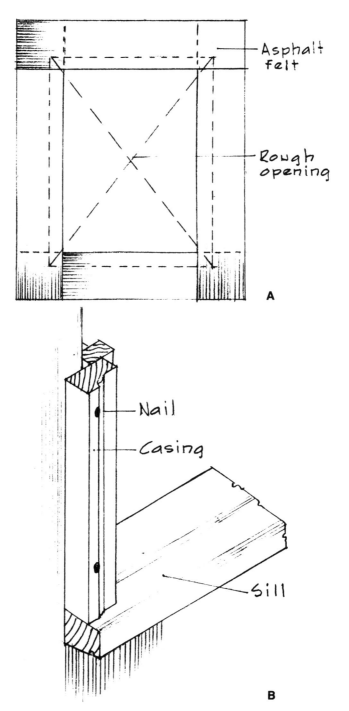

Fig. 72. Installing window frames.
A. Paper around opening.
B. Nailing (casing to edge studs and header).

INSTALLING THE EXTERIOR DOOR FRAME

Strips of asphalt felt should also be used around exterior door openings. In most cases, the sole plate, subfloor, and a portion of the joists and header must be removed at the bottom of the opening, Fig. 73. This can be done with a saw and a hatchet. The top of the door sill should be flush with the top of the finish floor. A full bearing for the sill on the floor framing is a must so strive for a good fit. A nailing block (2- by 4-inch member) can be used under the edge of the subfloor between joists if required, Fig. 73. After the door sill has been fitted, the frame is leveled and then fastened to the wall by nailing the casing to the studs and header. Use twelvepenny nails spaced 12 inches apart. After the finish floor or other covering is in place, a threshold with its weatherstrip is nailed over the joint between the sill and the finish floor, Fig. 73. Any nailing of the door sill to the floor framing now necessary should be done so that the threshold covers the nails.

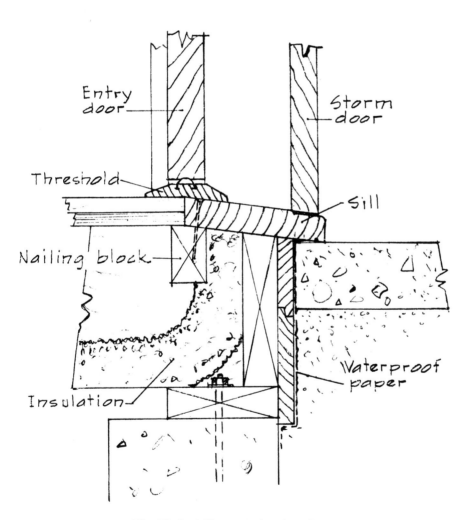

Fig. 73. Installing exterior door frame.

16
Exterior Coverings

There are many types of wood and nonwood materials available for exterior coverings. Of course, if you have selected the same material as is on the house proper, this choice has already been made. Horizontally applied sidings may consist of bevel wood siding in various widths, medium density hardboards, matched (tongued and grooved or shiplapped) boards in 1- by 6-inch and wider sizes, and metal or plastic sidings. Many of these materials may be used vertically and provide good service when applied properly. Rough-sawn boards with battens in several patterns are also applied vertically. Such applications, however, require nominal 1-inch wood boards or $\frac{1}{2}$-inch and thicker plywood sheathing unless horizontal nailers (blocking between studs) are used. Rough surfaced plywood in 4- by 8- or 4- by 9-foot sizes can also be applied vertically. Masonry veneers such as brick or stone are other nonwood coverings; however, a ledge must have been incorporated into the foundation wall to support these finish materials.

Species most commonly available for wood sidings are redwood, western red cedar, and cypress. These species have the essential properties required for siding such as good painting characteristics, easy working qualities, and freedom from warp. Other species containing these properties but perhaps not as readily obtainable are eastern white pine, cedars other than western red, sugar pine, and western white pine. Western hemlock, the spruces, ponderosa pine, and yellow-poplar have these properties to a fair degree. Perhaps one of the most important from the standpoint of best paint holding properties and minimum warping is to select material with vertical face grain. Rough-sawn boards or other sidings which are to be stained do not require as rigid properties.

HORIZONTAL SIDING

Bevel Siding

Perhaps the most common wood siding used is the bevel or lap siding. One side has a smooth paintable surface and the other a rough-sawn surface which can be stained. Bevel siding can be obtained in sizes from $\frac{1}{2}$ by 4 inches to $\frac{3}{4}$ by 10 inches or wider. The exposure width is usually $1\frac{1}{2}$ inches less than the finish width. The finish width is normally $\frac{1}{2}$ inch less than the size you order because of machining requirements. For example, a 10-inch bevel siding is actually $9\frac{1}{2}$ inches in width and exposure distance is usually 8 inches. This distance can be adjusted slightly between the window sill and the top of the drip cap. This is to insure that one butt edge is even with the bottom of the sill and another with the top of the drip cap, Fig. 74A. If you are matching the siding of the house, it is desirable to have the siding courses match those of the house. When a cornice provides protection, the siding course at the drip cap is sufficient. However, under other conditions, a flashing over the drip cap is recommended.

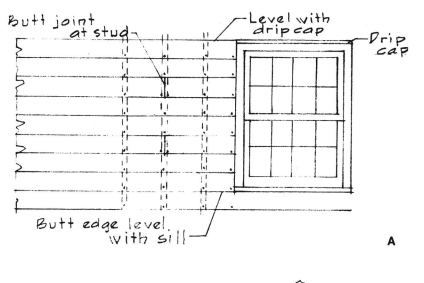

Butt joint at stud
Level with drip cap
Drip cap
Butt edge level with sill

A

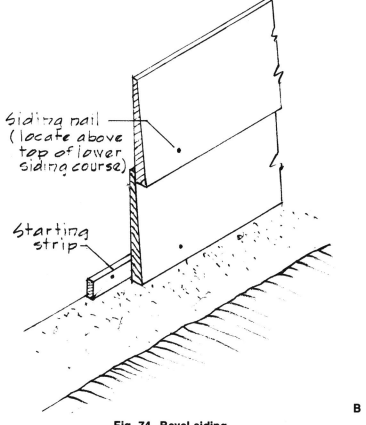

Siding nail (locate above top of lower siding course)

Starting strip

B

Fig. 74. Bevel siding.
A. Butt (end) joints.
B. Starting course.

A sheathing paper, such as 15-pound asphalt felt, will minimize air infiltration when wood board sheathing is used. Apply it horizontally in shingle lap fashion and tack or staple in place. Such paper is normally not necessary when plywood or fiberboard sheathing has been used (except around windows and door openings). However, it is good practice, when sheathing paper is not required, to place a strip at each corner. Use an 18-inch-wide strip of 15-pound asphalt felt, fold along the center, place and staple at each corner—foundation to top of wall. This will greatly reduce air infiltration in this area. When full covering of sheathing paper is used, mark location of the studs on the paper with chalk lines for easier nailing of the siding.

Begin application of bevel siding by first nailing a $\frac{3}{8}$- by 2-inch starter strip at the bottom of the sheathing or floor framing member, Fig. 74B. The first siding course can now be nailed in place. Locate the butt of this siding slightly below the starter strip to provide a good drip edge. It is desirable to locate all nails at the stud lines. End joints should always be made at a stud. Predrill if there is a tendency for the siding to split.

The junction of the siding with the outside corner of the existing house has been previously described in the Chapter "Wall Framing" and shown in Fig. 31B. The new siding terminating at an inside corner of the house can be fitted in two ways, against an inside corner board, scribed against the siding of the house. When using a corner board, a $1\frac{1}{4}$- or $1\frac{1}{2}$- by 4-inch member is recommended. First place it against the house siding and temporarily nail it in place. Now use a guide strip as wide as the

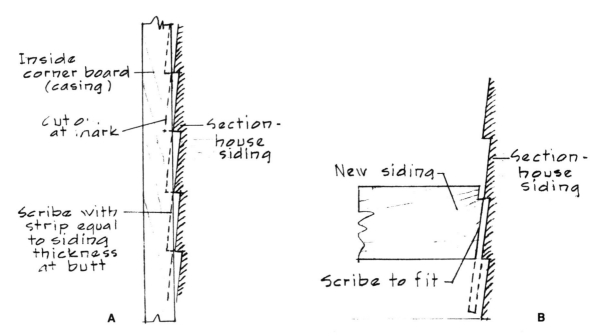

Fig. 75. Fitting siding at house wall.
A. Scribing corner board.
B. Scribing siding.

butt thickness of the house siding and mark the slope and the butt edge, Fig. 75A. Cut out these sections and, after applying calking along the inner edge, nail the corner board in place. When a corner board is used, a stud can be added on the wall of the addition to provide a nailing base for the siding, Fig. 31A.

If a scribed siding joint is desired, without a corner board, a similar marking system can be used. Place the end of the siding against the siding of the house and mark to conform to the slope, Fig. 75B. Apply calking to the inner edge and nail in place.

Nails

As brought out in the previous Chapter "Fastening," *always* use a galvanized or other rust-resistant siding nail for all exterior nailing including siding. Select a standard siding nail with its medium sized head. When nailing is not into a stud (not usually recommended), a threaded (ring shank) nail should be used.

The length of the nail depends on the thickness of the siding and the type of sheathing. Nails should have at least $1\frac{1}{2}$ inches of penetration into the wood behind the siding unless ring shank nails are used. For example, if the combined thickness of the sidings (at the lap) is $\frac{3}{4}$ inch and a $\frac{3}{4}$-inch fiberboard sheathing is used, the nails should be $1\frac{1}{2}$ plus $1\frac{1}{2}$ inches or 3 inches long to penetrate into the stud. Thus a tenpenny plain shank nail should be used. An eightpenny or ninepenny ring shank nail can be substituted. If plywood or wood board sheathing is used, a sevenpenny or eightpenny plain shank nail is satisfactory. When bevel siding is $\frac{1}{2}$ by 4 inches or wider, a sixpenny or sevenpenny nail can be selected when the sheathing is wood. Drive the nails flush with the surface of the siding but *do not* overdrive. This can leave an undesirable hammer mark on the surface.

The nails for 8- and 10-inch wide sidings should be located above the butt edge enough to clear the top of the siding below, Fig. 74B.

Exterior Corners

Exterior corners for bevel, lap, or similar wood sidings are perhaps best terminated by metal corners, Fig. 76A. These primed metal corners can normally be obtained for each type of siding used. The siding should be trimmed flush with the corners. Do not nail the siding at the corner until the metal corners are installed (from the bottom course up).

Corner boards can also be used, Fig. 76B. They should be of $1\frac{1}{4}$- or $1\frac{1}{2}$-inch-thick material depending on the siding thickness.

A miter cut for corners of bevel siding is difficult to make and is usually not recommended for a paint finish. If siding warps slightly forming an opening, a paint failure will often occur. Such a corner joint is more adaptable to nominal 1-inch-thick sidings, especially when a stained finish is used.

Siding at Roof Slope

Siding on dormers at the intersection of a roof slope should be cut to provide about 1-inch clearance above the shingles. Thus allow about $1\frac{1}{2}$ to $1\frac{3}{4}$ inches above the rafters when framing the roof, Fig. 44. Treating the bevel edges of the siding with a water-repellent preservative or a prime paint coat before nailing the siding in place will usually provide better paint retention along these edges.

Hardboard Siding

Hardboard siding is usually available in $\frac{7}{16}$- by 12-inch by 16-foot size and is prime coated ready for installation. It is applied like bevel siding, Fig. 74A, B, usually with a 10-inch exposure distance (2-inch lap). Use small to medium headed siding nails and nail at every stud. Primed metal corners can be obtained for the exterior corner finish.

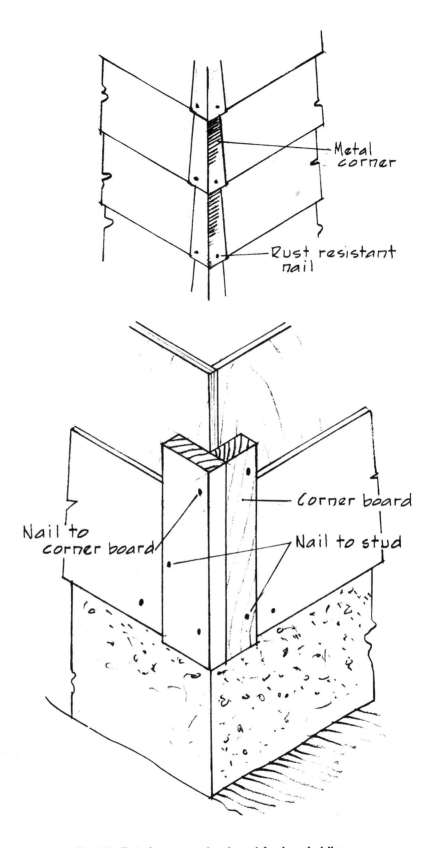

Fig. 76. Exterior corner treatment for bevel siding.
A. Metal corners.
B. Corner boards.

108

Matched Siding (Paneling)

Matched siding in $\frac{3}{4}$ by 6, $\frac{3}{4}$ by 8 inches, and wider sizes is often used as an exterior covering. A dressed and matched pattern (tongued and grooved) has more resistance to the entry of wind-driven rain than a shiplap pattern, Figs. 77A, B. However, because it does not have as watertight a joint as lap siding, water-resistant paper such as 15-pound asphalt felt, should be used over the sheathing. Nail siding through the tongue to each stud with a rust-resistant finish nail, Fig. 77C. Set the nail slightly with a nailset so it does not interfere with the next siding course. For 8-inch and wider siding, a face nail can be added near the bottom of the siding, Fig. 77C.

This type of exterior covering as well as lap siding is sometimes used diagonally (45°) for a contemporary pattern. Apply in the same manner as horizontally. Be sure that the tongue is along the upper edge and that a waterproof paper is used over the sheathing.

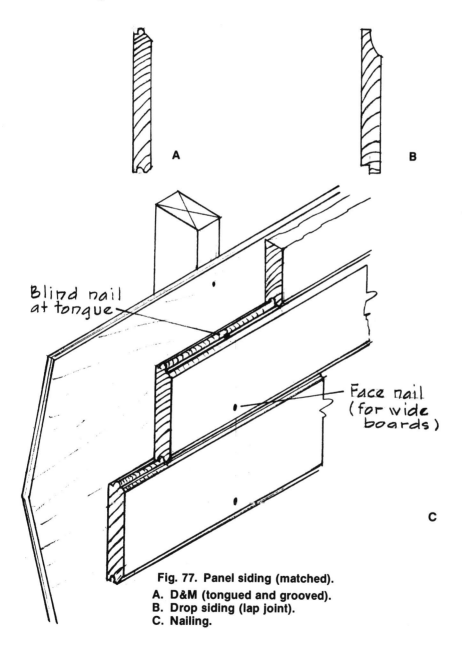

Fig. 77. Panel siding (matched).
A. D&M (tongued and grooved).
B. Drop siding (lap joint).
C. Nailing.

Miscellaneous Sidings

Metal, plastic, and plastic-coated sidings are also available for use as covering materials. Their greatest appeal is perhaps the need for minimum maintenance. Some types can be applied by the handyman; others only by the supplier.

VERTICAL SIDINGS

Rough-Sawn Vertical Boards

Rough-sawn boards in various widths are applied in three general patterns: (1) board and batten, Fig. 78A; (2) board and board, Fig. 78B; and (3) batten and board, Fig. 78C.

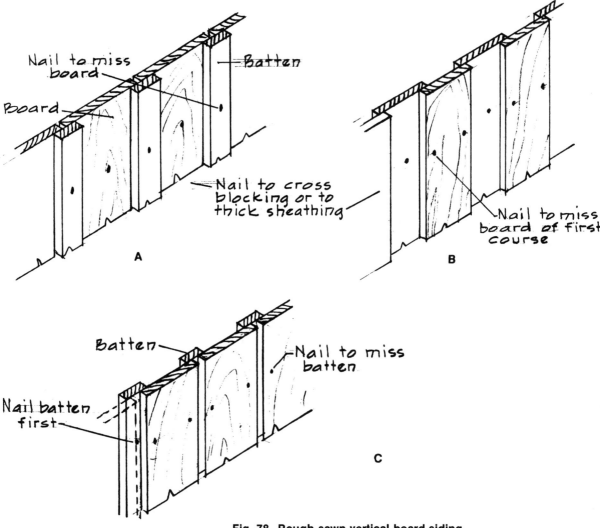

Fig. 78. Rough-sawn vertical board siding.
A. Board and batten.
B. Board and board.
C. Batten and board.

In such exterior coverings, and in most vertically applied sidings, some type of undernailing surface must be present. Such nailers can consist of: (1) 1-inch wood board sheathing; (2) $\frac{5}{8}$-inch or thicker plywood sheathing; (3) horizontal nailing strips (1 by 2's or 1 by 3's) nailed to the studs over the sheathing and space *no more* than 24 inches apart, and (4) 2- by 4-inch nailing blocks nailed between the wall studs. Regardless of the subnailing surface, a waterproof paper such as 15-pound asphalt felt should always be used under the finish siding. Use a lap joint in shingle fashion when installing the paper.

Board and Batten Pattern

Rough-sawn boards in 1- by 6-inch and wider sizes are usually spaced about $\frac{1}{2}$ inch apart. Use one nail at the center for 6- and 8-inch-wide boards, Fig. 78A, and two nails for 10-inch and wider boards. Space these about 3 to 4 inches apart. The battens, of 1 by 2 or wider sizes, should be fastened with nails that are about 1 inch longer than those used for the boards. Use threaded nails if they are available.

Board and Board Pattern

The first layer of boards for board and board patterns are spaced so that there is a 1- to $1\frac{1}{2}$-inch lap of the top boards, Fig. 78B. Use one nail at the center of 1- by 6- and 1- by 8-inch first course boards and two for the wider boards. The two nails for the top boards are spaced so they miss the edge of the first course of boards.

Batten and Board (Reverse Board and Batten)

The batten and board pattern is applied in the same manner as the board and board design. Use one nail for the battens and two for the boards, Fig. 78C.

Matched Siding (Paneling)

The vertical application of this tongued and grooved siding (dressed and matched with a V-bead) is much the same as the horizontal application in Fig. 77C. Use a galvanized finish nail and blind nail (nailing at the tongue). An additional face nail should be added for 8-inch and wider boards. The sheathing or other backing for the nails should be the same as those required for the rough-sawn vertical boards.

Exterior Plywood Siding

Rough-sawn plywood in 4- by 8- and 4- by 9-foot sheets is used with or without sheathing. It can be obtained in several patterns such as, a plain rough surface, a vertically grooved pattern, or a reverse board and batten design. When this plywood siding is used without sheathing, a $\frac{5}{8}$-inch thickness is required and must be applied vertically with perimeter nailing. The $\frac{3}{8}$-inch thickness can be used when sheathing is used on the walls. Always use sheathing paper for a wood board sheathing backing and also when the $\frac{5}{8}$-inch plywood siding serves both as sheathing and finish siding.

For $\frac{5}{8}$-inch plywood, space the edge nails about 6 inches apart and interior nails (always at studs) about 8 to 10 inches apart. The top and bottom nails (at top plates and joist header or stringer) should be spaced about 6 to 8 inches apart. Eightpenny galvanized nails are satisfactory for this nailing.

Plywood panel siding in $\frac{3}{8}$-inch thickness should always be applied over some type of braced sheathing with eightpenny or ninepenny nails. Space them about 6 to 8 inches apart at side, top, and bottom edges and at interior studs. A shiplap pattern is usually provided at vertical edges, and care should be taken to prevent splitting of this joint.

Termination of the siding at the cornice usually includes a frieze board or frieze molding. At the gable ends a frieze board of proper thickness (usually $1\frac{1}{8}$ inches) is normally used.

WOOD SHINGLES AND SHAKES

Wood shingles and shakes can be applied in a single or a double course pattern. They may be used directly over wood or plywood sheathing, but 1- by 3- or 1- by 4-inch nailing strips must be provided when sheathing has inadequate nailholding capacity (such as polystyrene or fiberboard sheathing). It is good practice to use sheathing paper under the shingles since it greatly reduces air infiltration and resists water penetration.

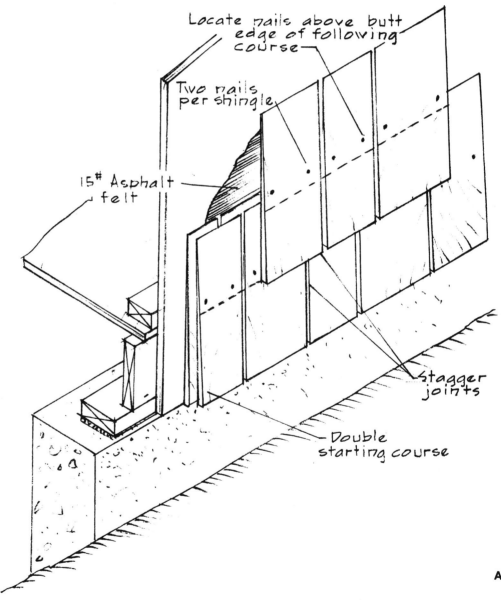

Fig. 79. Wood shingle siding.
A. Single course.

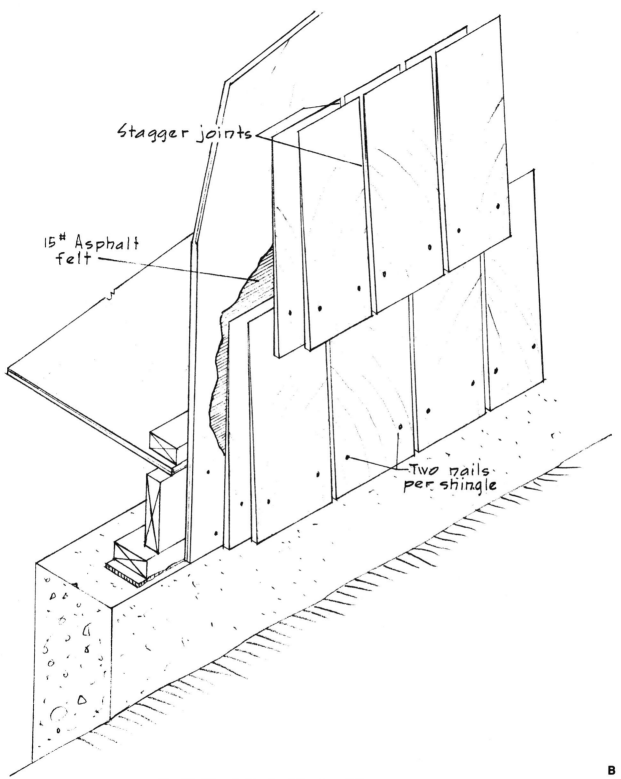

Stagger joints

15# Asphalt felt

Two nails per shingle

Fig. 79. Wood shingle siding (*cont'd*).
B. Double course.

B

In single course application, one course is laid directly over the other as lap siding is applied. The exposure distance for the 16-inch shingle is about $7\frac{1}{2}$ inches and $11\frac{1}{2}$ inches for the 24-inch shake. No. 1 or No. 2 grade shingles can be used for this method. Use two nails, placed $\frac{3}{4}$ to 1 inch from the edge, for each shingle locating them so the following course will cover the nails, Fig. 79A. The bottom course should be doubled. As in roof shingling, space the shingles so that the joints do not coincide. When plywood sheathing is only $\frac{3}{8}$-inch thick, it is good practice to use threaded (ring shank) nails rather than the standard galvanized shingle nail. Nails should be long enough to penetrate through the undernailing surface (sheathing or nailing strips).

The double course system has the usually desirable effect of a wide exposure distance. Furthermore, a third grade shingle can be used as an undercourse. The first course is nailed directly to the sheathing, projecting the bottom $\frac{1}{4}$ to $\frac{1}{2}$ inch below the top of the foundation wall. Nail only enough to hold the shingle in place. The top course, usually No. 1 grade, is then face nailed over the undercourse with $\frac{1}{4}$- or $\frac{3}{8}$-inch projection to provide a good drip edge, Fig. 79B. The normal exposure distance for a 16-inch wood shingle is about 10 to 12 inches. For 24-inch wood shakes you can use up to a 20-inch exposure for the No. 1 grade shake. Most shakes are handsplit and resawn. Use the split face as the exposed side. Two nails are used for each shingle and shake placed near the edge and above the butt, Fig. 79B. A straight piece of shiplap sheathing can be used as a guide in laying up double course shingles. An underlayment of 15-pound asphalt paper is a must.

Corners can be finished with metal corners which can usually be obtained in colors to match the color of stain used for the shingles. Other corner designs consist of overlapping of the shingle courses in alternate patterns or using a corner board.

17
Special Framing Details

Floor and wall framing details vary somewhat when plumbing and other utilities are involved. Without this special framing it is often necessary to cut floor joists excessively after they are installed to accommodate closet bends, etc. Fig. 80A shows a

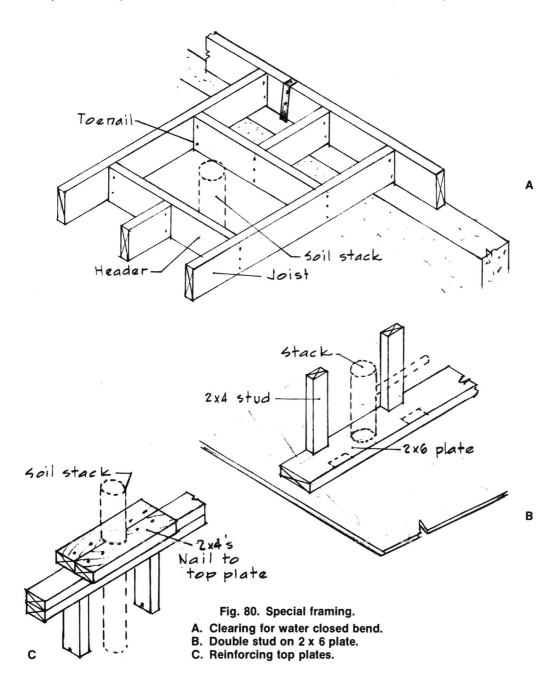

A

B

C

Fig. 80. Special framing.
A. Clearing for water closed bend.
B. Double stud on 2 x 6 plate.
C. Reinforcing top plates.

framing detail which might be used to provide clearance for a water closet bend. Good end nailing and toenailing are important.

Holes can be drilled in joists for water pipes when necessary. The hole should not be over 2 inches in diameter and drilled in the center of the joist, allowing $2\frac{1}{2}$ to 3 inches of undisturbed wood above and below the hole. This eliminates the use of holes in 2- by 6-inch joists because too great an amount is removed. Holes near the center of a span are especially critical.

It is good practice at tub locations to double the joists at the outer edge of the tub when joists are parallel to the length of the tub.

Wall framing for the plumbing wall (wall which provides space for water supply and vent stack) is usually framed with 2- by 6-inch bottom and top plates. Studs are spaced 16 inches on center and placed flatwise at each edge, Fig. 80B. Drain pipes and water supply pipes are located in this area. The spaced studs together with an insulation between will provide an excellent sound-resistant wall.

If a 3-inch plastic vent stack might be located in a 2 by 4 stud wall, the top plates should be reinforced. Two 2- by 4-inch scabs, cut around the stack, should be nailed to the top plates, Fig. 80C.

18
Thermal Insulation and Vapor Barriers

Adequate insulation is perhaps the most effective way to save on home heating costs. An uninsulated home loses twice as much heat as one properly insulated, and doubles fuel consumption and costs. Attic insulation is a big money saver and in most houses is easy to apply by the homeowner. Thus, whether you are insulating a new addition or adding insulation to your present home, the investment will pay for itself in lower fuel bills.

THERMAL CONDUCTIVITY

The thermal conductivity (insulating value) or various materials is normally expressed in their k (conductivity) value. The k values or heat conductivity are defined as the

TABLE 10. Thermal conductivity values of common insulating materials.[a]

Insulating Group		k Range (Conductivity)[b]
General	Specific Type	
Flexible	Standard materials	0.25–0.27
Fill	Standard materials	.28–.30
	Vermiculite	.45–.48
Reflective (2 sides)	Aluminum foil on each side of paper backing	[c]
Rigid	Insulating fiberboard	.35–.36
	Sheathing fiberboard	.42–.55
Foam board	Polystyrene	.19–.29
	Urethane	.15–.17
Wood	Low density (Cedars, soft pines, etc)	.60–.65

[a]Data from U.S. Dept. of Agriculture Handbook No. 73.

[b]k is the amount of heat, in British thermal units, that will pass in 1 hour through a sq ft of material 1 in. thick per 1°F temperature difference between faces of the material. (Thus the lower the k value, the better the insulation.)

[c]Values slightly better than 1-in. of flexible insulation. Reflective side must face a *space* to be effective.

Note: (1) Single glass has a U value of 1.13; with a storm sash a U value of 0.53. Insulated glass $U = 0.61$. (2) An 8-in. concrete block wall has an only slightly greater insulating value than 1-in. thickness of low-density wood.

amount of heat, in British thermal units, that will pass in 1 hour through 1 square foot of material 1 inch thick per 1°F temperature difference between faces of the material. Simply expressed, k represents heat loss; the lower this numerical value, the better the insulating qualities of a material.

Insulation is also rated commercially on its resistance, or R value, which is merely another expression of its insulating value. The R value is usually expressed as the total of the wall or a thick insulating blanket or batt, whereas k is the rating per inch of thickness. For example, a k value of 1 inch of insulation is 0.25. Then the resistance, R, is $\frac{1}{0.25}$ or 4.0. If the insulation blanket is $3\frac{1}{2}$ inches thick, the total R is $3\frac{1}{2} \times 4.0$ or 14.0. The insulation you buy at building supply firms usually has the total R stamped on the material. Thus the higher the R value (for any insulation thickness), the better the insulating value.

The thermal conductivity values of some of the most commonly used insulating materials is shown in Table 10.

WHERE TO INSULATE

Insulation should be used on exterior walls, ceilings, and floors that are exposed to unheated areas. This normally includes:

1. All exterior walls.
2. Walls adjacent to an unheated garage, porch, or attic stairway.
3. Ceilings under an unheated attic space.
4. Ceilings that are rafter spaces in flat or low-slope roofs.
5. In floors over unheated crawl spaces.
6. Around perimeter of walls when a crawl space is used as a heat chamber.
7. Around perimeter of concrete slabs (heated porch or room).
8. Between floor joists (a) over foundation walls in houses with basements and (b) between first and second floor in two-story houses.

While insulation is used mainly to reduce heat loss, it also serves to reduce heat gain in the hot summer months.

HOW TO INSULATE

Insulation is normally placed in wall, ceiling, and floor areas after wiring, heat and cold air ducts, and other utilities have been "roughed-in."

Wall Insulation

Flexible insulation in blanket or batt form should be placed between studs. It should be placed so that the vapor barrier covering is facing the inside of the room with the tabs overlapping the edge of the studs, Fig. 81A. This will minimize movement of water vapor to the outer cold surfaces. However, there is a different procedure when friction fit (unfaced) batts are used or the vapor barrier on the insulation is not felt to be adequate or is torn. A full covering of 4- or 6-mil polyethylene film should then be used over the insulation, studs, plates, headers, etc., Fig. 81B. Before applying the polyethylene (called enveloping), fill the open spaces between window and door frames with loose insulation. This includes areas between jambs and sill at the window and door framing members. These areas will be protected by the "enveloping" of polyethylene. However, when the enveloping is *not* used, strips of 4- or

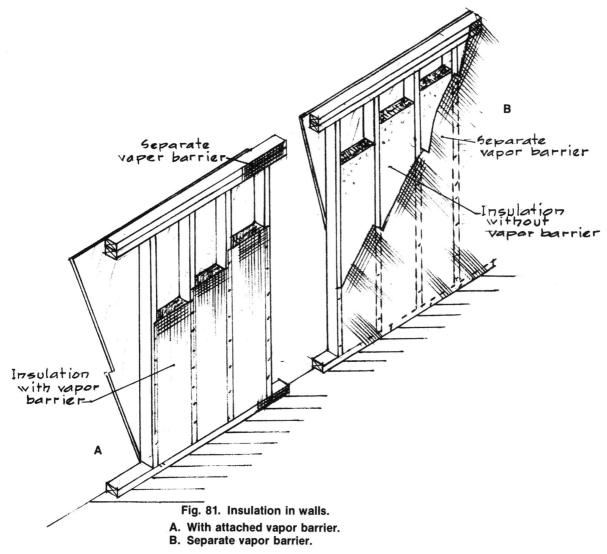

Fig. 81. Insulation in walls.
A. With attached vapor barrier.
B. Separate vapor barrier.

6-mil polyethylene or other good vapor barrier materials should be used around the frame. This includes the unprotected window and door headers. Staple the film enough to hold it in place until interior coverings have been applied.

Ceiling Insulation

Ceilings can be insulated with fill type or batt insulation. A thickness of 8 to 12 inches is commonly used to reduce heat loss. When a vapor barrier is a part of the insulation, place it face down toward the room. One method used for ceiling (attic) insulation consists of using $3\frac{1}{2}$-inch- or 6-inch-thick blanket or batt insulation (vapor side down) followed by a 6-inch unfaced batt or fill insulation for a total of $9\frac{1}{2}$ to 12 inches. When the attic space is hard to reach, the insulation can be placed before the ceiling finish is installed. Lay the upper batts across the joists and the lower batts between the joists. Be sure to allow space at the eave line for air circulation.

Floor (Crawl Space) Insulation

When the crawl space is unheated, insulation between floor joists might generally be installed after the addition has been enclosed. Use friction fit or similar insulation

119

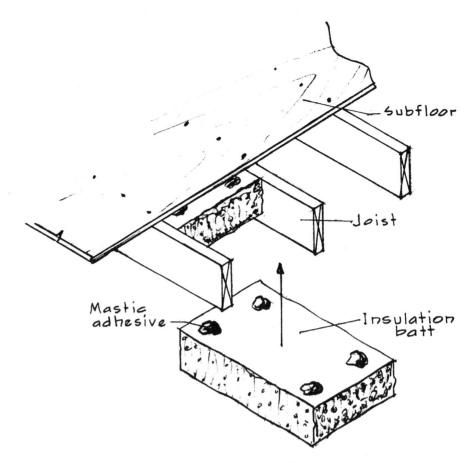

Fig. 82. Floor insulation.

batts between floor joists. Apply gobs of mastic or asphalt adhesive to the top surface of the insulation so that it adheres to the underside of the subfloor, Fig. 82.
Most batt insulations of this type are made to fit snugly between frame members.
When the crawl space is not roomy enough for this type installation, the tabs of the
vapor barrier on the insulation can be stapled to the top edge of the joists before
subfloor is placed. When a vapor barrier is desired, place it between the subfloor and
the finish floor.

If the crawl space is used as a plenum (heat) chamber, the inner faces of the
masonry wall should be insulated with a least 2 inches of a foam-type or similar
insulation. Carry the insulation about 6 inches below the ground surface. Also
insulate between joists around the perimeter of the foundation.

Attic Room Insulation

When an attic is remodeled to include several rooms, insulation should be used
in all areas between heated and unheated spaces. This might include ceilings, roof
slopes between rafters, new knee walls, and floors outside of the room proper,
Fig. 83. Apply the insulation as previously described for walls, ceilings, and floors.
It is important to leave a space above the insulation at the roof slope for a ventilating
airway. A full thick ($3\frac{1}{2}$-inch) insulating blanket for 2 by 6 rafters will provide a
2-inch airway. Use double batts in the ceiling area, 6-inch batts in the knee walls,
and 8 to 10 inches of insulation in the floor area outside the rooms proper, Fig. 83.

120

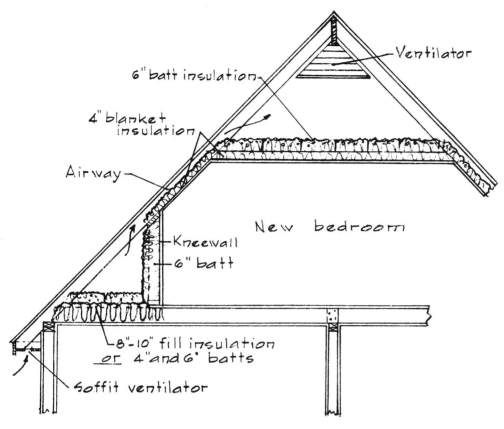

Fig. 83. Attic room insulation.

Insulation for Concrete Slabs

A concrete slab floor should have some type of insulation when the rooms above are to be heated. Such insulation is placed in a manner so as to minimize cold floors and heat loss. Support for the slab can consist of a masonry wall or concrete piers supporting a concrete grade beam, Fig. 19A and B. After the grade beam has been poured, a rigid waterproof insulation such as a cellular-glass insulating board or a foamed plastic is used along the inside of the grade beam, Fig. 84. For cold climates a 1-inch-thick by 18-inch-wide sheet of insulation should be placed along the inside face of the grade beam. After a sand and gravel tamped fill is placed, a 6-mil poly-ethylene vapor barrier should be used to prevent moisture penetration. The insula-tion is then placed over this vapor barrier. When a masonry wall is used for slab support, insulation is placed in the same manner.

Additional insulation can be used to advantage on a concrete slab. A foam insula-tion with an asbestos board facing is placed around the exterior of the slab, Fig. 84. It extends from under the siding to below ground level. This material can be applied with a mastic-type adhesive.

Another method which reduces heat loss is, of course, through the use of storm windows and doors. A storm window over a single glass window (double-hung, casement, etc.) reduces the heat loss by almost 100 percent. Even adding a storm window to a picture window having insulated glass will reduce heat loss of the opening by over 70 percent. Because windows and doors represent 15 to 20 percent of exterior walls, such extra protection becomes very important.

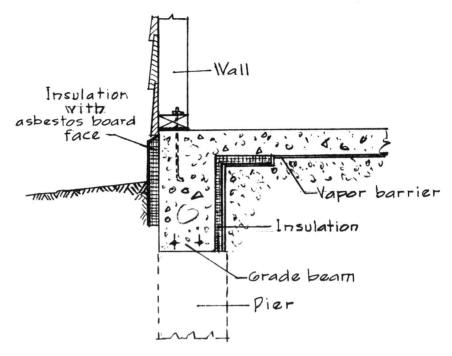

Fig. 84. Insulation for concrete slab.

VAPOR BARRIERS

Vapor barriers have been discussed in previous sections on insulation because they are normally an integral part of such materials. The importance of good vapor barriers cannot be stressed enough, especially in those houses which have systems producing "controlled" humidifiers. As the outside temperatures go well below freezing, the vapor pressure differences increase between the inside and outside. Thus, the colder the outside temperature, the greater this force which moves water vapor through the walls or openings around frames. This vapor can condense on a cold inner surface of the siding resulting in eventual paint peeling. The vapor barrier is thus the one deterrent in minimizing this vapor movement.

Some insulations do not have a vapor barrier which many consider adequate. A paper-backed foil and 4- or 6-mil polyethylene have good resistance to the passage of water vapor. *Some* asphalt-coated papers may be satisfactory under normal conditions if application of the insulation is properly done. As important as the quality of the vapor barrier is the method of application. This has been brought out in the previous sections and include: (1) enveloping of the entire inner surfaces of exposed walls; (2) providing vapor barriers around all areas of framed openings (windows and doors); (3) stapling the tab of the vapor barrier on insulation to the edge of the studs for a positive seal; and (4) care in providing a good vapor barrier for a concrete slab and crawl space.

Providing a vapor barrier for walls which have had insulation added (older houses) is sometimes a problem. The use of a prime coat of aluminum paint or a good sealer coat followed by decorative coats of paint will result in some protection. In moisture-producing bathrooms, for example, the use of several prime coats of aluminum paint is good practice.

Vapor barriers can be an advantage as soil covers in enclosed crawl spaces. They reduce the movement of soil moisture to wood members used in the floor system. A layer of 6-mil polyethylene with lapped edges provides an excellent soil cover. Roll roofing is also excellent and is very resistant to mechanical damage. Bricks or small sections of concrete block may be used to hold the soil cover in place.

19
Ventilation

Ventilation in house construction is normally required in unheated areas such as attics, crawl spaces, and spaces under roof surfaces in a flat roofed unit. Its main purpose is to exhaust, by natural or mechanical means, excessive moisture vapor which may accumulate in these areas.

Under some conditions, condensation of moisture vapor can occur in unheated spaces unless adequate ventilation is provided. Ventilation is also important in enclosed crawl spaces when floors are insulated. Attic ventilation together with good ceiling insulation will minimize the melting of snow on the roof. This water can cause ice dams at the cornice overhangs and possible moisture entry into the walls of the house. Thus good insulation and adequate ventilation will not only eliminate moisture problems in the winter, but also provide a cooler attic and a cooler house during summer months.

LOCATION OF VENTILATORS

In sloped roofs (gable or hip) with space above the ceiling, it is good practice to include both inlet and outlet ventilators. Thus, inlet ventilators in the soffit and outlet ventilators at the ridge provide a "stack" effect. This will result in a natural air movement and the exhaust of moisture vapor. Outlet ventilators alone are not as efficient and therefore require greater areas. Inlet ventilators are best located in the soffit area of the cornice and should be distributed along the length (and width) of the addition. Outlet ventilators can be located at the top of a gable end or at the ridge line in hip roof houses. A number of commercial ridge ventilators are available, varying from the simple "eyebrow" ventilator to power-driven types. Such ventilators should be located to the rear of your addition or where they are less conspicuous. The soffit area of a gable end overhang can also contain ventilation slots or holes.

AMOUNT OF VENTILATION

The ratios in the following chart may be used as a guide in determining the amount of ventilation required for your addition:

Type of Roof	Ratio of Total Minimum Net Ventilating Area to Ceiling Area[a]	
	Inlet	Outlet
Gable (outlet only)	0	1/300
Gable (inlet and outlet)	1/900	1/900
Hip (inlet and outlet)	1/900	1/1600
Flat or Low Slope (inlet–outlet combined)[b]	0	1/250

[a]Screened openings reduces ventilating by $\frac{1}{2}$.
[b]Ventilators located at flat roof overhang.

When ventilators are screened for insect protection, the total required area should be doubled as air movement through these screens is restricted. For example, if the ceiling of your gable roof addition has an area of 900 square feet, the total gross area for the inlet and outlet ventilators should be 2 square feet ($900 \times \frac{1}{900} \times 2$). Thus a total of 2 square feet of outlet ventilation and 2 square feet of inlet ventilation is required. This can be distributed along the ridge or at the gable end and along the soffit area.

TYPES AND LOCATION OF VENTILATORS

Outlet ventilators for gable roofs are normally located at the open gable ends. They can consist of preformed metal ventilators which allow for variable roof pitches or of rectangular forms made of metal or wood, Fig. 85A. Rectangular ventilators are available in sizes from 8 by 8 inches to 14 by 18 inches. They should be located as close to the ridge line as possible, Fig. 85B. Roof ventilators should be located near the ridge line to be most effective. They consist of the simple eyebrow type or the wind-driven turbine ventilator. Power-driven types are also available.

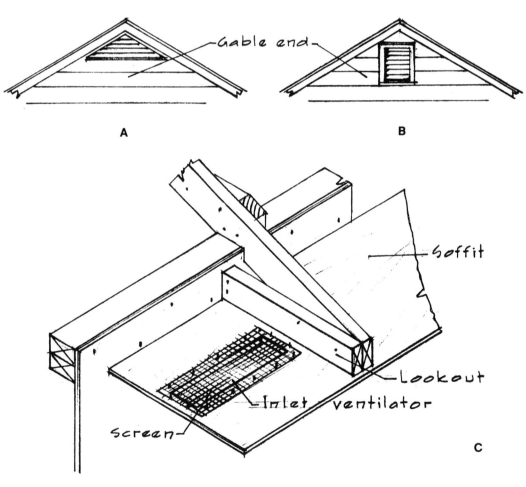

Fig. 85. Ventilators.
A. Outlet.
B. Outlet.
C. Inlet ventilator.

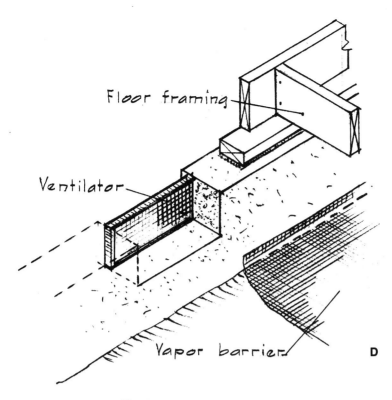

Floor framing

Ventilator

Vapor barrier

D

Fig. 85. Ventilators (*cont'd*).
D. Crawl space ventilator.

Inlet ventilators are best located in the soffit area of the roof overhang). They should be distributed along each side for gable roofs and along all sides for hip roof houses, but out from the wall to prevent entry of wind-driven snow, Fig. 85C. Such ventilators can be obtained in sizes from 4 by 16 inches to 8 by 16 inches. They are designed to fit in the spaces between rafters and the soffit lookouts (nailing blocks). A continuous screened slot is sometimes used along the soffit area. Such slots are often used in the overhang of flat or low-sloped roofs.

Unheated crawl spaces should normally have some type of ventilation. A soil cover greatly reduces this need, however. The total net area when a soil cover is used should be $\frac{1}{1600}$ ($\frac{1}{800}$ for screened ventilators) of the floor area. These ventilators can be located in the foundation wall, Fig. 85D. Place one on each side of the addition.

20

Sound Insulation

AIRBORNE SOUND INSULATION

Sound insulation is perhaps more important in walls and floors of apartments than in single dwellings. However, walls (and floors) might be sound insulated in bathrooms and in walls between bedrooms and activity rooms. For example, the resistance of a wall to the passage of airborne sound is rated by its Sound Transmission Class (STC). Thus the higher this value, the better the sound barrier. A rating of 45 or higher might be considered a reasonably good wall or floor from the standpoint of sound transmission in a single family house.

An 8-inch concrete block wall, for example, has an STC value of 45. A single stud wall with $\frac{1}{2}$-inch gypsum board on each side has an STC rating of 32. This latter construction does little in providing sound resistance between rooms. The following chart lists some typical wall and floor constructions and their STC ratings, Fig. 85E.

	Detail	Description	STC[1/]
A		8-inch concrete block	45
B		1/2-inch sound insulation board 1/2-inch gypsum board (each side)	46
C		1/2-inch gypsum wallboard	45
D		1/2-inch gypsum wallboard plus 1-1/2 inches flexible insulation	49

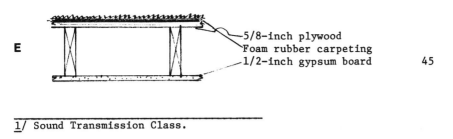

E   5/8-inch plywood
        Foam rubber carpeting
        1/2-inch gypsum board   45

1/ Sound Transmission Class.

Fig. 85E. Sound insulation of walls and ceilings.

A. **8-inch concrete block.**
B. **Frame wall with sound insulation board and gypsum board on each side.**
C. **Staggered studs (2 by 6 plates.) with ½-inch gypsum board on each side.**
D. **Staggered studs (2 by 6 plates) with 1½ inch flexible insulation filler and ½-inch gypsum wall board coverings.**
E. **Floor system with gypsum board under and plywood subfloor and foam rubber carpeting above.**

SOUND ABSORPTION

Another system of sound insulation involves the use of materials which absorb sounds. House furnishings such as drapes, carpeting, etc., have sound absorption qualities. Construction materials which can be used consist mainly of acoustic tile. These materials with perforated or roughened surfaces are used in ceilings and on walls where they are not subjected to mechanical damage. They may be applied with mastic to an underlayer of sheetrock, stapled to nailing strips, or with mechanical suspension systems.

21

Basement Rooms

Remodeling of existing basements or new basements for living areas is an economical method of acquiring extra space. To provide good living conditions during both summer and winter, the walls and floors should be treated and insulated properly. While more costly than a casual remodeling, good construction methods will pay off in better living conditions and savings in heating costs.

FLOORS

In those new additions which might incorporate an open framed wall (sloping lot) at one end and two sides with masonry walls, floors can be constructed as shown in Fig. 86A. After the soil (sand fill) has been leveled, a good vapor barrier is then applied over the entire surface of the basement. A 2-foot-wide strip of rigid insulation such as 1-inch polystyrene should be used around the perimeter. A 3- to $3\frac{1}{2}$-inch concrete slab is then poured over the entire surface. The finish surface of the basement can consist of asphalt tile, or a wood floor nailed to wood screeds leveled and anchored to the floor, Fig. 86A.

Remodeling of floors in existing basements with a concrete floor should include the use of insulation and a vapor barrier. One such method is shown in Fig. 86B. After a good vapor barrier has been placed on the concrete surface, install 2- by 3-inch screeds on 24-inch centers. They can be leveled, then anchored to the floor with masonry nails or anchors. After perimeter insulation has been applied, a $\frac{5}{8}$- or

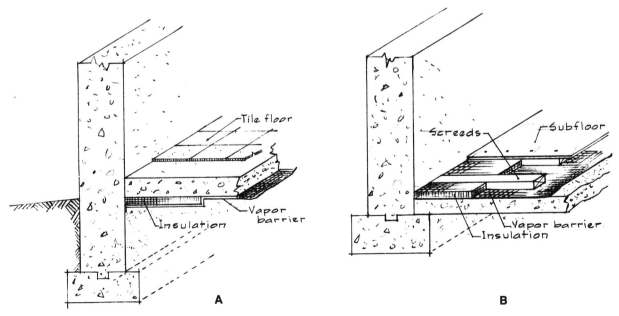

Fig. 86. Basement floors.
A. New floor treatment.
B. Existing floor treatment.

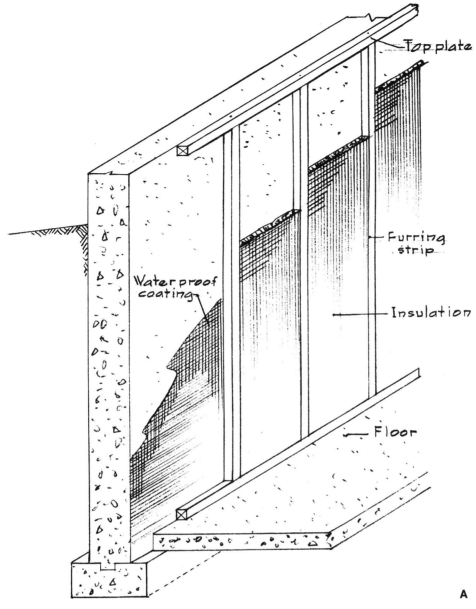

Fig. 87. Basement wall treatment.
A. Wall insulation.

$\frac{3}{4}$-inch plywood subfloor can be nailed to the screeds. Floor tile or carpeting can be used over the plywood. It is good practice to provide blocks for edge nailing or to use tongued and grooved plywood for a single subfloor.

WALLS

Perhaps the simplest method of supplying nailing surfaces for the finish and at the same time space for insulation is by the use of studs or furring strips. It is good practice to first apply a waterproof coating on the inner surface of the masonry wall. Top and bottom plates and 2- by 2-inch vertical furring strips spaced 16 or 24 inches on center form the framework against the wall, Fig. 87A. A construction adhesive or masonry nails can be used to fasten the furring strips to the wall between

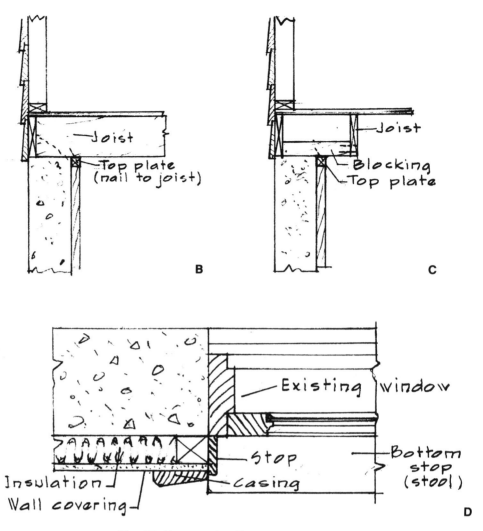

Fig. 87. Basement wall treatment (*cont'd*).
B. Top plate to cross joists.
C. Top plate to parallel joists.
D. Detail at window.
     (plan view).

top and bottom plates. When the top plate is at right angles to the joists, it can be nailed directly to the underside of these floor members, Fig. 87B. When the plate parallels the joists, use nailing blocks between the stringer joist and the first inside joist, Fig. 87C. Cut lengths for a driving fit and nail through the joist into the end of the block. Blanket insulation $1\frac{1}{2}$ inches thick or foam insulation can now be installed between the 2 by 2's. The finish can consist of plywood, gypsum board (sheetrock), hardboard, or paneling.

For carpeting or a finish wood floor, the trim along the basement floor may consist of a wood baseboard. If the finish floor is a vinyl tile, for example, a vinyl cove base can be used. The junction of the wall and ceiling can be finished with or without a small crown or cove molding. Trim around a basement window can consist of window stops and casing, Fig. 87D. The bottom stop can be in the form of a wide stool which can be used to hold decorative items, plants, etc.

130

22

Interior Wall and Ceiling Finish

Finishes most adaptable for covering interior framed areas by other than professionals are the "dry wall" materials. These include gypsum board (sheetrock), prefinished hardboard, wood paneling, plywood, and similar materials. Plastered walls and a ceiling finish over a gypsum lath base normally requires a professional craftsman. However, most dry wall finishes can be easily applied by the average skilled homeowner.

Bathtub enclosures in homes built by contractors are usually plastered and finished with ceramic tile. However, there is a special waterproof sheetrock material used around tubs that serves as a base for ceramic and similar tile which is installed with special adhesives. Plastic-faced hardboard with corner and edge moldings is also available for use around tub enclosures.

The minimum thicknesses of the various wood and wood-base materials used for interior coverings are shown in Table 11.

TABLE 11. Minimum thickness for wood and wood-base interior finishes.

Frame Member Spacing (in.)	Minimum Thickness (in.)			
	Plywood	Fiberboard	Wood Paneling	Hardboard
16	$\frac{1}{4}$	$\frac{1}{2}$	$\frac{3}{8}$	$\frac{1}{4}$
24	$\frac{3}{8}$	$\frac{3}{4}$	$\frac{5}{8}$	–

When wood panel boards or similar materials are applied vertically in 6- to 12-inch widths, some type of horizontal nailing base must be provided. Blocking between studs or horizontal nailing strips are commonly used.

GYPSUM BOARD

Gypsum board is a sheet material composed of a gypsum filler faced with paper. The paper face can be painted in several manners including the use of a base coat which simulates plaster. Other gypsum boards are prefinished with embossed and similar surfaces. These latter prefinished materials are normally applied in two layers with an adhesive over a nailed base of $\frac{3}{8}$-inch gypsum board to eliminate surface nails.

Gypsum board can be obtained in 4-foot widths and lengths up to 16 feet. The 4- by 8-foot sheet is most commonly used, however, and is applied vertically. The edges along the length (and sometimes the ends) are tapered, allowing for a filled and taped joint between sheets. A thickness of $\frac{1}{2}$ inch is usually recommended for new single construction when frame members are spaced 16 inches on center. Laminated construction consists of two layers of $\frac{3}{8}$-inch gypsum board; the first

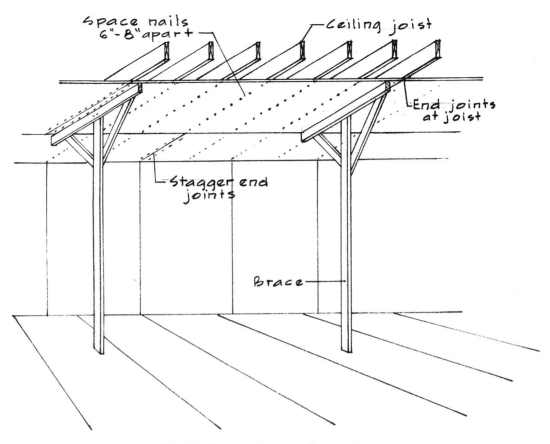

Fig. 88. Gypsum board-ceiling application.

nailed and the second applied with a wallboard adhesive. Vinyl-coated gypsum boards in various patterns are sometimes face nailed to studs with nails which match the color of the facing.

Ceiling Application

The ceiling finish is normally applied before the wall finish is installed. Use $1\frac{5}{8}$-inch dry wall nails spaced 6 to 8 inches apart. If a ring shank dry wall nail is used, a $1\frac{1}{2}$-inch length is sufficient.

To aid in holding the sheetrock in place on the ceiling while nailing, use a brace, Fig. 88. The brace consists of a 2- by 4-inch by 4-foot horizontal member with a braced vertical member. Total length should be slightly greater than ceiling height. Use one brace at each end of the sheet for easier application. Place the length of the sheets across the ceiling joists. Stagger end joints at least one joist spacing. All end joints should be made at a ceiling joist.

Vertical Application on Walls

Gypsum board applied vertically should be nailed around the perimeter and at intermediate studs with dry wall nails. Use $1\frac{5}{8}$-inch lengths for $\frac{1}{2}$-inch sheetrock. It is important that the moisture contents of the studs and ceiling joists be low enough to prevent "nail pops." These are caused by the drying out of frame members and results in small bulges at the nail locations. So if there is any question of this problem, delay the application of the gypsum board until members are drier. However, the use of ring shank nails will greatly reduce this problem.

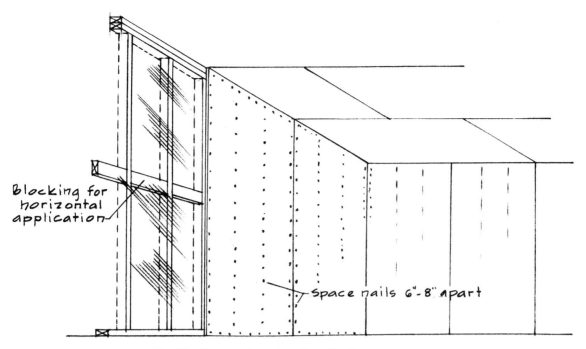

Fig. 89. Gypsum board-wall application.

When applying the gypsum board, use light contact between the sheets and space nails 6 to 8 inches apart at each stud, Fig. 89. The nails should be driven so as not to rupture the paper surface but enough to leave a small dimple which can be filled later with joint cement. The sheets are also nailed at the sole plate and top plate. Another nailing method sometimes used is called the "floating top." In this system, the top horizontal row of nails is eliminated allowing the top 6 or 8 inches of the sheet to be free. This is said to prevent fracture of the gypsum board if there is a movement of the framing members.

Horizontal Application on Walls

Horizontal application of gypsum board requires the use of nailing blocks cut between the studs at midheight of the wall, Fig. 89. As in other applications, center the ends (and edges) of the sheet on the center of the nailing members. Use 6- to 8-inch nail spacing. The advantage of this method is that full room-length sheets can be used, eliminating all intermediate vertical joints. This method is usually used for the undercourse in two-ply laminated construction. The top ply is applied vertically with a wallboard adhesive eliminating the need for nails. In such application, the horizontal nailing blocks can be eliminated.

Joint Treatment

Joints of gypsum dry wall are finished with a joint cement, "spackle," and a perforated tape. Nail "dimples" are also covered with the cement. Joint cement can be obtained in powder form and mixed with water to the right consistency. It should be in a soft putty form so as to be easily spread with a trowel or putty knife. Joint cement can also be obtained in a premixed form ready to use. A latex joint compound is also available at most building supply companies. Joint tape with a perforated face and thin tapered edges is used at all joints, and can be folded along the

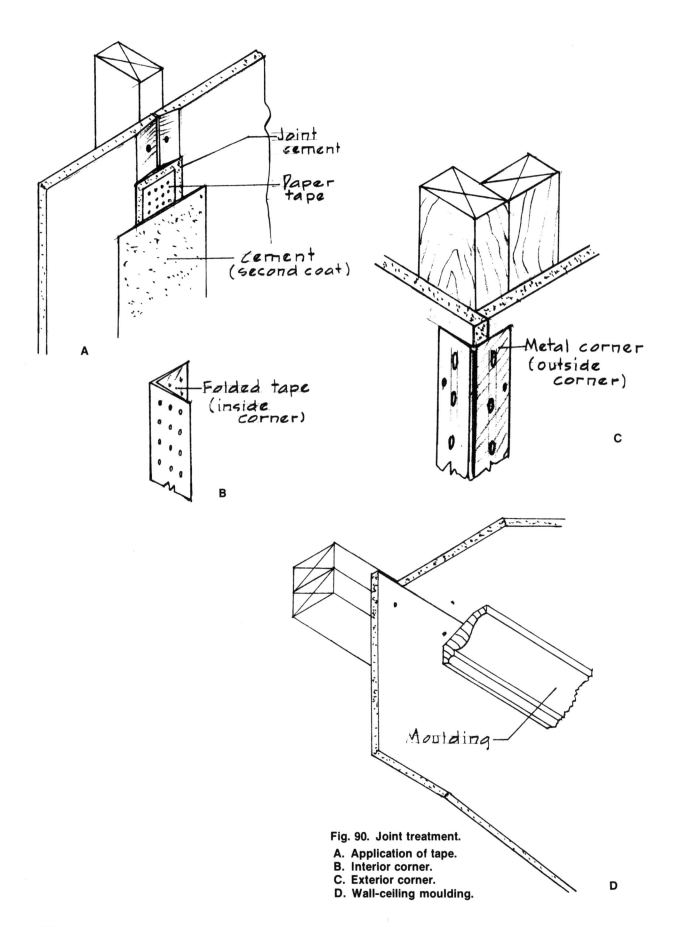

Joint
cement

Paper
tape

Cement
(second coat)

A

Folded tape
(inside
corner)

B

Metal corner
(outside
corner)

C

Moulding

D

Fig. 90. Joint treatment.
A. Application of tape.
B. Interior corner.
C. Exterior corner.
D. Wall-ceiling moulding.

134

center and used at interior corners and at wall and ceiling intersections. A dry wall corner bead of metal is commonly used at exterior corners. It is tacked in place and serves as a guide in providing a straight and impact-resistant edge.

The general procedure for taping joints (Fig. 90A) is as follows:

1. Use a wide (5 to 6 inches) spackling knife and spread the cement across the tapered edges of the gypsum board, starting at the top of the wall.

2. Press the tape in the recess with the spackling knife until the cement is forced through the perforations. Here is where too dry a compound mix will show up. If there are spots of poor or no tape adherence, it is a good indication that the mix is too dry. Remove and retape these sections.

3. Cover the tape with additional cement, feathering the outer edges.

4. Allow the cement to thoroughly dry and sand lightly. Apply a second coat, feathering the edges again. A steel trowel can be used for leveling and spreading if a third coat is necessary. Sand lightly between each coat and after the final coat.

5. The hammer dimples are also filled with several coats of cement (or more if necessary).

Interior corners and the wall–ceiling intersection can be finished with the tape, folding it at right angles before application, Fig. 90B. Use the same method of application as described for joints. For exterior corners use the metal edge previously described, Fig. 90C.

The wall–ceiling intersection can also be finished with a molding. A simple quarter-round molding or a more elaborate crown molding can be used, Fig. 90D. When a molding finish is used, the wall–ceiling joint need not be taped.

PLYWOOD

Prefinished plywood is available in a number of species and finishes and should not be overlooked as an accent wall or for the entire wall area of smaller rooms. It can result in a pleasing combination with a painted gypsum board ceiling. It is normally applied vertically in 4- by 8-foot sheets. A minimum thickness of $\frac{1}{4}$ inch when studs are spaced 16 inches on center is a good rule to follow. Small $1\frac{1}{4}$-inch colored coded nails can be obtained to match the finish of the plywood. They should be spaced 8 to 10 inches apart along each stud and at the top and bottom edges. Use only a light contact between sheets. Some plywoods are manufactured to simulate wood planking in various widths. Shallow routings are arranged so that small grooves are located on 16-inch centers. For example, these may consist of two 8-inch-wide "planks," one 12-inch- and one 4-inch-wide planks, and two 4-inch- and one 8-inch-wide plank for the 4-foot width. Nails are then located at those grooves over the stud locations.

Another system which might be used to cover existing smooth plaster walls for an accent area with plywood consists of the following: (1) Cut 8- by 8-inch squares from a thin hardwood plywood; (2) chamfer edges of tile slightly; (3) spread panel adhesive on plaster and apply the plywood squares, alternating face grain direction. The finish can be applied before or after the tiles are applied. To prevent cupping of the tile, use a good sealer on the back face.

Adhesives can also be used in fastening plywood and similar covering to the studs. Their use (always according to the adhesive manufacturer's directions) eliminates all nails except several guide nails at the top. Installation normally consists of the following: (1) apply two guide nails at the top after positioning; (2) remove ply-

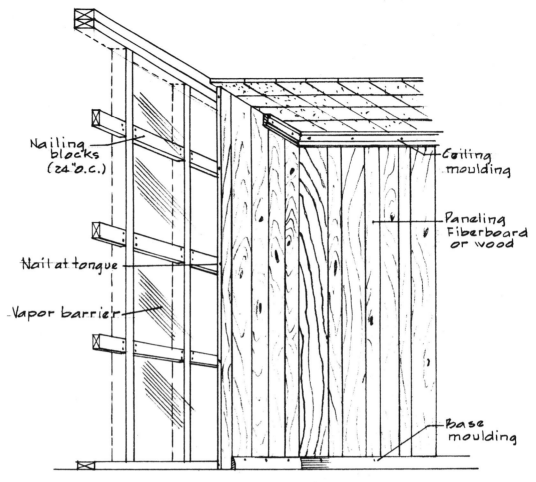

Fig. 91. Wall paneling—fiberboard or wood.

wood and spread the adhesive on frame members (in ribbons); (3) use guide nails in returning the plywood to the original position and press against the frame members to spread the adhesive on plywood and frame members; (4) pull the plywood away from the studs and after the adhesive has dried, press in place and tap along all frame members with a rubber mallet. Thinner plywood can be installed with adhesives over a solidly nailed backing, such as $\frac{3}{8}$-inch gypsum board.

HARDBOARD AND FIBERBOARD

Hardboard ($\frac{1}{4}$-inch thickness for 16-inch frame member spacing) can be installed in the same manner as plywood. Many types and finishes are available, some with printed surfaces to simulate plywood.

Fiberboard in plank or sheet form should be at least $\frac{1}{2}$ inch thick when frame members are spaced 16 inches on center. Tongued and grooved fiberboard planking in widths from 6 to 12 inches requires horizontal blocking between studs or nailing strips when applied vertically. Blocks or strips should not be more than 24 inches apart, Fig. 91. Use $1\frac{1}{2}$-inch brads or finish nails at the tongue portion. In the wider planks it might be advisable to face nail at the groove edge or to use a bit of adhesive against the nailing strips or blocks. The use of a 4- or 6-mil polyethylene vapor barrier over the studs and nailing strips on exterior walls is a must when not a part of

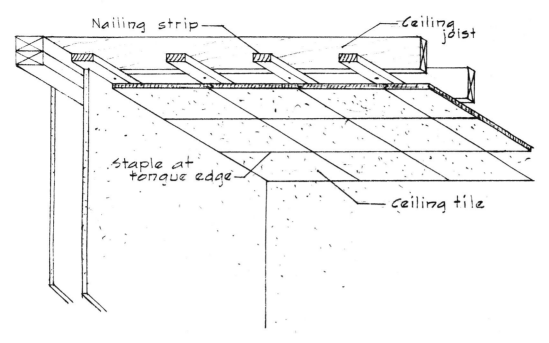

Fig. 92. Installation of ceiling tile.

your wall insulation. Because fiberboard is not too resistant to mechanical damage, use it on upper portions of the wall.

Fiberboard tile in 12- by 12-inch or larger sizes can be used as a ceiling finish. Such tile usually has two tongued and two grooved edges so that they lock in place when fastened. They are ordinarily installed on nailing strips spaced 12 inches on center. Strips are nailed to the undersides of the ceiling joists, Fig. 92. Use a staple gun for fastening the tile to the strips.

Suspended ceilings, which consist of a light metal framework suspended from the ceiling, can also be used. They are most useful when applying a lower ceiling in older houses. Tile sizes vary but a 2- by 4-foot size is commonly available.

Installation instructions usually accompany each suspended ceiling system but normally they consist of the following steps: (1) attach wall angles to each wall at the new ceiling height, and fasten to studs if possible; (2) use screw eyes in ceiling joists above location of main runner tees; (3) use wire to support the tees (holes are located at the top of the metal members for the wires); (4) attach cross tees at marked slots and lay in the 2- by 4-foot prefinished fiberboard panels. Because the metal tee grid members are exposed, such a ceiling is perhaps most adaptable to the casual family room.

WOOD PANELING

Wood paneling is applied in much the same manner as vertical fiberboard planking, Fig. 91. It can also be applied horizontally, for example, below a chair rail. The upper portion can then consist of a prefinished plywood, fiberboard planking, or vertically applied wood paneling. Use one fivepenny or sixpenny casing or finish nail at each stud or nailing strip. Table 11 should be used in selecting the proper thickness. When used vertically, nailing strips or blocking between studs is required.

23

Floor Coverings

Wood strip flooring or wood tile flooring is usually installed after the wall and ceiling finish is in place. This is also true of resilient floors such as vinyl, rubber, and other types. This does not apply to carpeting, however, as such materials are the last to be installed in your new addition. The type of finish floor you have planned has determined the height of the floor joists and subfloor. The level of the new floor should preferably be the same as that of the floor in the house proper to eliminate awkward thresholds. However, doors to the exterior or to an unheated addition such as an open porch usually requires some type of threshold for a good seal at the bottom of the door.

WOOD FLOORING

Strip Flooring

Wood strip flooring can be obtained in softwood or hardwood species. The softer species such as Douglas fir, hemlock, and southern pine in $1\frac{5}{8}$- to $5\frac{1}{8}$-inch widths are satisfactory where excessive wear is not anticipated. For best results, edge grain in a B and better grade is recommended. Use a $\frac{3}{4}$-inch thickness when installing over $\frac{1}{2}$-inch plywood subfloor or over diagonally laid wood boards.

Hardwood strip flooring is higher in cost than the softwood flooring but has a greater resistance to hard use. At least one of such species as oak, beech, birch, maple, or pecan can normally be obtained at your local lumber dealer. Edge grain in a clear grade is the most costly but a select grade (second grade) with small stains and grain variations will provide good service. The most common size for strip flooring is $\frac{3}{4}$ by $2\frac{1}{4}$ inches. Hardwood strip flooring in $\frac{3}{4}$-inch thickness can also be used over wood board subfloor or $\frac{1}{2}$-inch or thicker plywood. Thinner strip flooring, such as $\frac{3}{8}$ inch, should be installed over a tongued and grooved nominal 1-inch board subfloor. A tongued and grooved plywood subfloor in $\frac{5}{8}$- or $\frac{3}{4}$-inch thickness is also satisfactory.

Installing Strip Flooring

The subfloor should be clean and dry and well nailed. Look for nail projections or slightly loose areas and renail if necessary. Use a building paper such as 15-pound asphalt felt or a deadening felt over the subfloor. This will not only deaden sound but also minimize drafts and dust penetration from basement or crawl space areas. Paper can be used over a plywood subfloor as well as a wood board subfloor. Nailing through the subfloor into the joists provides a better floor, so use a chalk line on the paper to mark their location.

Flooring is usually delivered in a dry condition and care should be taken to keep it dry. Moisture absorbed after delivery is one of the most common causes for open joints between strips that appear several months after the heating season begins. Moisture contents should be about 8 to 9 percent over most of the country except the Southeast where 10 to 11 percent is recommended. In the dry Southwest a moisture content of 6 to 7 percent is a normal standard.

Strip flooring is usually laid with the lengths across the floor joists. Start at one side of the wall and face nail the inner edge, allowing a $\frac{3}{8}$- to $\frac{1}{2}$-inch space at the wall line, Fig. 93A. Use eightpenny flooring nails for $\frac{3}{4}$-inch flooring. This face nailing will be covered by the baseboard (and base shoe if one is used). Now nail (blind nail at each floor joist) the outer edge of the flooring (tongue side). Slope the nail about 45° to 50° with the horizontal, Fig. 93B. Use a scrap piece of flooring to drive the strips in place. Continue laying and nailing the flooring, now only into the tongue portion. End joints of the flooring should be alternately tongued and grooved to give good rigidity to these joints. Stagger the end joints. Use a large nailset to drive the nail the last $\frac{1}{8}$ inch or so and avoid hammer marks. If nails are difficult to drive or if slight splitting occurs (especially at ends), predrill or use a blunt-pointed nail. The last strip of flooring against the opposite wall must also be face nailed at the edge. Here again leave a $\frac{3}{8}$- to $\frac{1}{2}$-inch space. These spaces will allow the flooring to expand slightly during the humid seasons without causing damage to the wall or buckling of the floor.

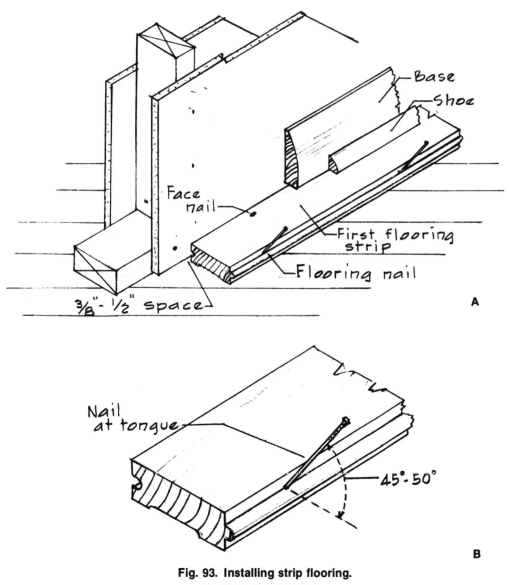

Fig. 93. Installing strip flooring.
A. First flooring strip.
B. Nailing detail.

Strip Flooring on a Concrete Slab

Strip flooring laid over a concrete slab is normally fastened by nailing to furring strips or to screeds anchored to the floor. One of the better methods commonly used consists of the following:

1. Use a heavy waterproof coating over the entire slab area.
2. Anchor or use a good mastic adhesive for 1- by 4-inch furring strips spaced on 16-inch centers, Fig. 94. Level by wedges, if necessary.

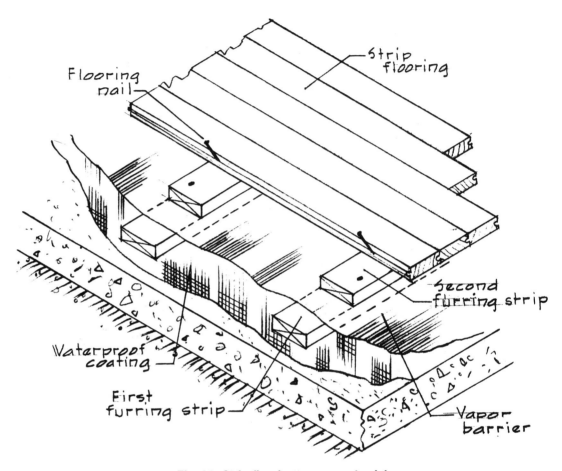

Fig. 94. Strip flooring on concrete slab.

3. Spread a vapor barrier such as 4-mil or heavier polyethylene over the furring strips followed by the second layer of 1- by 4-inch furring strips. Nail these to the first strips with fourpenny common, cement-coated or screw shank, nails. Space the nails about 10 inches apart at alternate edges.
4. Nail strip flooring in the normal manner previously described.

Wood Tile Flooring

Many types of prefinished hardwood tile or parquetry floor coverings are available. They are usually made of plywood with tongued and grooved edges and in thicknesses from $\frac{3}{8}$ to $\frac{5}{8}$ inch. Such flooring tile is usually fastened by nailing from the tongued side into a $\frac{5}{8}$-inch or thicker subfloor. Small screw shank flooring nails can be obtained for these flooring tile. To provide an interesting pattern, tile can be laid with alternating face grain directions and with various border designs. Because such tile are square, usually 8 by 8 inches in size, there is no problem of changing directions of the face grain. A long straight-edge can be used to start laying the tile along one side of the room. Joints between tile should be in line in both directions. A plywood underlayment should be used over a wood board subfloor. Plywood underlayment should be laid up with $\frac{1}{16}$-inch edge (side) spacing and $\frac{1}{32}$-inch end spacing. Be sure the joints of the tile do not occur over those of the underlayment.

RESILIENT TILE FLOORING

Resilient tile flooring in vinyl and similar materials (some with a rubber cushion backing) can be easily laid by the homeowner who has a little skill. Adhesives are normally used in applying these floor finishes. Tile is also available in prepasted form requiring only stripping of a covering material. Linoleum or similar materials in 6-foot-wide rolls is, of course, more difficult to apply by the average person than are the tile floor coverings.

The type of subfloor used under resilient tile is important. Tile should not be installed over a wood board subfloor. An underlayment of plywood, particle board, or hardboard should be used. If the top surface of the tile floor must be level with the adjoining wood floor of the house, use $\frac{5}{8}$-inch plywood or particle board underlayment, Fig. 95A. Rough or uneven edges of the subfloor or underlayment should be sanded for a smooth surface. Large cracks should be filled with a wood filler. Nails in the subfloor should be checked so that no nailheads protrude above the surface. Some treatment or sealing of the underlayment may be necessary especially for the prepasted tile. Follow the manufacturer's directions for each type of material.

MISCELLANEOUS FLOORS

Ceramic tile which can be installed with adhesives is laid over a double plywood underbase such as a $\frac{3}{4}$-inch subfloor and a $\frac{3}{8}$-inch plywood underlayment. Both should be well nailed, preferably with ring shank or screw shank nails. Be sure the joints of the tile do not coincide with the plywood joints.

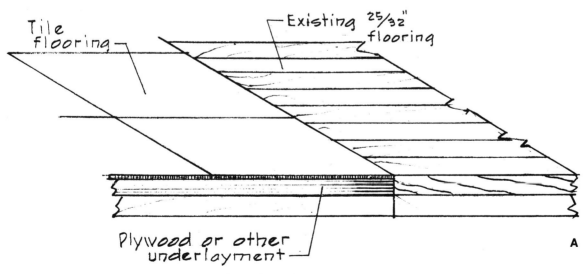

Fig. 95. Other finish floorings.
A. Resilient tile flooring.

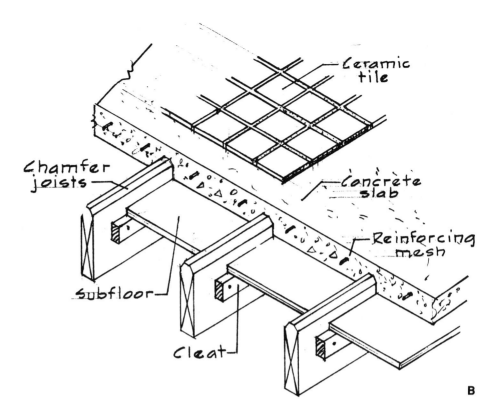

Fig. 95. Other finish flooring (cont'd).
B. Ceramic tile in bath.

If a concrete base is required for ceramic tile, the subfloor should be placed below the top of the joists supported by cleats, Fig. 95B. Joists should be chamfered to minimize cracking of the concrete and a $1\frac{1}{4}$-inch minimum thickness used above the tops of the joists. Use a mesh reinforcing wire in the concrete slab.

Carpeting also requires some type of underlayment over the subfloor. This ordinarily consists of plywood, particle board, or a medium-density hardboard. If the subfloor consists of 1-inch wood boards, use the length of the underlayment sheets (4 by 8 feet or longer) across the board direction. When the wood boards are applied diagonally, the direction of the sheets can be across the joists.

24

Interior Doors, Windows, and Trim

Interior door frames, doors, and trim for doors and windows are normally installed after the finish floor is in place. This does not apply to floors which may be carpeted. Cabinets, bookcases, fireplace mantels, and other interior millwork are also placed and secured at this time. Some contractors install the interior door frames *before* the walls are plastered, using the edges of the jambs as ground for the plaster finish. This is *not* desirable, however, as the jambs are not only subjected to excessive moisture but also to possible damage.

The standard width of door jambs is $4\frac{5}{8}$ inches for $\frac{1}{2}$-inch gypsum board finish and $5\frac{1}{8}$ inches for plastered walls for $3\frac{5}{8}$-inch-wide studs. However, if studs are $3\frac{1}{2}$ inches wide, the jambs might have to be ripped to the correct width. The width of jambs of doors between existing rooms and a new addition might be as much as 6 inches in width because of the exterior sheathing and siding.

SELECTION OF WOOD SPECIES

The treatment for interior millwork may consist of a paint finish, a clear (unstained) finish, or a stained and varnished finish. Some wood species used for trim are more adaptable to a paint finish than a natural finish. Wood to be painted should be smooth, close grained, and free from pitch streaks. Table 1 lists those species most desirable for a paint finish. These may include ponderosa pine, northern white pine, and similar species. When hardness is an additional desirable factor, select such species as birch, gum, and yellow-poplar.

For a natural finish, a pleasing figure, hardness, and uniform color are usually desirable. Species with these requirements include white and red oak, ash, maple, birch, cherry, and similar species. Those without distinct color or grain can be stained for their best appearance. Use Table 1 as a guide in selecting the wood species most desirable for your use.

The recommended moisture content for interior finish varies from 6 to 11 percent depending on climatic conditions. The southeastern states can use wood trim as high as 11 percent with good results. Other areas except the dry Southwest, where moisture content should be 6 percent, should use wood trim that has an 8 to 9 percent moisture content.

TRIM PARTS AND INSTALLATION

Door Frames and Trim

Interior door frames consist of two side jambs and a head jamb. They can be obtained with the head jamb rabbeted for easy assembly or in a preassembled form. Such units

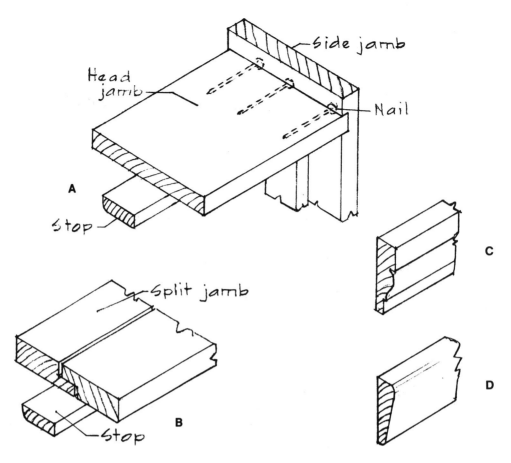

Fig. 96. Door frame members.
A. Assembly of jambs.
B. Split jamb.
C. Colonial-style casing.
D. Ranch-style casing.

often include a prefitted door with routing on door and jamb ready for hinges and locks. Stops and casings are other trim members used for door openings. Figures 96A to D show typical jambs and casing styles commonly used. Assembly of un-assembled jambs consist of nailing the side jambs to the head jamb with three seven-penny or eightpenny nails, Fig. 96A. A cross piece can be temporarily nailed at the bottom of the side jambs to retain the correct interior width. Split jambs, Fig. 96B, might be used where there is a variation in wall thickness. This can often occur in older houses. In such jambs, the casing on one or both sides is sometimes fitted and nailed in place.

Place the assembled door frame, with side jambs trimmed to the proper length, in the rough opening. If the jack stud (inner stud) at one side is perfectly plumb and straight, the side jamb of the frame can be nailed directly to this member. If not, use wood shingles as wedges, the tops sliding past each other, to align the side jamb. Space the wedges about 20 to 24 inches apart. Now nail this side jamb temporarily in place, Fig. 97A. Be sure the edges of the jamb are flush with the surface of the wall finish (gypsum board, plywood, etc.). Locate top and bottom pairs of wedges 6 to 8 inches from the ends of the frame. Space the other three pair equally between.

Use the same shingle wedge system at the opposite jamb. In driving the wedges from each side of the jamb, use a guide board cut to the exact length as the inside width of the clear opening. This will prevent bowing of the jamb and provide a straight and plumb alignment. Now nail the jambs in place with eightpenny finish nails. Use a pair of nails at each shingle wedge, placing one where the stop will cover it, Fig. 97A. Use a carpenter's square at the head and side jamb to be sure the frame is being installed correctly. Casings, as well as jambs, can be stained (and varnished, if desired) before they are installed. Thus after puttying the nailholes and applying the final coats of varnish, the finish will be completed.

Casings at the side and head jambs can now be installed. Locate the side casings $\frac{3}{16}$ inch back from inside face of the jambs, Fig. 97A. If the casing is molded, such as Figs. 96C or D, a miter joint is used at the intersection with the head jamb, Fig. 97B. A butt joint can be used for a square-edge casing, Fig. 97C. Use casing or finishing nails to fasten the casing to the jamb and to the edge (jack) studs of the opening,

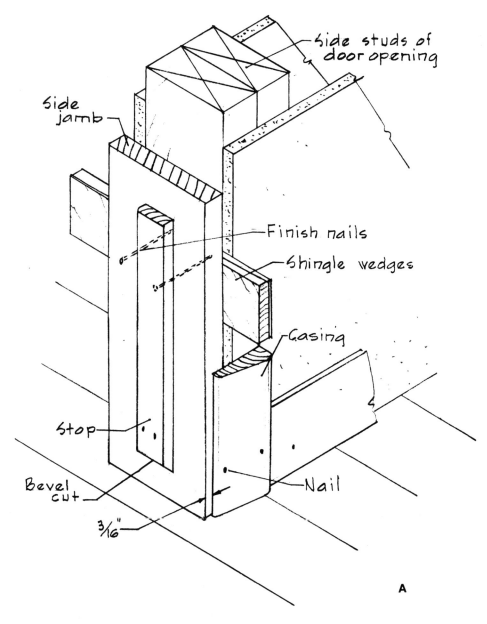

Fig. 97. Installing interior door frame.
A. Side jamb detail.

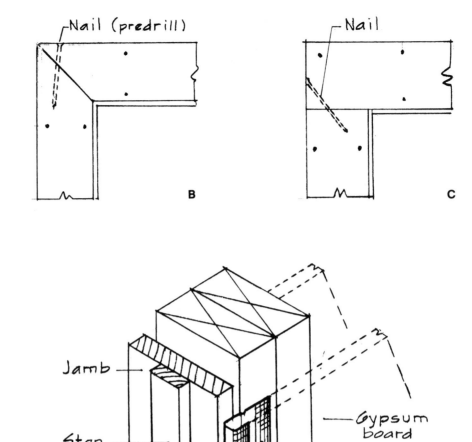

Fig. 97. Installing interior door frame (*cont'd*).
B. Miter corner.
C. Square-cut corner.
D. Metal casing.

Fig. 97A. For thin $\frac{7}{16}$-inch hardwood casing with $\frac{1}{2}$-inch gypsum wallboard, use $1\frac{1}{2}$-inch nails at the jamb and 2-inch nails (sixpenny) at the wall. For $\frac{5}{8}$-inch and thicker casing, use $1\frac{3}{4}$-inch nails at the jamb and $2\frac{1}{4}$ or $2\frac{1}{2}$-inch nails at the wall. The length depends on the thickness of the wall finish. For example, an eightpenny nail might be used for a plaster finish and a sixpenny nail when a $\frac{1}{2}$-inch gypsum wall covering is used. Before nailing the casing to the wall (at the miter corners), place a nail into the miter when the casings are $\frac{5}{8}$ inch or thicker, Figs. 97B and C. (This is likely to be impractical for thin casings, however.) Predrill before nailing the head casing. This will provide a smooth even joint. Use the same procedure in applying the casing to the inside of your exterior doors. Then set all nails. A metal casing for gypsum board is also available, Fig. 97D. Nail in place before installing the dry wall.

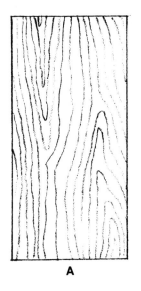 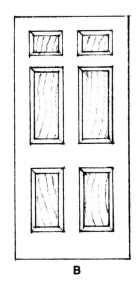 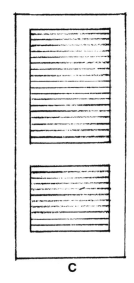

A   B   C

Fig. 98. Interior door types.
A. Flush.
B. Panel.
C. Panel with louvers.

Doors

The types of interior doors commonly used are the flush (with plywood or veneer faces) and the panel door. Panel doors have solid stiles (vertical members) and solid rails (cross members) and can be obtained in a number of designs, Fig. 98. The standard thickness for interior doors is $1\frac{3}{8}$ inches. However, sliding or cabinet doors might be $1\frac{1}{8}$ inches thick. Minimum size for passage doors is normally 2 feet 6 inches in width (all doors are 6 feet 8 inches in height). Doors for bathrooms and lavatories should be 2 feet 4 inches in width. Closet doors, depending on the size of the closet, may vary between 1 foot 8 inches and 2 feet 6 inches in width. Wardrobe doors of the sliding or folding types are available in many widths.

Exterior doors are $1\frac{3}{4}$ inches thick. They can also be obtained in flush design with a solid core or in panel design. Main entry doors are usually 3 feet 0 inch wide; secondary doors 2 feet 8 inches wide.

Doors should be fitted into the openings with the approximate clearance shown in Fig. 99A. The clearance at the bottom can vary somewhat as more space is required when carpeting is used. Doors ordinarily are slightly wider and higher than the framed opening (30 by 80 inches, for example) so some fitting is required. If the difference in width is only $\frac{1}{8}$ inch or so, the excess can be removed be planing only on one side or at one end. The following sequence might be used in fitting your doors:

1. Place one edge of the door along the hinge side and plane (jack or longer plane) to fit any jamb variations that might be necessary.

2. Place in opening and mark the opposite side at top and bottom. Now draw a line between and plane to the line. Bevel the inner edge slightly so that the door will swing freely, Fig. 99B.

3. Place blocks under the bottom of the door for the clearance you might desire ($\frac{1}{4}$ to $\frac{1}{2}$ inch above finish floor when carpeting is not used). If the bottom is not parallel to the floor, plane it to fit.

4. With the door in place, mark each side at the top in line with the head jamb. Draw a line between and on each side.

147

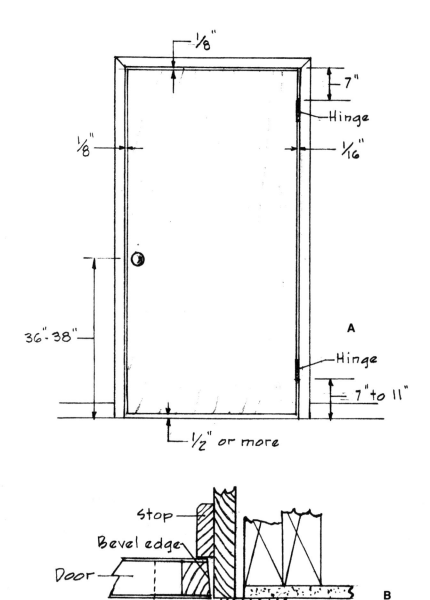

Fig. 99. Common door details.
A. Perimeter clearances.
B. Bevel edge on latch side.

5. The length may be trimmed to this line with a plane, a circular saw, or a handsaw. In sawing a flush door with a handsaw, make a sharp cut with a knife along the line on the underside. This will prevent chipping of the face veneer when sawing.

6. If an excessive amount must be removed from the top of a hollow core flush door, take one-half the required amount off the bottom first. Such flush doors have narrow stiles and rails under the face veneer. Sawing too much off one side may remove these narrow members.

Outside doors have a threshold between the door sill and the finish floor which normally contains a weatherstrip or stop. Weatherstrip is also placed on the side and head jambs of exterior door frames to eliminate drafts. If your frame is not supplied

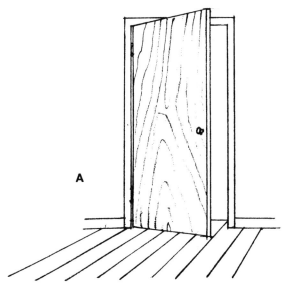
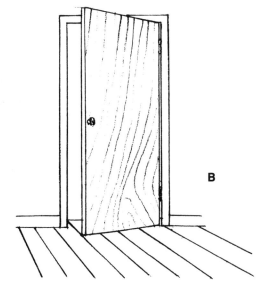

Fig. 99. Common door details (*cont'd*).
C. Left hand hinged door.
D. Right hand hinged door.

with stripping or you are renovating an old door, it certainly is worthwhile to install such weather protection.

After the door has been fitted, cut and temporarily nail the door stops in place so that the face of the door is flush with the edge of the jambs. A bevel cut at the floor line eliminates a dust pocket, Fig. 97A. Doors should swing into a room against a wall or closet. Never swing a door into a hallway! Doors are classed as "left hand" or "right hand" depending on the swing and location of the hinges, Fig. 99C and D. This must be specified if you are ordering prehung doors. In such units, jambs are nailed together, door fitted, and jambs and doors routed for hinges, lock sets, and strike plates. Exterior doors can also be ordered prehung.

Interior doors of $1\frac{3}{8}$-inch thickness usually are hung with two $3\frac{1}{2}$-by $3\frac{1}{2}$-inch loose-pin butt hinges. Hinges and other door hardware can be obtained in a number of finishes. Hinges can be located as shown in Fig. 99A or located to be in line with the top and bottom rail of a panel door.

With the door in place in the opening (blocked at the bottom), mark with chisel or knife on the door and jamb the location of the hinges. Hold the door in proper position at the sides by means of small wood wedges.

Now separate the hinges and mark the outline of one hinge half on the door edge as shown in Fig. 100A. Cut along the outline with a chisel and at the door edge. The depth of the cut should be equal or *very slightly* deeper than the thickness of the hinge leaf. Small shallow crosscuts with a chisel will allow easy removal of the wood, Fig. 100B. Fasten the hinge half in place with screws provided in the hinge set. Follow the same procedure on the hinge cutouts on the side jamb, Fig. 100C. Use square corner hinges (with loose pins) for hand tool routing. Use three hinges in 4- by 4-inch size for $1\frac{3}{4}$-inch exterior doors.

Machine routers and door and jamb butt template kits are available for fitting of hinges. Use the round corner hinges for machine cuts. Such units are accurate and provide the proper alignment and depth of the cuts. It may even pay to rent such units if they are available at your lumber dealer and you have a number of doors to install.

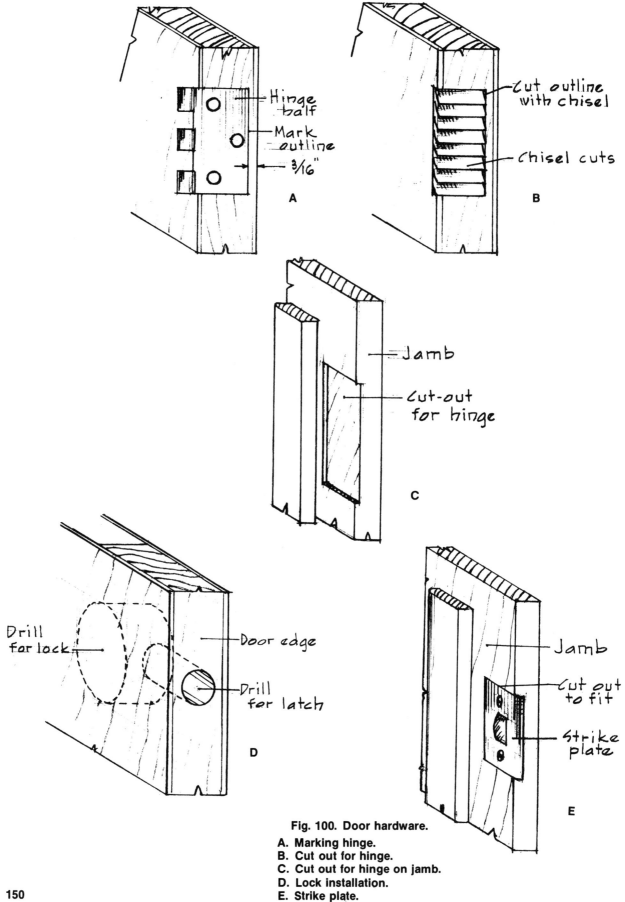

Fig. 100. Door hardware.
A. Marking hinge.
B. Cut out for hinge.
C. Cut out for hinge on jamb.
D. Lock installation.
E. Strike plate.

150

Doors for wardrobes (sliding or folding types) are mounted on tracks fastened to the head casing. Complete tracks and other hardware, together with instructions, are enclosed with each unit.

The installation of locks on the door and strike plate for the side jamb is now in order. Various types of locksets are available—the passage type (without a lock), a bathroom set with a lock on one side, privacy type, a "dummy" lock, and entrance locks of various types. All except the "dummy" lock (knob only) require drilling and fitting into the edge and face of the door. Tamperproof locks are available for exterior doors and can be used as a supplemental lock for existing doors.

Directions for drilling for the lock and latch, together with a folding template, are contained in each lockset. By following these instructions, a properly fitting lock is assured. These sequences are outlined generally as follows:

1. Fold the template and mark the center of the hole for the lock on the door face (this usually has a $2\frac{3}{8}$-inch back set).
2. Drill a 2- or $2\frac{1}{8}$-inch hole through the door. Use an expansion bit of some type but drill from each side to prevent damage to the face.
3. Drill the edge of the door for the latch (marked on template). Some locksets have a drive-in latch which requires no face plate routing, Fig. 100D.
4. Insert the latch and then the lockset. Fasten with screws. Before final tightening of the screws, try the knob to assure easy and free action.

When a small rectangular face plate is a part of the latch, it must be routed and fastened to the edge of the door with screws.

The strike plate is the last hardware item to be fitted. It is located in the face of the jamb so that the latch contacts the opening in the strike plate. Routing is required plus removal of additional wood for the strike plate, Fig. 100E. The edge of the jamb can be tapered slightly at the plate location to accommodate the curved edge of the strike plate.

Door stops can now be nailed in place permanently. Use $1\frac{1}{2}$-inch finish nails or brads and space about 12 inches apart, staggering slightly. Follow the recommended clearance shown in Fig. 101. Use a nail set to set all finish nails slightly below the surface to provide a space for putty or filler.

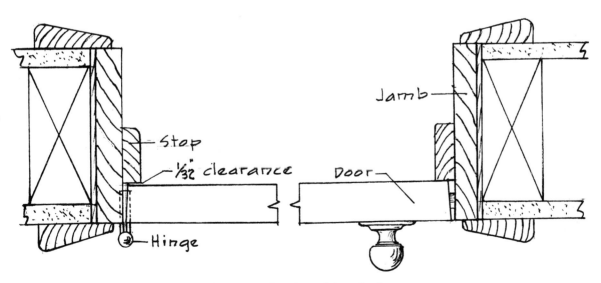

Fig. 101. Clearance for stops (plan view).

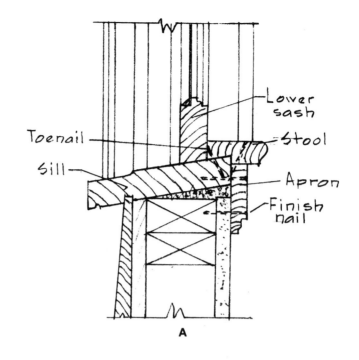

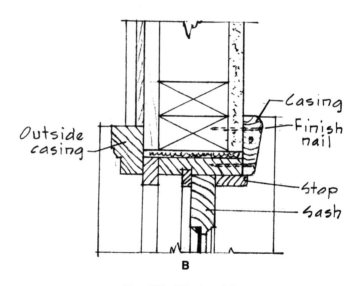

Fig. 102. Window trim.
A. Section through sill.
B. Plan view.

Window Frames and Trim

Interior trim around windows consists of stops, casing, stool, and apron, Figs. 102A and B. Figure 102A is a cross section through the window sill; Fig. 102B a cross section through the side jamb. Another method of trimming a window eliminates the stool and the apron, as such, and substitutes a casing and stop, Fig. 102C.

The stool is the first part to be installed, cutting the ends to fit against the side jamb and the wall finish. Toenail from the outer edge into the window sill and face nail at the location of the casing, Fig. 102A, where nails will be covered. The apron

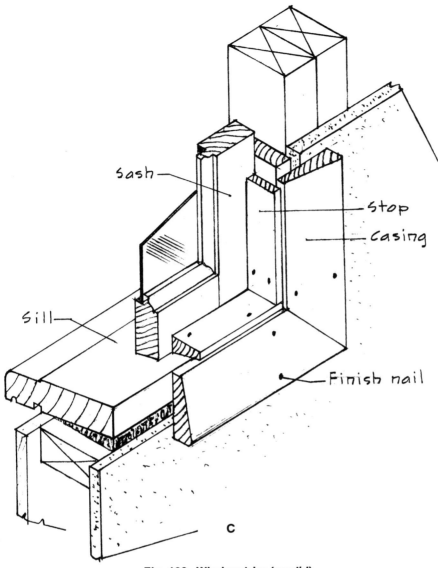

Fig. 102. Window trim (*cont'd*).
C. Overall view showing casing at sill.

can be installed next and is nailed to the window sill and 2- by 4-inch sill plate. Casing is cut and fitted as described for the casing around the doors except that the edges should be flush with the face of the jambs, Fig. 102B. Window stops can now be cut and fitted. Most window units are purchased with factory-installed weatherstrip and sash balances. Window stops are ordinarily placed against the edge of these weatherstrips and nailed to the jambs with $1\frac{1}{4}$- or $1\frac{1}{2}$-inch finish nails.

Windows with a full casing framing can be trimmed in the manner shown in Fig. 102C. The stop at the window sill has a slight bevel to conform to the slope of the sill.

Baseboard and Other Trim

Base moldings, in various combinations, serve as a finish between wall and floor. Depending on the design, they might consist of a three-piece unit—baseboard, base cap, and base shoe, Fig. 103A. They also can consist only of a base and shoe, Fig. 103B. When carpeting is used, the base shoe is often eliminated.

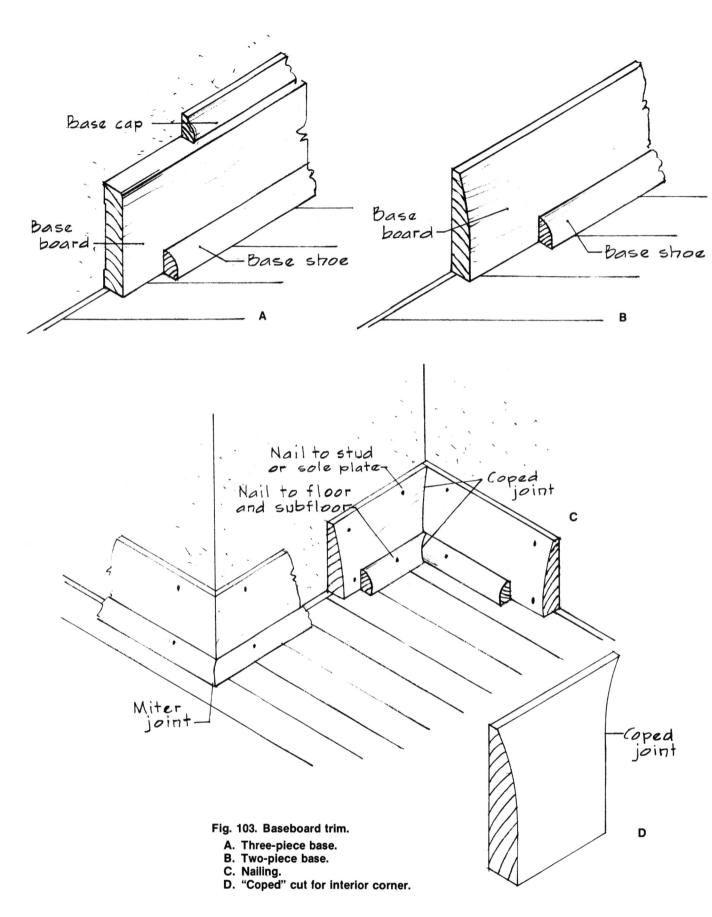

Fig. 103. Baseboard trim.

A. Three-piece base.
B. Two-piece base.
C. Nailing.
D. "Coped" cut for interior corner.

154

Outside corner joints for base units should be mitered, Fig. 103C. Interior joints should be butt joined for a square-edge base, for example. If the trim is molded with a curve or pattern, a combination of a square cut and a coped joint should be used. In such a joint, the baseboard is square cut against one wall. Then the meeting baseboard is beveled at a 45° angle and the bevel removed with a coping saw, Fig. 103D. This is called a "coped" joint and the member fits snugly against the baseboard of the opposing wall. Base shoe should be trimmed in the same manner. A coped joint at these inside corners eliminates or minimizes open joints that can occur with a bevel cut. Baseboard should be nailed into the 2 by 4 sole plate of the wall and into the stud. Use sevenpenny or eightpenny finish nails. When a base cap is used, nail with sixpenny or sevenpenny finish nails at each stud. Base shoe should be nailed into the subfloor and not into the baseboard. This will minimize the space between the floor and bottom edge of the base shoe if some shrinkage of the floor joists occurs. Predrill members, especially at the ends, if there is any chance that splitting might occur. This is especially true of small moldings in the dense hardwood species.

Ceiling molding, when a part of the design, can be installed in the same manner as the base molding, Fig. 90D. Inside corners can be treated in the same manner with a coped joint on the second member of the corner.

25
Cabinets and Other Millwork

Millwork, as a general term, normally covers those interior wood units (in addition to window and door units) which require manufacturing. They can include such items as simple shelving to an elaborate fireplace mantel. Interior stairs are also normally included. Most lumber companies supply fabricated cabinet units, unfinished or prefinished, which may meet your demands. If the construction of such millwork is somewhat beyond the skill of the amateur builder, it is sensible to purchase such units which may include vanities and medicine cabinets for bathrooms or lavatories, kitchen cabinets, and similar millwork. However, the construction of built-in shelving, for example, is normally much less difficult than hanging a door or installing trim around doors and windows. The fabrication of such parts can easily be done and can result in substantial savings.

KITCHEN CABINETS

While there are no hard and fast rules in sizes of built-in-place kitchen cabinets, it is a good idea to keep in mind the normal measurements shown in Fig. 104A. Base

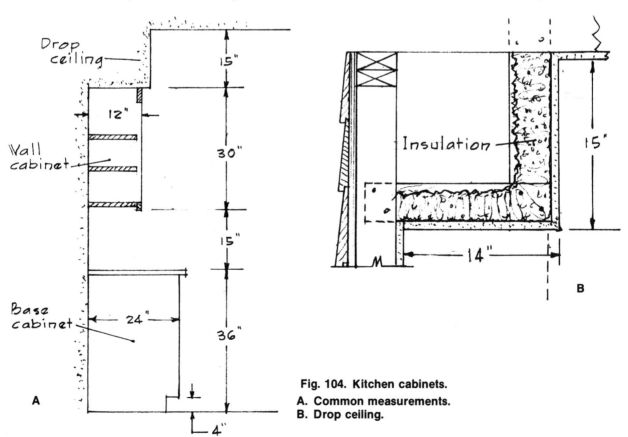

Fig. 104. Kitchen cabinets.
A. Common measurements.
B. Drop ceiling.

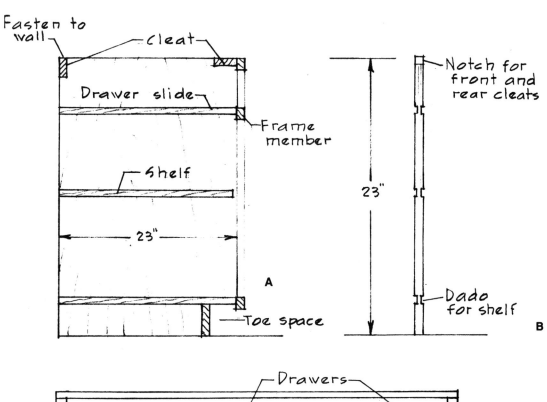

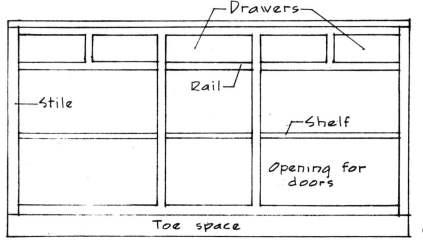

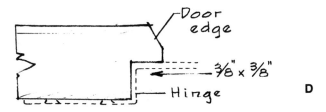

Fig. 105. Cabinet details.
A. Section through base cabinet.
B. Vertical support unit.
C. Typical front.
D. Door detail.

cabinets can be obtained in many combinations and sizes. They may vary in width from 24 to 48 inches and include several combinations of drawers and doors. The wall cabinets (upper wall units) are normally supplied with shelving and single or double doors depending on their width. They are installed below a drop ceiling or under a 12 to 18-inch wall cabinet fastened at the wall-ceiling line.

Drop ceilings above cabinets are framed before the interior finish is applied. Use 2- by 4-inch members and fasten them to the studs and ceiling joists, Fig. 104B. The horizontal and vertical members can be nailed together before fastening to the studs and ceiling joist. Exterior walls require insulation behind the drop ceiling.

If you are constructing kitchen cabinets yourself, use plywood or particle board for the basic framework which can then be faced with narrow 1-inch vertical stiles and horizontal rails. The vertical interior supports for shelving and drawer slides can also be made from plywood or particle board. For example, $\frac{3}{4}$-inch plywood sheet in 23- by 35-inch size can be used for the vertical framework, Fig. 105A.

Dado (rout) $\frac{1}{4}$-inch-deep grooves (the width of the shelving thickness) for the shelving in the pattern you choose, Fig. 105B. The end members would, of course, be routed only on one side if the cabinet is placed against a side wall. Shelving can be nailed in place and the cabinet "box" fastened to the back wall at the studs. Now use $\frac{3}{4}$- by $1\frac{1}{2}$- or 2-inch wood framing members and nail-glue them to the shelving and the vertical supports, Fig. 105C. Install the vertical stiles first and cut and fit the rails between them. Use a good glue and sixpenny or sevenpenny finish nails. Predrill if necessary. Drawers and doors can now be made to fit the openings. The back cleat, nailed to the rear edge of the vertical framework, is used to fasten the cabinet to the wall and also serves as support for the cabinet top. Wall cabinets are also supplied with a similar member.

Doors can be made (1) flush to fit into the door openings and hung with loose pin hinges or flush overlay hinges or (2) overlapping and hung with semiconcealed hinges. The overlapping doors should have an overall width and height $\frac{5}{8}$ inch greater than the framed opening. On a tablesaw, cut a $\frac{3}{8}$- by $\frac{3}{8}$-inch groove around the perimeter, Fig. 105D. The face edge may be tapered as shown or rounded as you prefer.

The countertop for the cabinet can be made of plywood and covered and edged with a rigid plastic or can be ordered from your building supply dealer.

Wall cabinets can be made in the same manner as described for the base cabinet. Construct the cabinet box on horses and mount on the wall before nailing on the facings (stiles and rails). The entire cabinet can also be assembled before mounting if desired. However, a better fit of the stile against a wall can be obtained by mounting only the box first.

KITCHEN LAYOUTS

If a kitchen is involved and is a part of your addition, various designs and layouts are possible. Figures 106A, B, and C show several designs that might fit your needs. Figure 106A is an "L" design and includes a corner eating area. Figure 106B is a partial "U" design and is somewhat similar to the "L" design except for the location of one door. The room is slightly larger and has more cupboard space. Figure 106C is a narrow Pullman or parallel wall type. The minimum width for such a design should be about 8 or $8\frac{1}{2}$ feet.

OTHER MILLWORK

Fireplace mantels and china cupboards in a colonial design are ordinarily made to order in a cabinet shop. Construction of a simple mantel, however, involving only a solid or built-up shelf above the fireplace opening is well within the skill of the amateur builder. Built-in shelves or bookcases are also easily constructed. In using plywood for shelving, for example, it is always a good policy to nail-glue a $\frac{3}{4}$- by $\frac{3}{4}$-inch or wider strip of solid wood to the outside edge for a finished appearance.

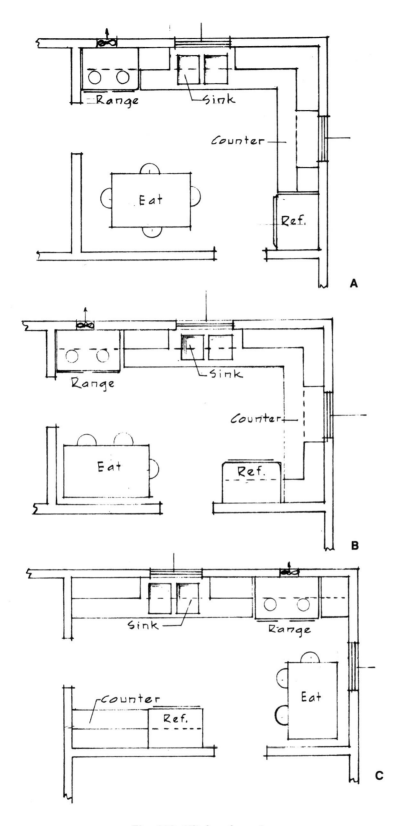

Fig. 106. Kitchen layouts.

A. "L" Design.
B. Partial "U" design.
C. Pullman design.

26
Stairs

INTERIOR STAIRS

Stairs may or may not be involved in the construction of your new addition. If they are, you have already framed the stairway opening to accommodate them, Fig. 26A. Perhaps the most important factors in stair design are adequate headroom and the correct ratio of riser height to tread width (rise to run) to achieve this headroom. Minimum measurements which might be followed are shown in Fig. 107. Total rise

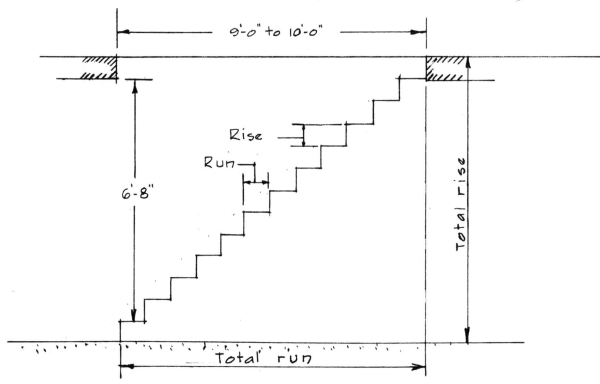

Fig. 107. Typical stair measurements.

from one floor to the upper floor is ceiling height plus floor framing depth. This may vary between 8 feet 8 inches and 9 feet 0 inch for 8-foot ceiling heights (104 to 108 inches). The framed stair opening may vary between 9 feet 0 inch and 10 feet 0 inch.

The *minimum* tread width and riser height for primary stairs is usually 9 inches and $8\frac{1}{4}$ inches, respectively. A rule of thumb which can be used for the relation of the tread width to riser height is as follows:

The tread width multiplied by the riser height should equal 72 to 75. Thus the minimum measurements previously outlined would be $9 \times 8\frac{1}{4} = 74$. A 10-inch tread should therefore have a $7\frac{1}{2}$-inch riser or an 11-inch tread about a $6\frac{3}{4}$-inch riser.

Another rule sometimes followed is tread width plus twice the riser height should equal about 25 inches. However, whichever of the two methods is used to determine the riser and tread sizes, a satisfactory stairway should result.

These suggested riser heights should also be used to determine the number of steps between floors and still allow adequate headroom. A minimum number of 14 risers is commonly used between first and second floors with an 8-foot first floor ceiling height. For basement stairs, 13 risers can be used. If 13 risers are used, the riser height would be about $7\frac{3}{4}$ inches when the total rise is 100 inches (first floor to basement floor or $100 \div 13$). Using the rule of thumb of riser times tread equals 75, the tread (run) should then be about $9\frac{3}{4}$ inches ($75 \div 7\frac{3}{4}$). Twelve treads would be required for the basement stair (for 13 risers). Thus, the total run (horizontal length of stair) would be $9\frac{3}{4} \times 12 = 117$ inches which would be well within the limits in providing headroom for a 9- to 10-foot floor framed opening. A clear height above the step to the underside of the opening of 6 feet 8 inches is required, Fig. 107.

Stair carriages are used to carry the stair load and also provide fastening areas for the treads and risers. For basement stairs they normally consist of a minimum of two 2-inch-thick members (usually 2 by 12's). The carriages are normally notched for the treads and risers. These carriages are, in turn, fastened to the floor framing of the first floor and rest on the basement floor. When treads are nominal 1 inch thick, use an extra carriage at the center when the width of the stair is over 24 inches. However, treads are normally much thicker. Carriages are marked to conform to the selected tread and rise measurements and notched with hand or electric saw. A ledger may be used against the stair header to support the upper ends of the stair carriages, Fig. 108. A 2- by 4-inch "kicker" plate can be anchored to the basement floor to act as a means of fastening the bottom of the carriages. A treated member or decay-resistant species can be used for this plate. Toenail the top of the carriages to the header and ledger, and to the kicker plate (at the basement floor) with tenpenny nails.

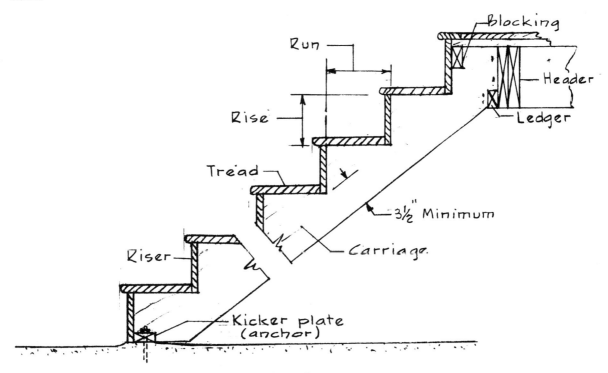

Fig. 108. Stair carriage.

Prepared treads and risers are available at your lumber company if you do not choose to use 2-inch plank treads and 1-inch board risers. Commercial treads are machined from $1\frac{1}{4}$ material and have a finish thickness of about $1\frac{1}{8}$ inches. They are available in $11\frac{1}{2}$-inch widths and in 3- and 4-foot lengths. They can be ripped to the width your stairway requires. Species commonly available are oak, Douglas fir, and southern pine. For a primary stairway, risers can consist of clear lumber in 1-inch nominal thickness in the same species used for the treads.

One method used in fastening risers and $1\frac{1}{8}$-inch treads to the carriages starts with the bottom riser as follows. Nail the riser to each carriage with two eightpenny or ninepenny finish nails. If necessary, plane or trim the tops of the riser to be flush with the horizontal top edge of the carriage. Now nail the tread to each carriage with three ninepenny or tenpenny finish nails, Fig. 109A. The projection of the nosing of the tread should be at least $1\frac{1}{8}$ inches beyond the outer face of the riser. Continue nailing risers and treads in the same sequence.

Another method which might be used consists of nailing first and second risers in place and nailing first (bottom) tread in place and nail second riser to the back edge of the tread, Fig. 109B. Continue to the top. This method can provide better stiffness to the treads.

The top of the stair can be finished with a nosing, Fig. 109C. Depending on the finish floor, this may consist of a portion of a tread or a routed nosing, Fig. 109D. A good combination for a secondary or a basement stair (if uncarpeted) might consist of oak treads (for wear) and a less dense wood species for the risers.

For enclosed stairways the sides (against the walls) might be finished with stringers which are notched to fit the treads and risers. Another method consists of the following: (1) nail the stringers to the wall (at the studs); (2) nail the stair carriages over the stringer; and (3) install treads and risers, Fig. 110.

Primary stairs from the first to the second floor ordinarily consist of housed stringers with treads and risers fastened with glued hardwood wedges. Risers are also nailed to the back edges of the treads. In this type of stairway, assembly of the treads and risers is done from the underside of the stair before the finish covering is applied. Such units are custom built at a lumber supply company and are sometimes pre-assembled ready to install in the stairway opening.

Handrails should be used on at least one side of the stairway. They are easily mounted to the wall with hardware designed for such use.

When the attic is used primarily for storage and space for a fixed stairway is not available, the use of a folding stair should be considered. This may be especially true in remodeling an older house which has some usable attic space for storage. Ceiling joists should be capable of carrying some live load when such an access is considered. The opening for a folding stair is finished in the same manner as a doorway, with perimeter jambs and casing. Opening sizes vary somewhat but are usually about 26 by 54 inches. These folding stairs are completely assembled ready for installation. Instructions are included.

EXTERIOR STAIRS

Exterior stairs are normally exposed to the weather, such as those which serve an open wood deck; therefore, they should be constructed with treated wood or with a decay-resistant species. Fasteners should be rust-resistant. Any details should be such that are no pockets which trap and hold moisture. It is also desirable that exposure of end grain be kept to a minimum unless protected. Stair design, the relation of tread width or riser height, can generally be the same as those described for interior stairs.

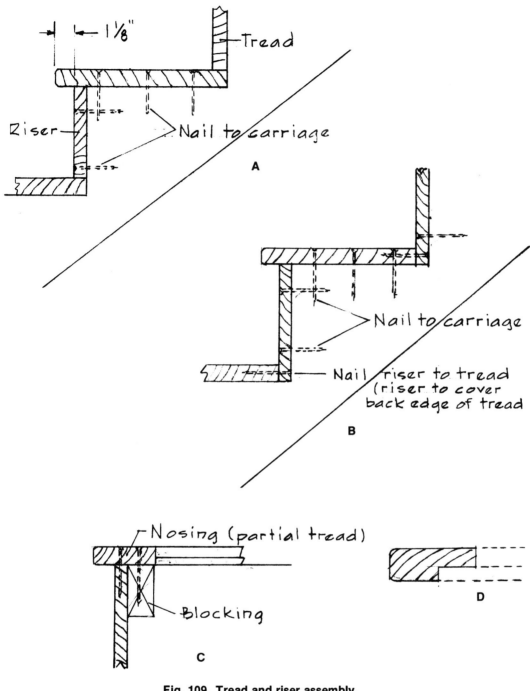

Fig. 109. Tread and riser assembly.
A. Method A.
B. Method B-extra nailing.
C. Top of stair.
D. Routed nosing.

Carriages

Stair carriages are normally supported by one or more floor joists of the deck. When the carriages are fastened at right angles to a joist, a 2- by 3- or 2- by 4-inch ledger can be fastened to the joist, Fig. 111A. Nail the ledgers to the joist with twelvepenny galvanized (or equal) nails. Notch the end of the carriage for the ledger. Toenail the

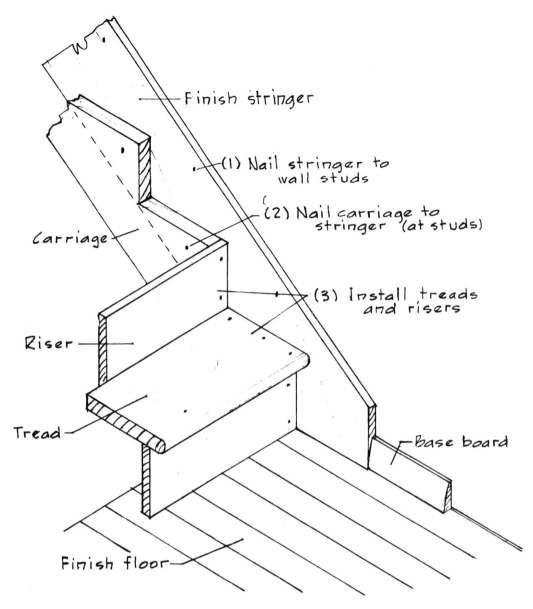

Finish stringer

(1) Nail stringer to wall studs

(2) Nail carriage to stringer (at studs)

Carriage

(3) Install treads and risers

Riser

Tread

Base board

Finish floor

Fig. 110. Enclosed stairway.

carriage into the ledger and joist with tenpenny galvanized nails. Two carriages can be used for spans up to 4 feet if 2-inch plank treads are used. When carriages are parallel to a joist or floor beam, they can be bolted to the ends as shown in Fig. 111B.

The lower end of the carriages should be fastened in some manner, preferably to a concrete slab, the surface of which is above the ground level. This can be done by anchoring an angle iron to the slab. Fasten the angle iron to the carriage with lag screws, Fig. 111C. This will prevent the bearing edge of the carriage from being in contact with the concrete.

One method of providing support for the treads consists of notching the carriages, Fig. 112A. Exposed cuts should ordinarily be treated with a water-repellent preservative.

164

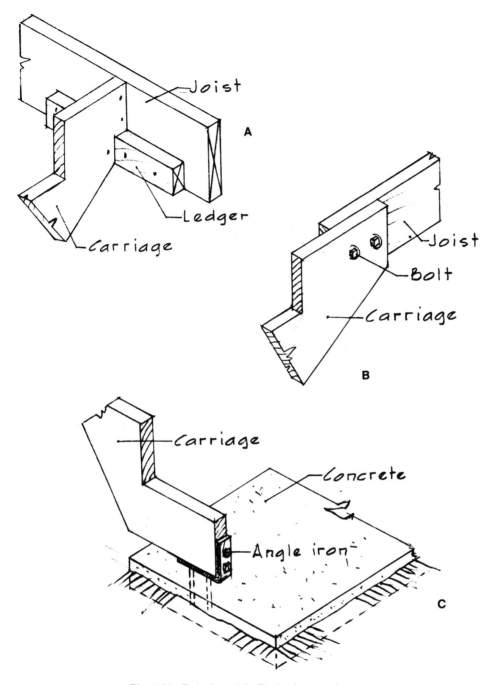

Fig. 111. Exterior stair-Fastening carriage.
A. Fastening carriage to face of joist.
B. Fastening carriage to end of joist.
C. Anchoring bottom of carriage.

A second method of tread support consists of providing 2- by 4-inch cleats along the inside faces of the carriages, Fig. 112B. They should be fastened with nails, bolts, or lag screws.

A third method consists of 2- by 4-inch cleats which extend beyond the edge of the stringer, Fig. 112C. These cleats should be fastened with bolts or lag screws. Sloping the horizontal notch cut of the carriages or the cleats slightly outward will

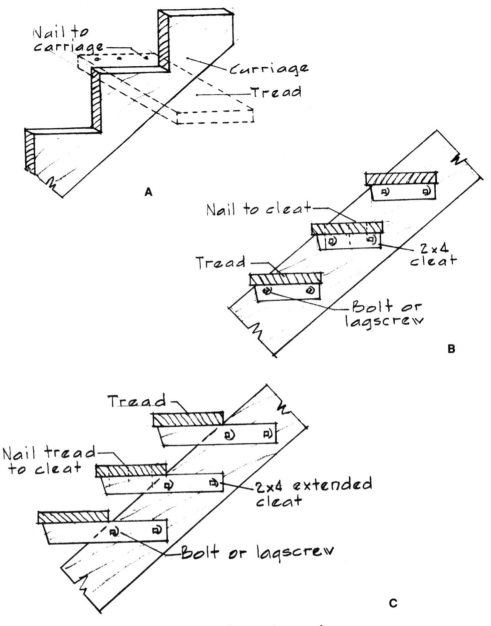

Fig. 112. Tread support on carriages.
A. Direct carriage support.
B. Cleat support.
C. Extended cleat support.

allow water to drain off. The use of small drain holes or two-piece treads spaced $\frac{1}{8}$ inch apart will also provide drainage.

Nail 2-inch plank steps to the carriage or cleats with sixteenpenny galvanized ring shank nails. Use three for 2- by 10-inch or 2- by 12-inch treads and two in each of the "split" (two-piece) steps. Large galvanized screws can be used in place of the nails. Allow a small clearance at the ends of the steps where they contact the carriage. This will allow all members to dry out more readily.

27
Flashing and Other Sheet Metal

In house construction, the sheet metal work consists mainly of flashing, gutters, and downspouts. Flashing over the drip cap in exposed doors and windows is normally recommended. However, where cornice overhangs protect these areas, the flashing is usually eliminated. The use of flashing in valleys, at the intersection of two slopes, is important. Flashing is sometimes used at gable ends, for example, when there is a change in siding materials. Gutters and downspouts are other metal materials used on roofs. They prevent water from running along the basement wall and entering the basement. Good drainage and a gravel bed below the cornice area often minimizes this problem.

MATERIALS

Materials most often used for sheet metal use are galvanized metal, aluminum, and terneplate (tin). Copper and stainless steel may also be used in certain areas of the country where corrosive atmospheres are a problem. Wood gutters, in redwood or similar species, are also used when there is a desire to provide a special architectural design.

Galvanized (zinc-coated) metal is normally specified as 26 gage for heavy use such as gutters and 28 gage for flashing and other uses.

Aluminum flashing have a minimum thickness of 0.019 inch, the same as for roof valleys. Gutters should be made from 0.027-inch-thick metal.

Tin flashing (terneplate) as used for shingle flashing and valleys is often prime coated on at least one side.

Metal fasteners used with flashing should be compatible to prevent corrosion when unlike metals are used together, i.e.: for galvanized and tinplate metal, use galvanized or stainless steel fasteners; for aluminum, use aluminum or stainless steel fasteners; and for copper flashing, use copper or stainless steel fasteners.

FLASHING FOR MATERIAL CHANGES

When a material change occurs at the gable end of a house, for example, some provision should be made for a good drip edge. These materials might consist of horizontal siding below and vertical boards above. When siding materials are on the same plane, a molding together with adequate flashing can be used, Fig. 113. The bottom of the vertical boards should clear the flashing by about $\frac{1}{2}$ inch for a good drip.

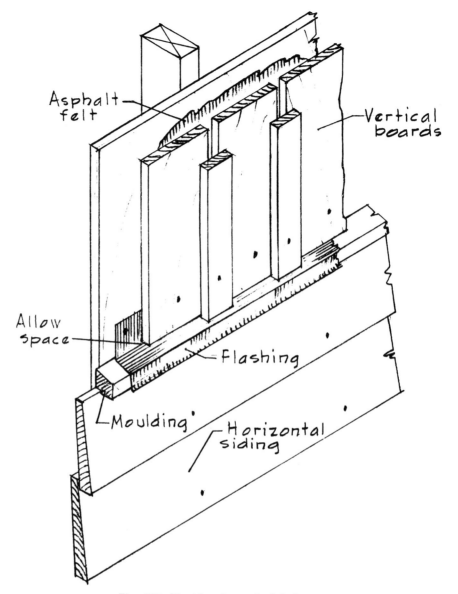

Asphalt felt

Vertical boards

Allow space

Flashing

Moulding

Horizontal siding

Fig. 113. Flashing for material change.

FLASHING USED FOR SHINGLES

Shingle flashing is normally used between the roof and a vertical surface. These and other flashing details have been covered in the previous Chapter "Roof Coverings." This includes: (1) flashing at gable roof edge, Fig. 62B; (2) shingle flashing at walls and chimneys, Figs. 65A and B; (3) valley flashing, Fig. 66; and (4) flashing at the cornice to minimize ice dam problems, Fig. 67.

GUTTERS AND DOWNSPOUTS

Gutters are normally available in prepainted or unpainted metal in a half-round form, Fig. 114A, or a formed pattern, Fig. 114B. Wood gutters have a molded face and a half-round "runway," Fig. 114C. Round downspouts are used for half-round gutters and a rectangular shape for formed gutters. A single downspout normally serves 30

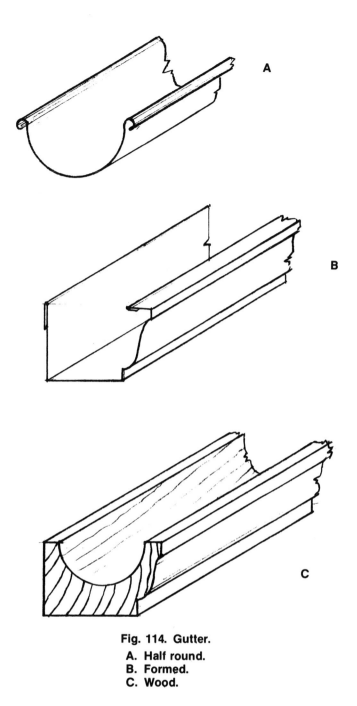

Fig. 114. Gutter.
A. Half round.
B. Formed.
C. Wood.

feet of a roof line. One rule sometimes used with respect to downspout is as follows: 1 square inch downspout area is required for 100 square feet of roof.

Round and formed gutters are fastened to the cornice by means of hangers. However, a spike and ferrule is sometimes used for the formed metal gutter. When using the spike, be sure they are located at the rafter ends if a nailing header (2-inch member fastened to the ends of the rafters) is not used.

The facia serves as a backing for the gutter to provide the correct location when necessary to prevent water from overflowing the edge, Fig. 115A. The spike, with a ferrule between the gutter, is driven into this strip and the backing, Fig. 115B. Slope the gutters a minimum of $\frac{1}{2}$ inch for each 10 feet of length (toward the downspouts).

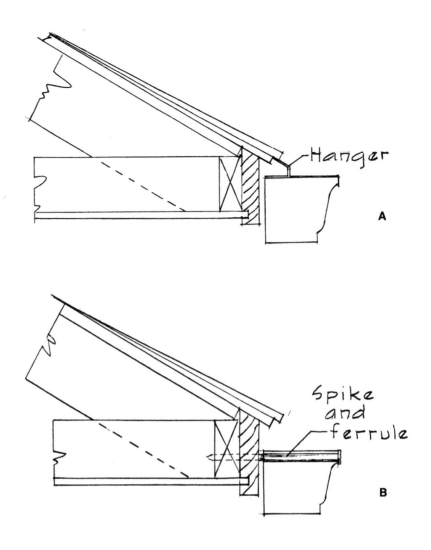

Fig. 115. Gutter hangers.
A. Metal hanger.
B. Spike and ferrule.

Downspouts are fastened to the side of the house with metal straps of various types. Those straps which provide a space between siding and downspout by the use of a small ferrule or collar are preferred, Fig. 116. Use one at the upper and one at the lower end of the downspout. An additional strap can be used for long downspouts. Elbow and downspout connections can be made with a sealant or with sheet metal screws.

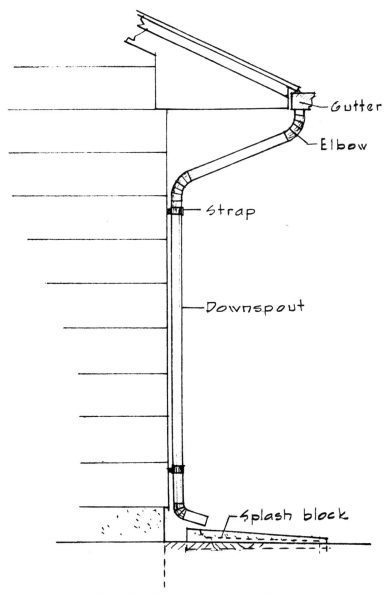

Fig. 116. Downspout arrangement.

The rainwater runoff must be guided away from the house by some means. Splash blocks or extended downspouts can be used. With such a provision, and a good slope of the ground away from the foundation, there should be no problem of water entry into the basement, Fig. 116.

28

Open Porches

ROOF DESIGN

An enclosed porch constructed from the ground up (footings, slab, etc.), has the same masonry, framing, and finishing details which have been covered in the previous chapters. However, the construction varies somewhat if you wish for a simple roof over an existing concrete slab. This could include only the porch roof and supporting posts. Such a unit could be fully enclosed, even as a heated room, in the future if desired.

We will assume that the slab is well constructed with a stable foundation and footings. One of the first needs is the assembly of a perimeter beam for the roof. The use of doubled 2- by 6-inch or 2- by 8-inch members may be assembled around the perimeter of the porch. Use $\frac{1}{2}$-inch spacers between the 2-inch members and overlap and nail the corners as shown in Fig. 117A. The thickness of this beam should be the same as the size of the supporting posts. A joist hanger for the doubled beam is now

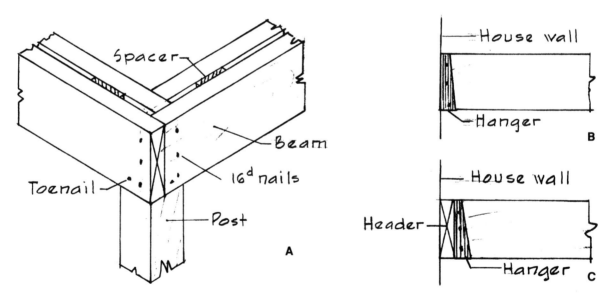

Fig. 117. Porch beam.
A. Fastening at corner.
B. Hanger to house wall.
C. Hanger to header.

mounted on the house wall, Fig. 117B. Hangers should be nailed to house studs or to a 2-inch header which has been nailed to the house wall at the studs, Fig. 117C.

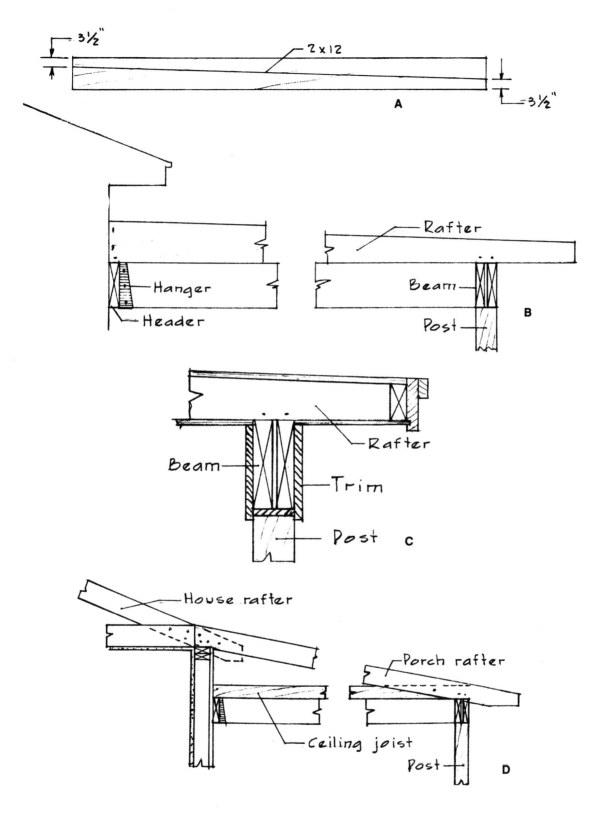

Fig. 118. Porch details.

A. Rafter layout.
B. Rafter assembly.
C. Trim at beam.
D. Porch rafters bearing on house wall.

The perimeter beam can now be raised in place, the outside supported by one or more 4- by 4-inch post at each corner. Temporary supports of several 2- by 4-inch posts can also be used.

Two simple systems of roof construction can be used for such a porch when the span is no greater than about 11 to 12 feet. The first consists of ripping, from 2 by 12's, two sloping members which serve as both ceiling joist and rafters, Fig. 118A. Use a guide and an electric handsaw, if available. The narrow end can be held at $3\frac{1}{2}$ inches. The wide end will thus be about $7\frac{5}{8}$ inches providing a 4- inch slope for the roof. Use a 2- by 12-inch member that is 2 feet longer than the width of the porch for a good overhang. These rafter joists can now be toenailed to the inside header and to the outside beam, Fig. 118B. Trim can be installed as shown in Fig. 118C. Joist hangers can also be used for support. Space the rafters 16 inches or less on center.

The second system consists of utilizing the top plates of the existing house to support the rafters, Fig. 118D. The cornice trim and part of the roof sheathing of the house must be removed. Use 2 by 4 ceiling joists spaced 16 inches on center when the span is not greater than 12 feet. Toenail them to the inside header and to the top of the outside beam. Then rafters, normally 2 by 6's, can be installed. Nail them to the top plate of the house wall and to the adjacent house rafter as well as to the outside beam, Fig. 118D. Trim can be installed as shown in Fig. 118C. Before installing the roofing, use a strip of heavy roll roofing at the junction of the old and new roof to prevent water entry.

A more involved roof system is that of a gable or hip roof design. Details for such construction can be found in the Chapter "Ceiling and Roof Framing."

In snow areas, the rafters for a low-slope roof should usually be restricted to 2- by 6-inch or larger members, depending on the span between the house and the outer beam. For example, if southern pine members in No. 2 grade (or equal) are used, the allowable span for 2- by 6-inch rafters is about 12 feet for 16-inch spacings.* The allowable span would be about $13\frac{1}{2}$ feet if a 12-inch spacing is used. Rafters of 2- by 4-inch size should be limited to very short spans. Roof sheathing, cornice, and other trim can be installed as described in previous chapters.

Metal angles or stirrups can be used to anchor the posts to the beam, Fig. 119A. This should be done before the cornice trim is applied. The base of the posts can be anchored to the concrete slab with "U" straps, Fig. 119B. Use anchor bolts in fastening the straps to the concrete. Space posts 5 to 6 feet apart along the outer beam.

RAILINGS

An open porch often requires the addition of some type of railing from the standpoint of safety or appearance. Such railings are best fastened between the posts supporting the roof. Railings can be made with wood horizontal rails and wood balusters. Metal balustrades or rail sections are available at many lumber supply dealers. A good combination includes the use of a metal rail section topped with a horizontal wood rail.

Wood rail sections machined from 2- by 4-inch members can be combined with 2- by 2-inch balusters. Such sections can be made and assembled in units to fit between the posts. The balusters can be toenailed to the top rail as shown in Fig. 120A. A long screw can be used through the bottom into each wood baluster. For long spans, it may be desirable to use a long screw (galvanized or cadmium plate) at both top and bottom. It is desirable, however, to minimize any exposed fastenings in railings of this type.

*For other grades and spans, refer to Southern Pine Technical Bulletin or similar span tables.

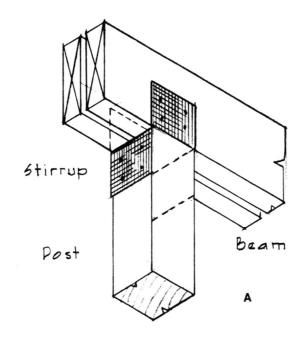

Stirrup

Post

Beam

A

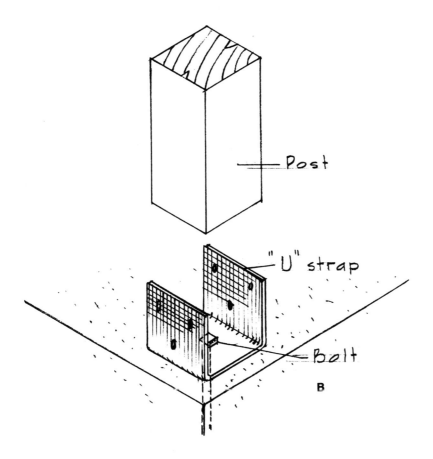

Post

"U" strap

Bolt

B

Fig. 119. Post connections.
A. Post to beam.
B. Post to floor.

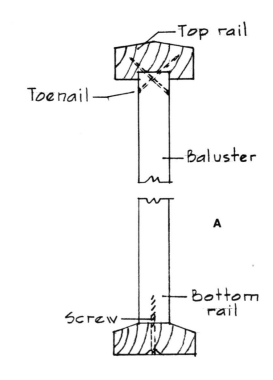

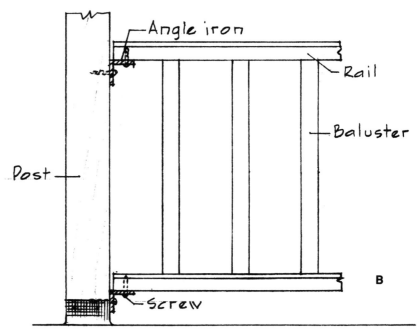

Fig. 120. Porch railing.
A. Railing assembly.
B. Railing to post.

Fasten the horizontal rails to the posts with galvanized angle irons and screws. First fasten the bottom angle iron to the rail and the top angle iron to the post, before mounting them in place. This will allow easy accessibility of the screws when mount-

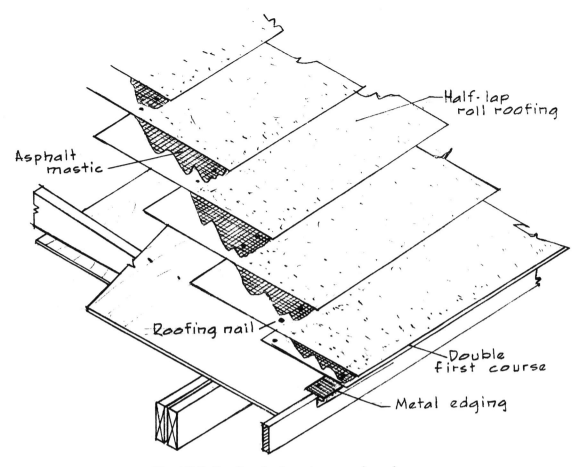

Fig. 120C. Roofing for low-slope porch roof.

ing each rail section, Fig. 120B. When a metal balustrade is used in combination with a wood top rail, assembly can be made in the same manner.

Cross members of 2 by 4's can also be used in place of the 2- by 2-inch balusters. They can be combined in a cross pattern alone or with one or more vertical balusters at each end.

ROOFING

A built-up roof consisting of a number of layers of 15- or 30-pound asphalt felt lapped and applied with hot tar is often used for low-slope roofs. Another system which is more easily applied consists of the following steps:

1. Nail a half-width (18 inches) 50-pound or heavier roll roofing at the cornice. Nail at top and bottom, Fig. 120C. A metal edging can be used under the lower edge.

2. A full width of half-lap 36-inch roll roofing (lower half surfaced) can now be nailed over the first. Use a full bed of sealant or asphalt mastic at the lower half. Nail just above the lap of the next layer so that nails will be covered (about 19 inches). Space the roofing nails 2 to 3 inches apart.

3. The next and each following layer is installed in the same manner, Fig. 120C. It is not good practice to use face nailing on low-pitch roofs. Nails can loosen and cause leaks.

177

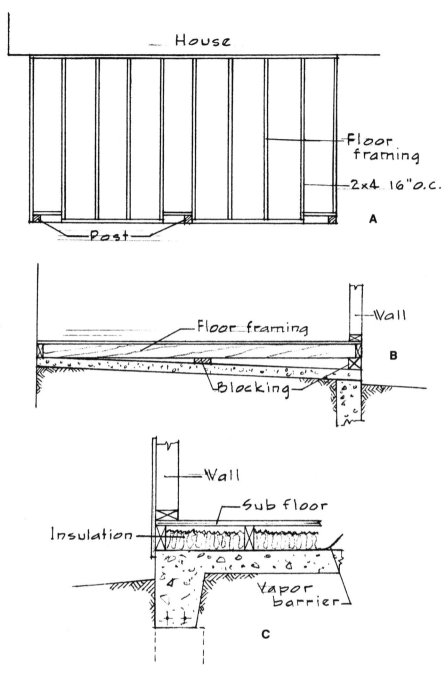

Fig. 121. Future porch enclosure.
A. Floor framing plan.
B. Blocking to level floor.
C. Insulation.

FUTURE ENCLOSURE

If in the future you wish to enclose and heat your now-completed open porch, the task is relatively simple. First lay 6-mil polyethylene film over the concrete slab. Then assemble a framework of 2 by 4's with a 2- by 4-inch header flush with the outside line of the posts. The 2 by 4 floor joists, spaced 16 inches on center, should be located perpendicular to the line of the house, Fig. 121A.

If the slab slopes outward, block up the outside edge (header) of the framework until the 2- by 4-inch joists are level. Anchor the framework to the concrete, the posts, and the house floor framing wherever possible. Because the concrete floor of a porch is normally sloped for drainage, supports at the center of the span are now placed under each joist, Fig. 119B. This might be a 1- by 4- or a 2- by 4-inch block depending on the slope. If the porch is more than 12 feet deep so that the span (between center blocking and outside or inside wall) is more than 6 feet, use 2- by 6-inch joists.

If the porch is to be heated (forced air), a cold air return duct can be installed from the house to the outer edge of the framed joists. In this case use $3\frac{1}{2}$-inch or thicker insulation batts between the joists. Subfloor, of 1-inch boards or $\frac{1}{2}$-inch or thicker plywood, can be nailed to the joists. Wall framing and sheathing with the desired openings for doors and windows should be ready for installation, Fig. 119C. After the wall enclosure is complete, install window and door frames and follow the procedures outlined in the previous chapters on siding, installation, etc.

29
Unattached Garage

A well constructed garage, whether connected to the house or unattached, should have a good foundation. The bottom of the foundation should be below the frost line to prevent movement of the concrete slab as frost leaves the ground. Form the foundation wall so that the top is well above the groundline, Fig. 122A. Use $\frac{3}{8}$- or $\frac{1}{2}$-inch anchor bolts around the perimeter (for the sill) spaced 6 feet apart and at each corner. Don't forget to provide for the door openings by blocking out the form at the side framing, Fig. 122B. The concrete floor and apron can be poured after the soil around the foundation settles and the sand and gravel fill is installed.

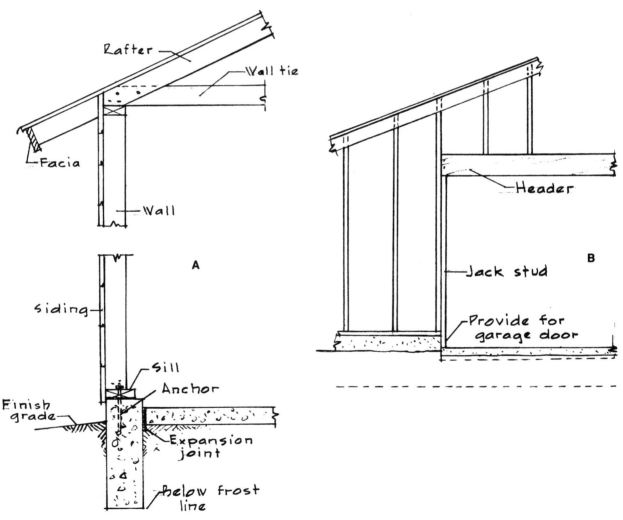

Fig. 122. Unattached garage.
A. Section thru wall.
B. Doorway detail.

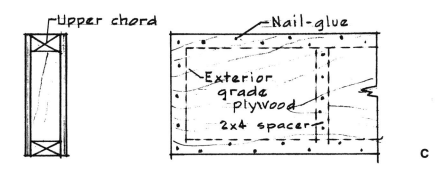

C

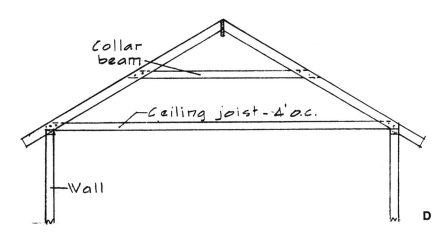

D

Fig. 122. Unattached garage (*cont'd*).
C. Plywood-faced beam.
D. Wall ties.

The wall framing can be assembled on the floor of the garage and erected as described in the Chapter "Wall Framing." Studs can be spaced 24 inches on center when siding is nominal 1-inch material or when sheathing is used under the siding. It is good practice, when moisture is a problem, to use a treated bottom plate. Drill holes to conform to the foundation anchor bolts.

The headers over the garage doors usually consist of doubled 2 by 10's for 8- or 9-foot-wide garage door openings when the rafters bear on that wall. A beam of sufficient depth for a 15- or 16-foot-wide door opening, which serves to support the rafters, might be built-up. A framework of 2- by 4-inch members should be covered with $\frac{1}{2}$-inch exterior grade plywood, Fig. 122C. Use a waterproof glue and nail-glue the plywood to the members. Use full-length upper and lower chords (2- by 4-inch horizontal members). Use 2- by 4-inch spacers every 2 feet. A 4 by 4 spacer should be used at plywood splices. Alternate these splices front to back. Be sure that the edges of the members are smooth and level so that full contact of the plywood is achieved. Space sixpenny nails about 4 to 5 inches apart. *These beams should be fabricated under shop conditions.* A steel beam or a deep laminated beam (such as three 2 by 12's) can also be used as a beam over wide garage doors.

A sill sealer (4-inch-wide pads of fiberglass) can be used over the foundation to provide a tight joint. The preassembled wall sections can now be erected and nailed together at each corner.

Roof framing can consist of wood trusses obtained at your lumber dealer or of rafters tied together at a ridge beam, Fig. 122D. Before the roof is started, plumb and brace each wall. Use two braces on long sides if necessary. When rafters are used, tie opposite walls together with ceiling joists spaced 4 feet apart. For garage widths up to about 16 feet, 2- by 4-inch ceiling joists can be used, Fig. 122D. Both rafters and trusses should be fastened together as described in the Chapter "Ceiling and Roof Framing."

Roof sheathing, roofing, and trim can be applied in the same manner as described in previous chapters. Use nominal 1-inch boards or $\frac{1}{2}$-inch plywood for roof sheathing when rafters are spaced no more than 24 inches on center.

Siding for the unattached garage can conform to that used on the house or to one of the following alternates: (1) 1- by 6-inch drop siding (for 16- or 24-inch stud spacing), (2) $\frac{3}{4}$-inch bevel siding, (3) $\frac{1}{2}$-inch hardboard siding, or (4) $\frac{5}{8}$-inch (4- by 8-foot) textured plywood siding (for 24-inch stud spacing) or other approved materials.

Garage doors can be obtained in sizes from 8 by 7 feet (width by height) to 16 by 7 feet. Overhead doors are normally supplied with hardware and doors are predrilled to accept these materials. About the only requirement for hanging these doors (in addition to studs and header) are door jambs and inside casing. Directions are complete for the erection of overhead doors and can be easily followed. The normal headroom required for the overhead track is about 12 to 24 inches but special low headroom brackets can be obtained which can be used when the headroom is only 3 to 4 inches. Automatic door openers are usually applied by specialists.

Precut materials for garages of various sizes can be obtained at most of the larger building supply companies. This requires only assembly of the various parts on the site over a proper foundation or concrete slab.

30
Chimneys and Fireplaces

Construction of chimneys and fireplaces might not be within the ability of the average homeowner. However, certain factors must be considered if such units are to be a part of your new addition. These are as follows: (1) proper footings, (2) clearance for wood framing members, (3) wall framing for fireplace opening, and (4) provision for the chimney at the roof framing or at cornice or gable ends. Most building supply companies have the "Franklin-type" fireplace available which requires only proper clearance at the walls and installation of an approved stovepipe kit. Such units can supply heat for a good part of the colder season if your house heating system is not extended into the addition. Such units might also be used as a supplemental heating source. True woodburning prefabricated fireplaces, using a minimum of masonry, are also available. They are made of steel with fireproof liners and an insulated stovepipe. They are normally designed for an interior wall. Check your local codes to determine the restrictions for these and similar units. The construction of chimneys and fireplaces must normally follow rigid codes and Fire Underwriter requirements.

CHIMNEYS

Chimneys are constructed of masonry units which might include brick, stone, or concrete block. A flue lining of some type is required in most building regulations.

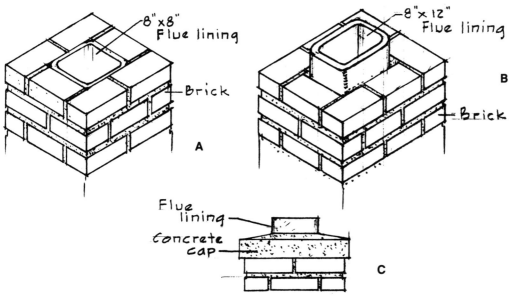

Fig. 123. Brick chimney.
A. For 8" x 8" flue.
B. For 8" x 12" flue.
C. Concrete cap.

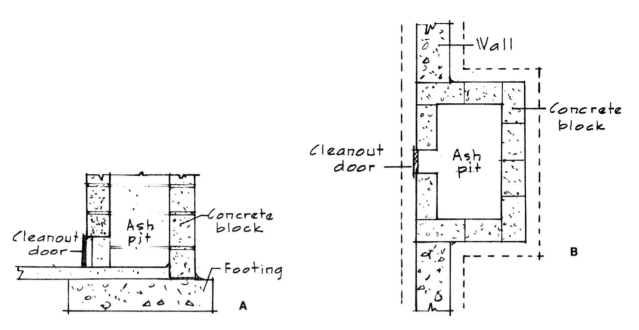

Fig. 124. Fireplace footing.
A. Section.
B. Plan view.

These flue linings may consist of rectangular or round shapes in a vitrified finish. An 8- by 8-inch or 8-inch round flue lining requires six bricks for each course, Fig. 123A. An 8- by 12-inch flue lining requires eight bricks per course, Fig. 123B. Prefabricated chimneys are available in several sizes eliminating the need for masonry. For the best results and to eliminate "down drafts," the top of the chimney should extend at least 2 feet above the ridge of your addition or clear a wall that is within 10 feet of the chimney. Masonry chimneys should be topped with a poured concrete cap, Fig. 123C. Use one flue liner for each fireplace or heating unit.

FOOTINGS

Footings for a chimney or fireplace should normally be about 10 to 12 inches deep and extend 6 inches beyond the perimeter of the chimney or fireplace base, Fig. 124A. The fireplace wall or chimney may be of poured concrete, of concrete block, or of brick. A poured basement wall is sometimes blocked out for the fireplace and chimney and finished to grade line with concrete block, Fig. 124B. A cleanout door should be included at basement floor level.

FIREPLACE

Wood framing members at chimneys or fireplaces should have at least a 2-inch clearance and the space firestopped with asbestos, fiberglass, or other similar noncombustible material. Prefabricated units of steel which incorporate inlet and outlet ducts for better utilization of the heat from the fire are available and require only enclosing with brick. The smoke shelf and damper are a part of the unit.

The layout for a typical masonry fireplace is shown in Fig. 125. The relation of the height to the depth of the opening should be a ratio of 3 (height) to 2 (depth). Such a ratio is generally followed in the prefabricated steel units. The height of the

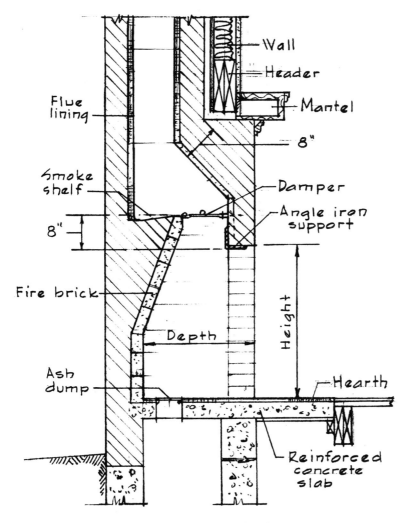

Fig. 125. Fireplace details.

smoke shelf should be 8 inches above the top of the fireplace opening. The inside area of the flue lining should be at least 10 percent of the fireplace opening. For example, a fireplace with a 30- by 26-inch opening (width and height) has a 780 square inch area and thus requires at least an 8- by 12-inch flue liner. The hearth (of masonry or tile) should extend at least 16 inches away from the face of the fireplace. Check your local code for other regulations relating to clearances, flue size requirements, etc.

31

Concrete Flatwork

Concrete flatwork consists of basement floors, driveways, sidewalks, and similar work. Driveways are ordinarily formed with 2- by 6-inch members which result in about a $5\frac{1}{2}$-inch-thick slab. To prevent cracking, 6- by 6-inch steel mesh reinforcing should be used. Asphalt-impregnated expansion joint material can be used for about every 20 feet of driveway and at junctions with sidewalks, masonry walls, etc. *Do not* pour over an area that has been filled until it has settled. A sand and gravel or gravel base, well tamped and settled, is desirable. In level areas, a crowned center for rain drainage is normally recommended. A minimum width of 9 feet for single driveways and 16 feet for double driveways allows room for garage entry and parking for two cars.

Sidewalks and basement floors should be formed with 2- by 4-inch members to provide about a $3\frac{1}{2}$-inch-thick concrete floor. Slope the basement floor toward a floor drain which has previously been installed and connected to your sewer line.

A $4\frac{1}{2}$ or 5 bag mix (number of bags of cement for each cubic yard of concrete) should be satisfactory for most conditions. Where there are severe winter conditions and consistent exposure to salt, a $5\frac{1}{2}$ or 6 bag mix containing an air-entraining mixture can be used for driveways.

32
Painting and Finishing

Wood and wood products in a variety of species, surface treatments, and colors can be used for the exterior and interior of dwellings. You may have used a few or a number of such variations in your addition. Paint is the finish normally used on materials such as primed hardboard siding, pine or other similar wood species used for trim, and other interior members. These items are usually not as adaptable to clear or lightly stained finished as are other species. Penetrating-type preservatives or pigmented stains might be used for smooth or rough surfaced siding species such as redwood or cedar. Such finishes are also used for plywood with either rough or smooth surfaces. Light stains (low pigmentation) or a clear varnish can be used on interior millwork and doors for such species as oak, mahogany, and other woods with grain variations.

Wood members, such as trim and siding, which have a vertical grain (edge grain) surface have better paint durability than the same species with flat grain surfaces. Thus, if your siding has an excessive amount of flat grain pieces, you should perhaps consider the use of some type of stain. The reverse side of the bevel sidings have a sawn surface which can be stained. You can specify vertical grain siding when ordering, but it is more costly than a more common grade. Plywood with a resin-treated paper-overlaid face is also well adapted to a paint finish.

EXTERIOR FINISHES FOR WOOD

Natural Finishes

Natural weathering of wood (without finish) usually affects the original color. Generally the dark-colored woods become lighter and the light-colored woods become darker. This may occur after several months or within a few years. As weathering continues, all woods become gray, but there is a gradual degradation of the wood cells at the surface. Therefore, it is good practice to provide some type of finish on your siding and trim. Weathered barn boards are sometimes used for an accent area and, when protected from rain by an overhang, will retain their original color for many years.

Rough surfaced woods, such as sawn or sandblasted surfaces, are best finished with a clear preservative or a pigmented stain. Clear preservatives most often used are the water-repellent types which can be obtained at most paint stores. They normally consist of the following: a preservative; a small amount of resin; a very small amount of a water repellent (wax-type material); a vehicle such as a paint thinner. This treatment, which penetrates the wood surface, retards the growth of mildew, prevents water staining, reduces warping, and protects those species which have low decay resistance. This type of preservative produces a clear golden tan color and, while more adaptable to rough sawn boards, can also be used on smooth surfaces. This preservative can be applied by brushing, dipping, or spraying. Rough surfaces will absorb more but are longer lived than when used on a smooth surface. While it is often necessary to apply such finishes every year for 2 or 3 years, the treatments will become more durable after this period. Pigmented colors can be added to water-repellent preservatives for special color effects. Two to six fluid ounces of colors in oil or tinting colors can be added to each gallon of treating solution.

Pigmented Stains

Pigmented stains are available in many colors and because they do not form a continuous film on the surface, they do not crack or blister. They can be lightly or heavily pigmented, the lightly pigmented materials allowing much of the grain pattern to show through. These materials can also be sprayed or brushed on exterior surfaces, but the heavily pigmented stains are perhaps best applied by brush. While the first coat may last only 2 to 4 years, the second application will normally last 8 to 10 years. Use two coats initially on rough surfaces.

An effective pigmented stain which is often used consists of the following materials: linseed oil vehicle; a fungicide-type preservative which protects the oil from mildew; and a water repellent such as paraffin wax. Red or brown iron oxide pigments can be used to simulate the natural colors of redwood and cedar.

Paints

Paints produce a nonporous film which retards penetration of moisture and reduces discoloration by wood extractives. Paint is not a preservative, however, and problems sometimes result when the film is broken. The latex and alkyd paints and the newer porous lead paints have the capacity to "breathe" which allows moisture vapor to pass through from the inner surfaces and areas of the house. However, these paints still retain resistance to the penetration of rain and dew. The modern paints are also fast drying and easy to apply with a brush (or roller) on smooth surfaced sidings.

Most paint manufacturers recommend the use of a primer before the finish coat is applied. Many of these prime coats consist of a nonporous oil-base primer paint which resists extractive staining. However, use the primer recommended in the directions included with your finish paint. Those woods free of colored extractives, such as pine and fir, can usually be painted without priming when using an acrylic-latex paint. Be sure to use a metal primer for such sheet metal items as gutters, downspouts, and metal siding corners. Galvanized metals should be washed with a light acid solution or left to weather before painting.

Apply the finish coat (or coats) of paint within 2 weeks after the application of the primer coat. A gallon of paint should cover approximately 400 to 500 square feet. Latex paints should not be applied during very hot weather or in direct sunlight, as they dry very quickly under these conditions. Not only is it difficult to apply an even coat, but the brush has a tendency to become heavily coated with paint.

Repainting should not be done until the old paint has worn thin. Faded or dirty paint can be freshened by washing. If there are exposed wood surfaces, spot prime with an approved primer paint before the new finish coat is applied.

INTERIOR FINISHES

Interior finishes normally include those for (1) woodwork such as trim, doors, cabinets, paneling, and floors and (2) walls and ceilings. Interior woodwork may be painted or treated with a transparent finish with or without staining. Walls and ceilings, whether plastered or covered with gypsum board, are normally painted.

Painting

Walls and Ceilings—Painting of new plaster or gypsum board walls and ceilings normally consists of a good prime coat sealer and one coat of finish paint. The sealer can be obtained in the same color as you have chosen for the final coat if you so desire. Some painters select a slightly lighter shade for the prime coat so that the final coat will eliminate "skips." Latex flat and semigloss paints are perhaps the most often used on walls and ceilings. They can be applied with a brush or roller or a combination of the two. A texture sealer, simulating a plaster finish, is available at most paint or lumber supply dealers for gypsum board. Sealers for plaster or dry wall should not be used for woodwork. Do not paint plastered surfaces until they are thoroughly dry. This is especially true of oil-base paints.

Woodwork—Before painting, woodwork should be extremely smooth. Sand planer marks or raised grain as such imperfections are accentuated with a high gloss paint. Hardwoods with large pores, such as oak, mahogany, and similar species, should be filled with a wood filler before the prime coat of paint is applied. Use the type of primer paint recommended in the instructions included with your finish paint. After the primer paint is thoroughly dry, sand the surface lightly and putty nailholes with putty of the same color as the finish coat.

Final paint coats on woodwork normally consist of a satin (semigloss) finish or a high gloss finish. These resist wear more than the flat finishes. Sand the first coat lightly if two finish coats are used.

Transparent Finishes for Woodwork

Transparent finishes with or without staining are used on most hardwoods and some softwood trim and paneling. Much of the plywood paneling now available, for example, is prefinished eliminating the need for staining and varnishing.

Stains most often recommended for hardwoods are the "nongrain-raising" ones which dry quickly when compared to the water stains. Some stains are pigmented and also serve as fillers for porous woods. Hardwoods with large pores, such as ash, butternut, chestnut, mahogany, oak, and similar woods, normally require filling when a smooth finish is desired. The filler may be transparent and thus will have no effect on the color of the finish. Putty or similar materials having the same color as the stained or natural finish of the wood should be used for nailholes after the staining process. As previously brought out, staining and filling such trim items as jambs, stops, casings, and baseboard before they are applied will save a great deal of work. Staining trim when it is in place is painstaking.

Sealers are normally thinned out varnishes or lacquers and are often applied to minimize absorption of subsequent finish coats. Satin or semigloss varnish or lacquer will produce a good wearing surface without a highly shiny surface. A high gloss finish, however, on grained woods seems to reflect the inner beauty of the wood. Try several different finishes on pieces of scrap wood to guide you in selecting the right type.

Interior Floors

Wood floors, except the prefinished types, normally require sanding before a finish is applied. If the flooring is somewhat uneven, a machine sander used at a 45° angle with the direction of the floor is normally the first step. The final step in sanding, with a fine grit such as 2/0, should be parallel to the direction of the strip flooring. Remove all dust before applying the finish.

Floors may be finished with a floor sealer or by using a filler and/or stain before the finish is used. Sealers, which are normally thinned out varnishes, can be applied with a brush. Then, using a coarse, lint-free cloth, rub the coating into the wood first starting across the grain and finish with the grain. Treat a 3-foot-wide strip along the length of the room before applying the sealer to the next strip. After the sealer has thoroughly dried, a second coat can be used. Some sealers might be applied differently and, if so, follow the directions on the container.

If a smooth glossy finish is desired for flooring with large pores, such as oak, a filler is normally used after sanding. A filler may be paste or liquid, natural or colored. It is applied by brushing first across the grain and then with the grain. Remove the surplus filler immediately by wiping across the grain (to fill the pores) and then lightly with the grain.

When the filler has dried, the final varnish coats may be applied. Varnish may be based on alkyd, phenolic, epoxy, or polyurethane resins. They all form a distinct coating over the wood and give a lustrous finish. Some provide better service than others where heavy use is anticipated. Recommendations are normally included with each type of finish. A wide brush, of the type designated for varnish, can be used in applying the finish. If two coats are desired, allow the first to dry thoroughly.

If a stain is desired because of uneven coloring of the strip flooring, it should be applied after the sanding process. Stain should be oil-based to minimize raising of the grain.

A final treatment with a paste or liquid wax might be desirable to provide good performance. Paste waxes generally give the best appearance and durability. Two coats of liquid wax are usually recommended.

Exterior Floors

Exposed flooring on porches and decks is commonly painted. Apply a heavy coat of water-repellent preservative so that it penetrates into the joints. After the preservative has thoroughly dried (usually 48 hour in warm weather), a good deck paint can be used. Two coats of paint are required for good coverage.

A rustic-type deck may also be finished with several coats of the water-repellent preservative, or with penetrating-type pigmented stain. Because these types of finishes penetrate the wood, they require refinishing more often than painted surfaces.

33

Protection Against Decay and Termites

GENERAL

Wood used in a dry condition so that it will not exceed a moisture content of 19 percent, or wetted only briefly and rapidly redried, will not decay. If, however, due to poor construction details, wood remains wet for long periods at temperatures favorable to the growth of decay organisms, decay will likely begin. Thus, by using good assembly details or by the use of treated wood in severe exposure conditions, decay will not be a factor in your new addition.

Subterranean termites and dry-wood termites which can infect wood in houses occur in the southern sections of the United States. The subterranean termites are the most common and require moisture in the soil and in their movement (shelter tubes) from soil to wood parts. These earthlike shelter tubes can be easily detected at foundation walls or in crawl space areas. They are more difficult to find if they travel from under a concrete slab to wood parts by way of openings around pipes.

SAFEGUARDS AGAINST DECAY

Some of the precautions which might be used to insure resistance to decay in wood parts are as follows:

1. Use pressure-treated wood for sills and plates on foundation walls when they are near the soil line.
2. Provide at least 8 inches of clearance from the ground to the bottom of the siding.
3. Slope the ground away from the foundation for good drainage.
4. Use a soil cover of polyethylene in crawl spaces.
5. Use flashing wherever necessary to eliminate water entry.
6. Use good overhangs at cornice and gable ends to keep rain away from walls.
7. Use gutters, downspouts, and splash blocks to carry water away from foundation walls.
8. Use good inlet and outlet ventilators for a dry attic.
9. Use dry lumber—under 19 percent for framing material and under 10 to 12 percent for interior wood parts.
10. Use a water-repellent preservative at siding joints (butt joints and juncture with casing) before painting under severe conditions.
11. Use a good vapor barrier on the interior side of all exposed walls to minimize movement of water vapor through stud spaces to cold exterior surfaces.
12. Do not retain a high humidity within the house during cold weather which results in surface condensation on window surfaces. Water can run down and soak into sash rails and window sills.

SAFEGUARDS AGAINST TERMITES

Some of the precautions which should be considered in the construction of your house (if it is in a termite area) are as follows:

1. Remove all wood items before backfilling or pouring a concrete slab.
2. Treat soil under a concrete slab and along foundation walls with an approved soil treatment designed for elimination of termites.
3. Use a termite shield (normally a rust-resistant metal) over foundation walls with inner and outer edges bent down to form a drip edge.
4. Pour tar around soil and water pipes in a concrete slab to close any openings.

Appendices
Minor Projects

INTRODUCTION

Is your house large enough and in a good neighborhood, but needs some work on the exterior or interior? Something can be done that is less complicated and costly than extensive remodeling of the interior or the construction of an addition. There are a number of simple improvements which can make your house more livable and less costly to maintain and heat. These projects may even consist of the addition of shutters, providing better foundation drainage, or adding mastic sealant to flashing and shingles. Somewhat more involved projects can consist of residing the house, erecting a simple roof to protect an exposed exterior door, or removing part of an interior wall to open the living-dining area. These and many more similar projects with helpful details and descriptions are presented in this section. Hopefully they will aid in the work of improving your existing home.

Appendix A
Outside Improvements

BETTER OUTSIDE DRAINAGE

Improving the drainage around your house will minimize the amount of rainwater entering the basement walls. Soil against the foundation walls often settles allowing rainwater or melting snow to follow the foundation wall to the footing where it can result in wet or damp basement floors. For better protection, add soil against the the wall to provide a slope away from the house. If a basement window is in the way of the fill, use a metal "area wall." They can be obtained in widths up to 30 inches. The use of a black polyethylene strip of film over the sloped ground followed by several inches of gravel or crushed rock is sometimes used in more difficult soil conditions. These precautions, of course, are in addition to the use of gutters, downspouts, and splash blocks (see Chapter "Flashing and Other Sheet Metal").

CALKING SHINGLES AND FLASHING

Do you have minor leaks in your roof during rainstorms with accompanying high winds? It may be that the shingle tabs (in nonseal tab asphalt shingles) lift up enough to permit the entry of rain. Does the area around a chimney become damp during a storm? Most of these problems can be remedied by use of a calking gun with an asphalt mastic compound. For loose shingles, use a small spot of mastic under each shingle tab and press in place. There might also be nail pops caused by roofing nails which are located at a knot or joint between roof coverings. These form a small hump in the shingles as the nail works out. The guilty nail should removed, the hole sealed, and the nail replaced in solid wood. Lift the shingle only enough to remove the nail and drive the new one in with a thin metal bar and a hammer.

Check the flashing around your chimney and at valleys and ridges. These areas can also be calked if there are any openings in the original sealant. A latex calk might be used for surface or for exposed areas. While on the roof, check the mortar joints in your chimney. They also might need some repointing. Use a rich mortar-sand mixture and apply with a small pointing trowel.

RESHINGLING YOUR ROOF

An asphalt shingle roof may provide good service for 18 to 20 years and a wood shingle roof for up to 35 years depending on exposure conditions. In most cases the asphalt shingles need not be removed before reshingling. Nail down any curled or loose shingles to provide a good level surface. Apply the shingles as described in the Chapter "Roof Coverings." If shingles are worn at the overhang, cut them flush with the facia molding. Use a metal overhang drip edge along the gable and eave lines before starting the shingling process. Roofing nails should be long enough to penetrate the roof sheathing ($1\frac{1}{4}$ to $1\frac{1}{2}$ inches). If valley or other flashing is in poor condition, replace it. The valley flashing can be placed over the old. Lift the old shingles along the valley, removing nails, if necessary, so that the flashing is well under existing shingles.

New wood shingles can also be used over an old wood shingle roof with some additional precautions. Again, nail down curled or loose shingles to provide a smooth surface. Most recommendations include the removal of the shingles along the gable edge and at valleys. Replace these shingles with a nominal 1- by 6- or 1- by 8-inch board. Extend the board slightly over the edge of the gable. This board can be prepainted at exposed edges, if desired. At the ridge, remove the Boston ridge shingles or metal ridge and replace with new ones. Check valley flashing as previously outlined for asphalt shingles. Galvanized shingle nails, $1\frac{1}{2}$ to 2 inches long, are usually required when reshingling. Use the same method of shingling as described in the Chapter "Roof Coverings."

Note: See next Section "Adding Roof Extensions" if remodeling of the roof overhang is desired.

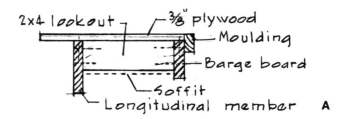

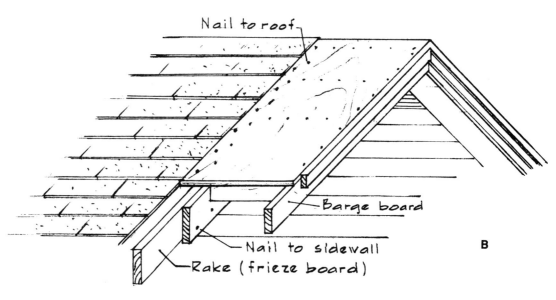

Fig. 126. Rake extension.
A. Fabrication.
B. Application.

ADDING ROOF EXTENSIONS

Many of the houses constructed in the late 40's and the 50's had little gable end and cornice extensions. These are classed as "close" rakes and "close" cornices. This type of construction reduced the cost to the contractor but did little to improve the appearance of the house. This does not necessarily apply to the "salt box" design once so popular in the New England areas in the 18th and 19th centuries.

A close cornice and a close rake is constructed without frame members extending beyond the side or end walls of the house. Only the trim moldings extend beyond the wall line. Roof extensions can enhance the appearance of many house designs as well as serve to protect side walls. If you plan to reshingle your house, consideration might be given to extending the roof lines before the shingling begins. The following suggestions will likely aid you in such a project.

Rake Extension

Select the extension you wish and nail short 2- by 4-inch lookouts to 1- by 4-inch or 1- by 6-inch longitudinal members to the ends, Fig. 126A. Space the blocks 24 inches apart. Now nail a strip of $\frac{3}{8}$-inch plywood to the framework, flush on one side (outside edge) and extending 5 to 6 inches beyond the inside edge. These frames can be made in 8-foot or longer sections. Remove any molding or trim on the house that might be fastened to the rake frieze board. Also cut and remove the shingles back from the edge a distance equal to the plywood projection. Raise the frames in place and nail the inner 1-inch member to the face of the frieze board. Then nail the plywood into the top edge of the rafter (through the roof sheathing), Fig. 126B. The barge board molding and the soffit can be installed. The $\frac{3}{8}$-inch plywood is about equal to the thickness of the asphalt shingle courses. If any adjustment is required, use thicker plywood.

Cornice Extension

A roof extension at the cornice can be made quite simply by nailing small brackets to the roof of the house. Remove facia moldings and gutters. Determine the amount of overhang desired and nail a sample bracket together using 2- by 4-inch members, Fig. 127A. After trying it at the cornice, assemble a number of the brackets (3 for each 4 feet). Nail a 1- by 6- or 1- by 8-inch backing board to the rafter extension blocks and a 1- by 4-inch facia board at each end of the lookout, Fig. 127B. Brackets should be placed on 16-inch centers. These frames can also be made in 8-foot or longer sections.

Raise the sections in place and nail the upper backer board to the facia of the house and the lower backer to the siding (at stud line) with tenpenny or twelve-penny nails. Trim the shingles 5 to 6 inches back from the edge and cover the framework with $\frac{3}{8}$-inch plywood. The plywood should extend up to the edge of the trimmed asphalt shingles. The plywood extension should be well nailed into the roof at the rafters as well as into the brackets and facia nailer, Fig. 127C. If thicker plywood is required to equal the shingle course thickness, make the necessary adjustments. Facia, facia molding, and soffit can then be installed, Fig. 127C. The roof should be ready for reshingling. It is good practice to provide vent in the old facia between rafters into the attic space. Inlet ventilators can then be installed in the soffit of the new cornice (see Chapter "Ventilation").

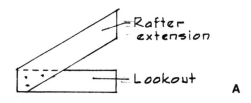

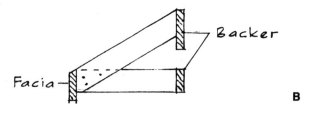

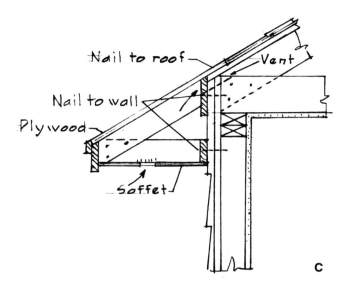

Fig. 127. Cornice extension.
A. Sample bracket.
B. Assembly.
C. Application.

Another method which might be used as an alternate to the bracket system consists of sawing sections out of the facia board on the house wall (and sheathing, if necessary). Remove a section of roof shingles and roof sheathing. Rafter extensions can now be added. A box cornice (with lookouts) or one without lookouts will complete the cornice extension (see Chapter "Cornice Framing and Trim").

RESIDING YOUR HOUSE

Residing your house is a somewhat involved project, but certainly not as difficult as many other house improvements. It is only a little more complicated than applying siding to a new house. Minor problems, such as siding joints at window and door casings, can be solved by the use of an additional member alongside or over the existing casing. Normally no changes or additions are required at the drip cap (top of windows and doors) or under window sills.

Select the type of siding most easily applied over the existing siding yet pleasant in appearace and in keeping with the architectural design of your house. Such sidings may include a primed hardboard which comes in $\frac{7}{16}$- by 12-inch by 16-foot sizes. Wide cedar or redwood siding can also be used to cover your old siding. These sidings can be prestained on the rough sawn side before applying over the old siding of your house. In low shingle-story houses, a rough sawn plywood siding in 4- by 8- or 4- by 9-foot sheets or a board and batten siding pattern may be desirable. Such sidings can also be prestained before they are used over the old siding.

In a lap siding pattern, it is good practice to have the nailing area coincide with a butt edge of the siding to be covered. For example, if your existing siding has an exposed distance of 5 or $5\frac{1}{4}$ inches, you can use the primed hardboard in 12-inch widths with an exposure of 10 or $10\frac{1}{2}$ inches, Fig. 128A. This will result in a $1\frac{1}{2}$- or 2-inch lap which is desirable. Thus one course of the new siding will cover two two courses of the old. Use galvanized ring shank nails as they provide superior holding power.

If the thickness of the existing casing at the sides of doors and windows is not sufficient to provide a good butt joint, an auxiliary casing can be used. One method consists of the following: With an electric circular saw and guide, saw a groove parallel to the casing only through the old siding. Remove any nails that might be in the way. After removing the siding, select $\frac{3}{4}$-, $1\frac{1}{4}$-, or $1\frac{1}{2}$-inch-wide material with sufficient depth to provide a good butt joint for the siding, Fig. 128B. Nail in place with galvanized nails.

An auxiliary casing might be used which does not require removal of the siding. With a table saw, form a back band so that it laps the edge of the old casing, Fig. 128C. Another simple system consists of nailing a 1- by 1-inch member to the edge of the existing casing, Fig. 128D.

Apply your siding in the same manner as described in the chapter "Exterior Coverings." Some care might be taken when a butt joint of a wide thin siding does not occur at a casing or a corner. If there is some space between new siding and the old, use a shim and nail the end of each siding piece, Fig. 128E.

Panel siding, such as large sheets of plywood, can be applied directly to your old siding. They can be prestained before being nailed in place. Use 16-inch spacing (horizontally) and place nails about 8 to 10 inches apart vertically. Use galvanized or stainless steel nails of sufficient length to penetrate well into the siding and wood sheathing or into the studs.

If your house has no wall insulation, what better time to add some type from the outside before you start your residing project. The following section contains several suggestions that might be helpful.

ADDING WALL INSULATION FROM THE EXTERIOR

Perhaps the most practical method of adding insulation to the exposed walls of your frame house is from the exterior. This normally involves drilling holes in the wall be-

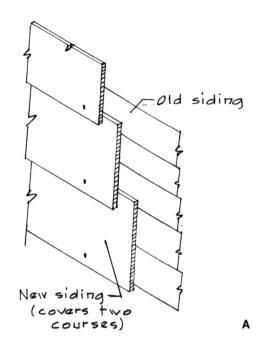

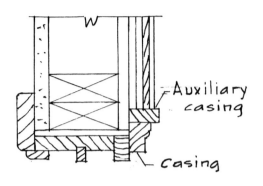

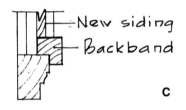

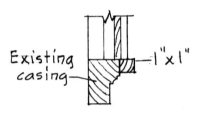

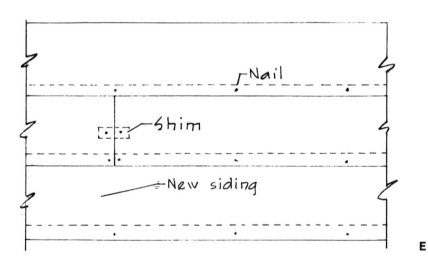

Fig. 128. Residing.
A. Double coursing.
B. Auxiliary casing.
C. Auxiliary casing.
D. Auxiliary casing.
E. Butt joint treatment.

tween the studs just under the top plates and under the window sills. If your home projects include residing the house, the holes may be drilled through both siding and sheathing. However, if this combination project is not planned, siding must be removed at the areas requiring the fill holes. Lift the siding at the butt edge and also the siding course above the one to be removed and pull the nails. Those that cannot be pulled can be cut off with a hack saw blade. Now drill holes between each stud and under the windows. A 2-inch-diameter hole is normally large enough. If your house is $1\frac{1}{2}$ or 2 stories, be careful of heat or cold air return ducts that might be located between studs. Check the interior wall for these duct spaces. These spaces, of course, cannot be insulated in this manner.

Several types of fill insulations are available. They include fiberglass, rock wool, or similar materials (in a form suitable for pouring), and also small pellets of vermiculite. For easier application, the fiberglass pellets normally require the use of a portable blowing machine to force the insulation into the stud spaces. The vermiculate can be poured by hand or can be applied with a blower. The fiberglass and rock wool have somewhat greater insulating value than the vermiculite.

After filling each stud space to the top, cover the holes with sheet metal or waterproof paper, such as asphalt felt, before replacing the siding.

A foamed-in-place insulation is available and is normally supplied by insulating companies using special equipment. This type is also applied through holes drilled between stud spaces.

ADD A NEW WINDOW

Replacing old windows, adding new ones, or providing an opening for sliding doors, normally means the removal of a good portion of an exterior wall. When this wall is load bearing (ceiling joists and rafters bear on it), some type of support should be provided at the wall line. This might consist of a beam with proper supports along the inside wall, Fig. 129A. When spans are quite long and rafter projections permit it, an extra support might be used along the exterior wall, Fig. 129A. The posts should be spaced outside the edge of the new opening. Some type of support should also be used at nonlead-bearing walls where windows might be added. If an existing window is involved, first take off the interior trim (casing, stool, etc.), loosen the outside casing, remove the frame from the outside.

When you select your new window or window combinations, you can obtain the required rough opening size. Mark this new width and height on the inside wall and carefully remove the plaster or gypsum board to these marks. The top finish line under the existing window header will have to be removed to the underside of the top plates to provide a space for the new header. The studs will now be exposed. The studs that require removal between the old and new openings should be sawed at the new window sill line and removed to the underside of the top plates. Use doubled 2- by 12-inch members for the new header unless the new opening is too wide to cause some deflection under normal roof loads. In such cases (usually for spans greater than 8 feet), the window design should incorporate intermediate supports. New or existing studs to support the header (jack studs) should be located as shown in Fig. 129B. Use short blocks between the header and the top plates if necessary. Fit and nail a 2- by 4-inch sill at the bottom of the opening. Now remove the siding and sheathing at a line to accommodate the new frame, Fig. 192C. After the frame is fastened in place, add siding where required. The interior covering and the window trim can now be completed.

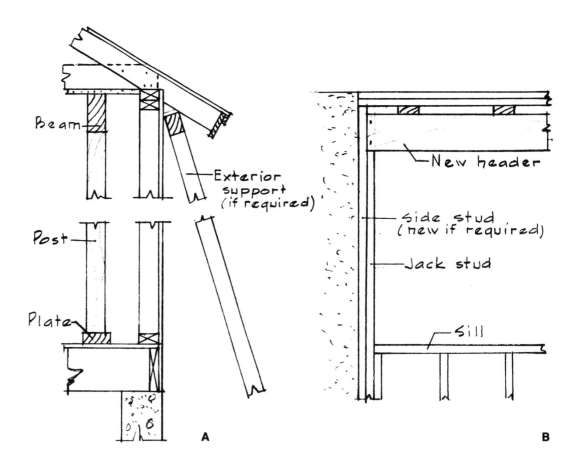

Beam

Post

Plate

Exterior
support
(if required)

A

New header

Side stud
(new if required)

Jack stud

Sill

B

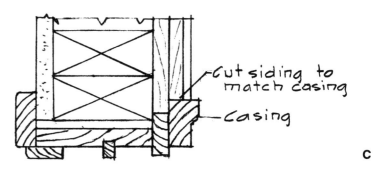

Cut siding to
match casing

Casing

C

Fig. 129. Adding a new window.
A. Support for exterior wall.
B. Framing at opening.
C. Plan view of new window jamb.

PROTECT THAT EXPOSED DOOR!

Do you have an exterior door that is exposed to the weather? If there is an entry platform, the construction of a simple hood or canopy is an easy and worthwhile construction project. One method consists of the fabrication of a frame about the same size as your concrete platform. For a simple "shed-type" slope, use a 1- by 6-inch rear member and a 1- by 4-inch front member, Fig. 130A.

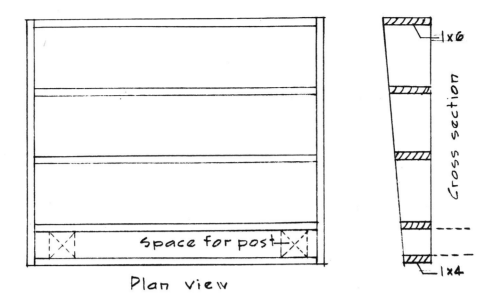

Plan view

Cross section

1x6

1x4

Space for post

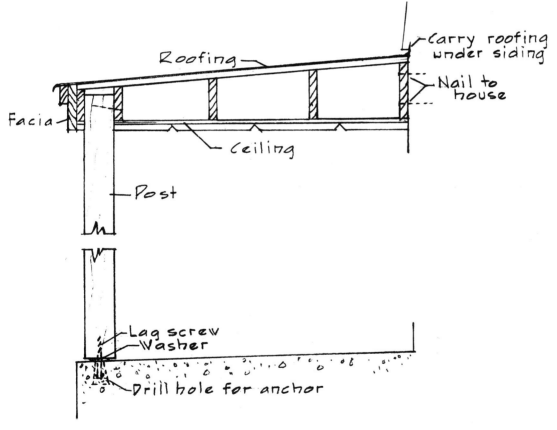

Roofing

Carry roofing
under siding

Nail to
house

Facia

Ceiling

Post

Lag screw
Washer

Drill hole for anchor

Fig. 130. Hood over entry door.
A. Frame work plan.
B. Installation.

Cross members can be nailed between the side members which are sloped from $5\frac{1}{2}$ inches to $3\frac{1}{2}$ inches (back to front). A cross member can be nailed $3\frac{1}{2}$ inches in back of the front member to accommodate $3\frac{1}{2}$- by $3\frac{1}{2}$-inch posts (nominal 4 by 4).

Fig. 130. Hood over entry door (*cont'd*).
C. Typical hood.

Place the framework on the stoop in its correct position and mark an outline on the concrete for the 4- by 4-inch posts. At the center of the post locations, drill a $\frac{3}{4}$- to 1-inch-diameter hole about $2\frac{1}{2}$ to 3 inches deep. Use a hand star drill if a power drill is not available.

Raise the framework in place above the door (2 to 4 inches above the top casing and drip cap) and nail the rear cross member (the 1 by 6) to the house siding at the stud lines. Use temporary braces to support the outer edge of the frame. The roof sheathing can be applied before or after the frame is in place. Use $\frac{3}{8}$- or $\frac{1}{2}$-inch exterior grade plywood.

Posts should be nominal 4 by 4's in redwood or similar species. Treated posts can also be used. Drill a lead hole and screw in a $\frac{3}{8}$- by 4-inch galvanized lag screw in the center of one end of each post over a large square galvanized washer. Use a rich cement-sand wet mixture or a waterproof filler in the holes and place the lag-screwed ends in the holes, Fig. 130B. After plumbing the posts, fasten them by nailing at the top through two or more sides of the canopy frame. Facia and facia molding can be added. In addition, a metal overhanging drip edge should be installed around the perimeter. Use 65-pound roll roofing ($\frac{1}{2}$-lap or similar material; several colors are available) and fasten down with generous ribbons of asphalt roofing cement. Roofing nails can be used where they are covered by next strip of roofing. Carry the roofing up against a siding course and apply a metal counterflashing over the roofing, Fig. 130B. Plywood or similar material can be used as a ceiling finish for the canopy. A typical protective roof for a formerly unprotected door is shown in Fig. 130C.

SHUTTER APPLICATION

Shutters are often used to enhance the exterior appearance of a house. This is true if they are used properly and in keeping with the general design of the house. A colonial or Cape Cod house is perhaps best accented by the louvered type shutter with its stiles and cross rails. The ranch and similar one-story houses can use a more rustic design. Such types are normally not available and must be made by hand. However, they can be fabricated quite simply. The louvered shutter can be purchased as their construction is somewhat complicated for the home workshop.

The rustic shutter can be made simply from grooved plywood siding or from tongued and grooved boards fastened together with two exposed or hidden cross cleats, Fig. 131A. Use screws to fasten the cleats to the vertical boards.

The length (height) of shutters should be about equal to the sash opening from the underside of top casing to the top of the sill, Fig. 131B. Use galvanized screws to fasten the shutter to the siding along the edge of the side casing. Locate the screws so that they enter the butt edge of a siding course. Use small rubber spacers, Fig. 131C, between the shutter and the wood siding. This will prevent rain pockets between the shutter and siding which can cause paint failure.

ADD A SIMPLE CARPORT

In northern climates some type of protection for your car is a big advantage during the winter months. The answer may be a carport. We will assume that the size of your lot is large enough to provide the construction of some type of shelter for your car or cars. Perhaps the lowest cost structure would be an open or semiopen carport. Such a unit can be constructed so that it may be converted to an enclosed garage at a future date, if so desired. The following details should aid in the construction of such units.

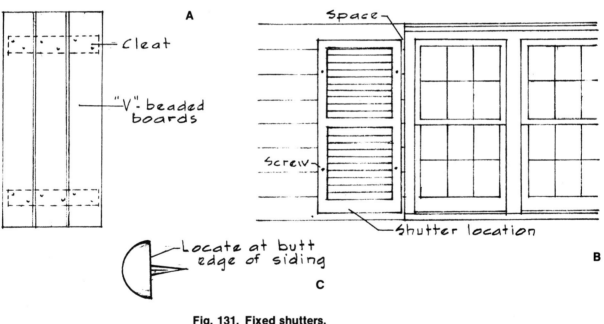

Fig. 131. Fixed shutters.
A. Rustic shutter.
B. Shutter application.
C. Rubber spacer.

An important factor in the construction of a carport is to provide resistance to "uplift" during periods of very high winds which can destroy the roof. These details should include good anchorage and ties as follows: (1) footing to posts, (2) posts to beams, (3) beams to roof framing (rafters), and (4) rafters to house framing (wall or roof).

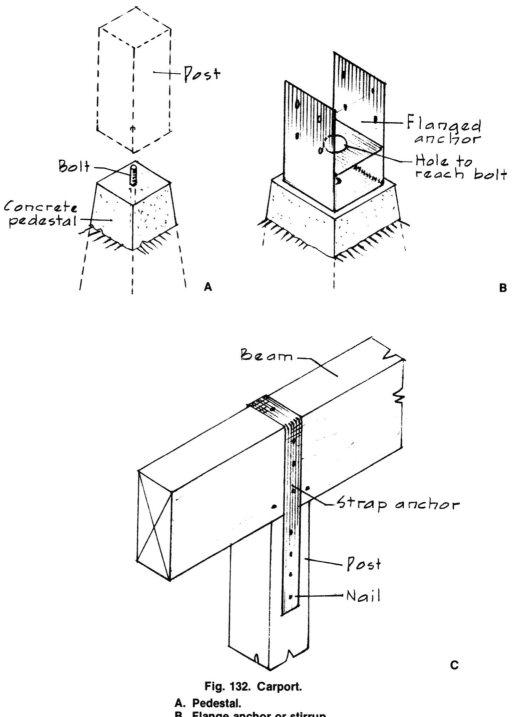

Fig. 132. Carport.
A. Pedestal.
B. Flange anchor or stirrup.
C. Strap anchor.

Post footings should be deep enough to be below the frostline. Holes can be dug with a posthole digger with the bottom spread out to form a wide base. Posts are normally spaced no more than 6 feet apart. A long ½-inch anchor bolt is placed in the pedestal during pouring operations, Fig. 132A. A flanged anchor for 4- by 4- or 4- by 6-inch posts can be fastened to the concrete pedestal, Fig. 132B. Use galvanized nails or lag screws in fastening the metal anchor to the post.

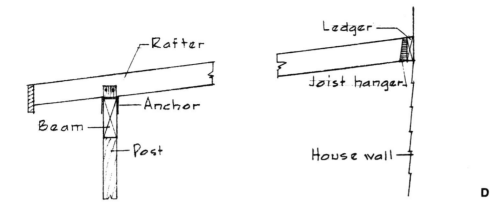

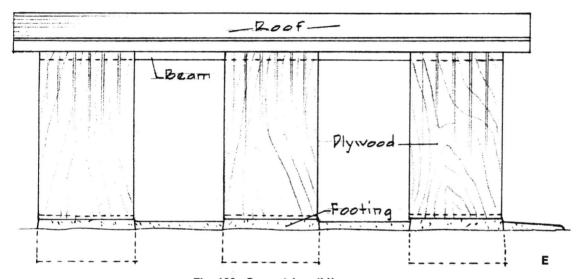

Fig. 132. Carport (*cont'd*).
D. Detail at rafter.
E. Side view of partially closed carport.

If the conversion to a garage is a possibility, the construction of a continuous foundation might be considered which would replace the post footings.

Beams are fastened to the posts by means of angle irons. Strap anchors could also be used over the top of the beam, Fig. 132C. Commercial anchors are usually available for such connections. Beams can be solid or of laminated construction (two 2-inch members). Spans for various beam sizes should confrom generally to the window header sizes listed in the Chapter "Wall Framing." This would determine the spacing of the posts.

The rafters, spaced 16 inches on center and slightly sloped for drainage, should be toenailed to the beam and, in addition, a metal strap or commercial anchor used at each rafter, Fig. 132D. A 2- by 6- or 2- by 8-inch ledger is lag screwed to the studs or top plates of the house wall (over the siding) and the rafters toenailed to the ledger. In addition, use joist hangers for additional ties, Fig. 132D. Rafters should be designed to carry any snow load common to your area. Local building codes normally specify the allowable spans for various sizes of rafters (see Chapter "Porches").

Roof sheathing, roofing, and flashing should conform to the details previously outlined in other chapters of this handbook.

Another system of constructing a side wall for your carport could consist of 4- by 8-foot panels anchored to a foundation wall and spaced 4 feet apart, Fig. 132E. Panels would consist of 2- by 4-inch vertical members spaced 16 inches on center and covered with exterior grade plywood in an attractive pattern. The beam, tying the panels together, might consist of a 4 by 6 or two 2 by 6's. Panels should be well anchored to both the foundation wall and to the beam. Use a 2- by 6-inch sill bolted to the foundation wall.

Appendix B
Basement Improvements

Satisfactory rooms can be provided in your basement if it is in a reasonably good condition. The information for such improvements has been covered in the Chapter "Basement Rooms." However, there are several less involved projects which can be done in the basement which will often be reflected in other rooms of your house. One or more of the following projects might accomplish such improvements.

STIFFER FLOOR JOISTS
(REDUCE DEFLECTION UNDER LOAD)

Do you feel the floor vibrate or hear a glass rattle in a tray when someone walks across your living room? It may be that the floor joists, while more than adequate from the standpoint of strength, could have less deflection under such use. In other words, the joists could be stiffer. There is a relatively simple method of stiffening the floor joists of your house while at the same time making them somewhat stronger. Adding a joist at every other joist is one method, but it is difficult to place them over the foundation wall and the center beam so that they are effective.

A simpler method consists of the use of a 1- by 4-inch or two 1- by 2-inch members nail-glued to the bottom area of each joist. If the bottom edge of the joists are unobstructed from the foundation wall to the center beam, a 1- by 4-inch member can be nail-glued to the bottom of each joist, Fig. 133A. The important factors to be considered are as follows:

1. Use full length 1 by 4's (from foundation wall to center beam).
2. The gluing surface of the joist must be smooth and clean.
3. Use a water-resistant glue and spread well on bottom edge of joist and on the 1 by 4.
4. Use sixpenny or sevenpenny nails spaced about 8 inches apart.
5. Nail rapidly while glue is still soft or liquid (pieces may be partly prenailed before application).
6. Do not load the first floor above while applying the reinforcing (excessive walking, etc.).

When there are obstructions at the bottom edge of the joists, use a 1- by 2-inch member at each side, Fig. 133B. These also should follow the same general rules as outlined for the 1- by 4-inch members. If cross bridging is in the way, remove and replace it after the project is completed. Laboratory load tests have indicated a marked improvement in providing additional joist stiffness with these nail-glued members.

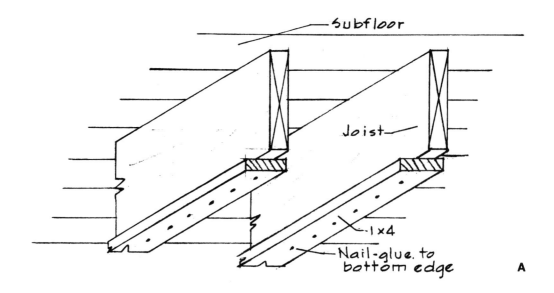

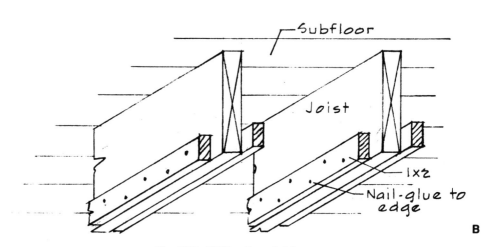

Fig. 133. Stiffer floor joists.
A. Using 1 x 4's.
B. Using 2- 1 x 2's.

MORE EFFICIENT WOOD BEAMS

If there is a noticeable deflection in your solid or laminated wood beam and the span between supports is quite long, it is likely that an additional post should be added to prevent further deflection. Use a steel jack post near the center of the span and tighten slightly each week. This might *slowly* correct some of the excessive deflection. Do not overtighten so as to disturb the ends of the beam. After several months or even a year, put in a permanent post if you so desire.

An existing wood beam might also be stiffened by adding an additional 2-inch member, the same depth as the beam. Cut it so that a part of each end is supported by the foundation wall and a supporting post. If the surfaces are smooth and not warped, spread a water-resistant glue on them and nail the members to the existing beam. Use twelvepenny nails and stagger them at 12-inch spacings along the length. This additional member can be used along the entire length of the beam for best results.

ELIMINATE THOSE SQUEAKY FLOORS

"Squeaks" in your floors may be caused by one or more of the following:

1. Flooring nails loosened or not nailed to a floor joist.
2. Flooring dried out, causing movement between floor pieces.
3. Subfloor loose at a joist.
4. Cupping or bowing of the floor or subfloor.

First determine the exact areas where this problem occurs. Then one of several methods might be used in minimizing this annoyance. Correcting this problem from the top surface can be done if the floor is not carpeted. However, it usually involves drilling a hole in the floor, then a lead hole for the screw. After the screw is placed, a plug matching the flooring grain can be installed.

Other methods consist of making the corrections in the basement. Thus, the floor above does not have to be disturbed. If your marked problem area shows that the subfloor has lifted above the top of the joist, nail-glue a 2 by 2 to, and flush with, the top edge, Fig. 134A. After the glue has dried, use long $2\frac{1}{2}$-inch screws from the bottom of the cleat into the subfloor and finish floor. A small lead hole might be used. (The screw length depends on the subfloor thickness.)

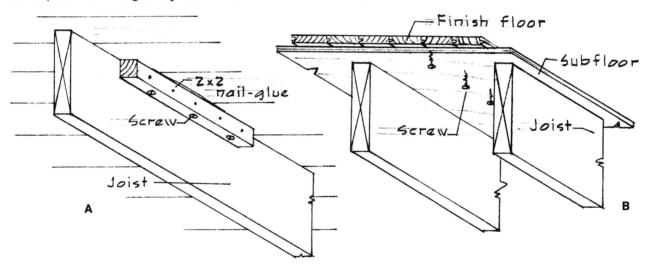

Fig. 134. Eliminate "squeaky" floors.
A. With 2 x 2 on joist.
B. With screws.

If there is no such indication of loose subfloor, use a number of screws along the problem area, Fig. 134B. Use lead holes and screws long enough to penetrate at least one-half the thickness of the finish floor. Do not use wedges between the top of the joists and the subfloor as this is likely to result in an uneven floor.

FOUNDATION INSULATION

An area in the basement that is sometimes uninsulated during construction of a

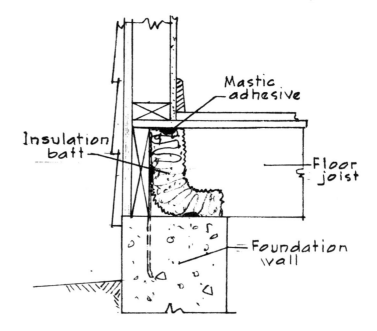

Fig. 135. Foundation insulation.

house is the area above the foundation wall. This perimeter area includes spaces between floor joists and along the stringer (band) joists. Use 16- to 20-inch-long sections of 3½- or 6-inch-thick batt insulation and place them in between each joist at the foundation wall, Fig. 135. If necessary use a dab or two of mastic adhesive against the header joist and/or subfloor to hold the batt in place. If there is a vapor barrier on the insulation, it should be placed to face the basement side. Use long sections of the insulation along those outer walls which are parallel to the joists. Insulation in these areas will not only reduce heat loss but will also result in warmer floors in the rooms above.

DRIER BASEMENTS

Perhaps the simplest method of having a drier basement is through the use of mechanical dehumidifers. They are controlled by a thermostat and should be located so that a drain hose leads to the floor drain. However, there are certain precautions which can be used to minimize moisture buildup in basements during humid summers. If a crawl space is involved or one is connected to a basement area, use a soil cover of 4- or 6-mil polyethylene to prevent ground moisture from entering the space above. Other factors which might influence moisture in the basement are as follows:

1. Prevent outside moisture from soaking masonry walls (previously covered and includes sloping of ground away from wall, etc.).

2. Use a waterproof coating on the inner surfaces of the wall and on the exterior if they are exposed. Many types are available, some being transparent. If there are small openings where water enters occasionally, they should be filled with a hydraulic cement before application of the waterproof coating.

3. If you wish to air out your basement, open the windows at night, not during the day. This is especially true during the hot humid days in the summer months.

Appendix C
Interior Improvements

There are a number of projects which you might select to improve the interior of your home. Furthermore, some can be completed with only a little effort, some assistance, and at a reasonable cost. If you need a more open living-dining area, more efficient insulation, or better kitchen cabinets, the following suggestions will hopefully aid you in the completion of such projects.

A GOOD ROOM FROM YOUR GARAGE

An existing attached garage can be adapted to a pleasant room usable in winter and summer when it is insulated and supplied with some type of heat. The floor level of an attached garage is normally from 16 to 24 inches below the floor level of the house. This might vary even more depending on the amount of exposed foundation wall. It is often desirable, when possible, in converting the garage to a room, to locate the floor joists so that the floor level is the same as that of the house. This is usually quite simple as the new joists can be attached to the garage and house walls at almost any desired elevation.

Joist sizes and spacings should conform to the suggested span tables shown in Table 7. Depending on the height of the new floor and the joist size, a ledger can be nailed to the band joist of the house to support the joists, Fig. 136A. A soil cover of 4- or 6-mil polyethylene should now be used over the existing garage slab. When

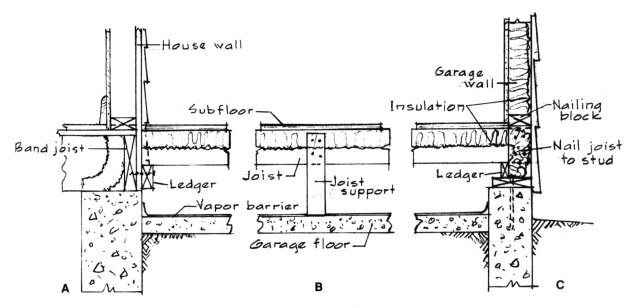

Fig. 136. A room from your garage.
- **A. Section at house.**
- **B. Section at center of span.**
- **C. Section at garage wall.**

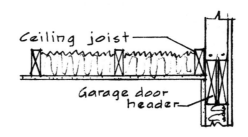

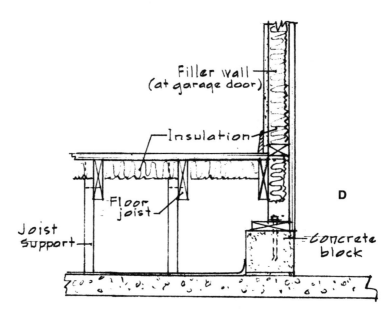

Fig. 136. A room from your garage (cont'd).
D. Section through garage door.

spans are long, use a 2- by 4-inch joist support at the center of each span, Fig. 136B. Spike to each joist. Now nail each joist to each garage wall stud with sixteenpenny nails, Fig. 136C. If the studs are spaced 24 inches on center in the garage wall, toenail the joists into the ledger member if the joist and stud do not coincide. Use a 2- by 3- or 2- by 4-inch ledger member to support joists that do not coincide with the studs of the garage wall, Fig. 136C.

Floor insulation can be installed before the subfloor is nailed in place. The same applies to any cold air return ducts or heat ducts that might be located between the joists. A nailing block can be used between studs to supply a fastening area for base trim, Fig. 136C.

A filler wall at the garage door location should be constructed with 2- by 4-inch studs supported on a sill plate, Fig. 136D. Use concrete block or poured concrete to fill the area at the door opening. The height should be the same as the concrete wall of the garage. The garage door area might also be suitable for the location of one large or several smaller windows if the garage door header is at the correct elevation. The size of the ceiling joists should conform to those recommended in Table 8. They are supported on one side at the top plate of the garage wall. A 2- by 6-inch ledger, nailed to the wall of the house after removing the siding, supports the other end of the ceiling joist. Toenail into the ledger with tenpenny nails or use metal joist hangers.

Insulation of walls, ceilings, and floor should follow the details outlined in the Chapter "Thermal Insulation and Vapor Barriers." Wall finishes, whether gypsum board, paneling, or other materials, can be nailed directly over the siding on the house side. Other construction and finishing details can conform to those outlined in the main section of this handbook.

REMOVING INTERIOR WALLS

Providing an opening between two rooms can be a relatively simple project if the wall to be opened is *not* a load-bearing wall. In single-story houses which are constructed with roof trusses, all walls are normally nonload bearing. However, any wall which supports ceiling joists is load bearing to some degree. If the ceiling joists are also floor joists for second floor rooms, the load on the wall is much greater than in a simple one-story house. Load-bearing walls ordinarily are those that are located at or near the center of the width of the house and parallel to the length.

Following are suggested allowable spans for interior walls which carry second floor loads. They are similar to the headers over windows in the Chapter "Wall Framing."

Span (ft)	*Nominal Member Size (Doubled)* (in.)[a]	
6	2	2 × 8's
7	2	2 × 10's
8	2	2 × 12's

[a]Better construction grades of such species as southern pine or Douglas fir.

These spans are much less than can be used in the normal single-story house. For example, a beam consisting of two 2- by 12-inch members is satisfactory for a 12-foot opening in a one-story house when the wall carries only normal ceiling loads.

It is necessary to provide temporary support for the ceiling loads at each side of a load-bearing wall before starting this project. Use a beam with suitable posts or adjustable jacks on each side of the wall, Fig. 137A. Be sure the beam is firmly positioned against the ceiling. Outline the proposed opening and remove the plaster and studs at each side and to the underside of the top plates. Assemble the doubled beam for the opening and jack it in place against the two top plates and between the side studs of the new opening. Toenail the beam to these studs and add a jack stud (supporting stud) under each end of the beam, Fig. 137B. These studs should be long enough to be tight against the beam and the sole plate. Nail them to the adjacent studs with twelvepenny nails. Remove the sole (bottom) plate between the supporting jack studs.

Gypsum board can be used to cover the beam and the side studs. If your walls have $\frac{1}{2}$-inch gypsum finish, use the same thickness. If there is a plaster finish, use $\frac{1}{2}$- and $\frac{3}{8}$-inch thicknesses for $\frac{7}{8}$-inch plaster and two $\frac{3}{8}$-inch thicknesses for $\frac{3}{4}$-inch plaster combinations. Place a dry wall corner bead at all exposed edges and spackle all joints.

An alternate treatment for the new opening consists of finishing it with side and head jambs. Casing can then be used at the sides and top of the opening.

Because the removal of the sole plate will expose the subfloor, this area in the opening must be filled to match the original floor. Carpeting can also be used.

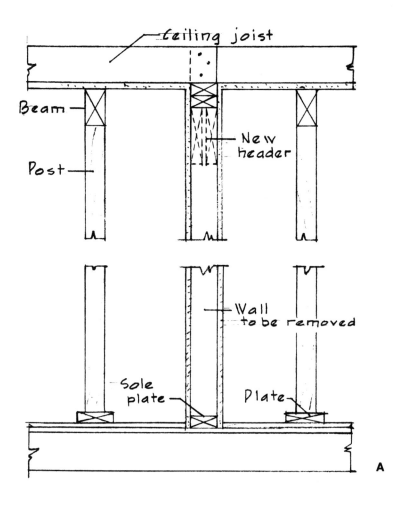

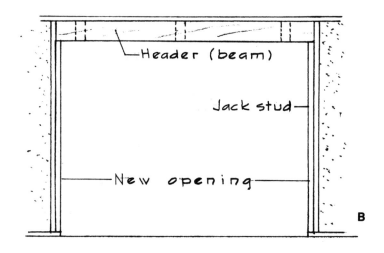

Fig. 137. Removing interior walls (partial).
A. Support.
B. New opening.

NEW CUPBOARDS FOR OLD

If your painted cupboards are reasonably well designed but need some renovating to make your kitchen more appealing, it is not necessary to invest in new cabinets. New doors can be made and the cupboard facings and sides can be covered with $\frac{1}{4}$-inch plywood in species such as mahogany, oak, or birch.

Remove the doors and hardware and sand the exposed painted surfaces of the cupboard. Using $\frac{1}{4}$-inch birch plywood, for example, cover any exposed sides or ends. Spread a good water-resistant glue on the parts and fasten them in place with $\frac{3}{4}$- or 1-inch brads. Now rip narrow strips of the $\frac{1}{4}$-inch plywood the same width as the cupboard facings (vertical stiles and horizontal rails). These can also be nail-glued to the face of the old cupboard, Fig. 138A.

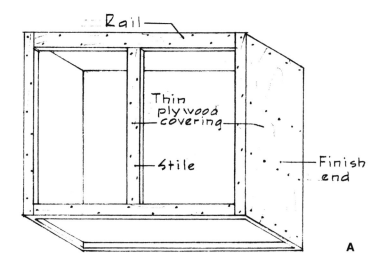

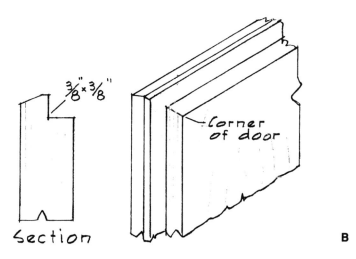

Fig. 138. Remodeling cupboards.
A. Facing old cupboards.
B. New door detail.

New doors can be made from lumber core plywood to match the size of the old doors. They can be made flush to fit between stiles and rails with loose pin hinge hardware (or concealed hinges) or with a routed edge for use with semiconcealed hinges, Fig. 138B. It might also be possible, and at less cost, to utilize the old cupboard doors by gluing on new plywood faces. These should likely be made for a flush fit. Decorative moldings can be used on the doors if so desired. Doors and cabinets can now be stained and finished and new hardware applied to give your kitchen a brand new look. Drawer fronts can also be treated in this manner.

WEATHERSTRIPPING FOR WINDOWS

Windows in many of the older houses were not supplied with weatherstripping when they were constructed. There are several types of weatherstrip materials which will make the windows and doors more draft free. One type of unit which serves not only as weatherstripping but also as a balance is designed for the double-hung window. It is a full-width, full-height unit for the jambs made of a spring metal and fits over the existing jamb, Fig. 139A. This weatherstrip can be obtained to fit each double-hung window size with the bottom edge cut to fit the slope of the sill.

In applying this type of full jamb weatherstrip, first remove the side and head window stops. Then remove the lower sash, the side and top parting strips (a $\frac{1}{2}$- by $\frac{3}{4}$-inch strip between the sash), and finally the upper sash. To be sure that each weatherstrip fits against the jamb, try it out by first placing the bottom against the sill and swinging it in place.

If the sash is not machined along the center of each stile, it must be routed to accept the spring-contained portion of the weatherstrip, Fig. 139A.

Place each sash in one weatherstrip placed on the floor, pulling the balance spring clips to the bottom of the sash. Next place the other strip over the sash and repeat the process, Fig. 139B. Holding the entire unit with both hands, place it in the window opening, bottom end first. Anchors provided with the strip can now be driven into the sill and the top jamb. Cut new window stops (or use the old if undamaged) and install so there is some pressure on the edge of the weatherstrip, Fig. 139C.

A metal spring weatherstrip is available and is adaptable to both casement windows and exterior doors, Fig. 139D. Use small rust-resistant nails to fasten them in place. A new threshold with vinyl inserts will stop drafts under your exterior doors.

While improving the weatherproofing of your windows and doors, it is likely that combination storm windows and doors might be added on the exterior. If you have no storm windows or storm doors, remember that their addition will not only reduce air infiltration but will also reduce heat loss through these units by 100 percent! Metal conbination windows (painted or unpainted) and doors, with self-storing features for the inserts, are available. They can be obtained to fit almost any type opening you might have in your house.

Also available are combination units with wood frames and metal or vinyl inserts. Installation for window units is simple, as it requires only a bead of calking compound and the use of screws around sides and top.

NEW CASING AND DOORS

Another method of creating a pleasant look to your door openings is to install new casings, doors, and hardware. Depending on the general style of your interior, and assuming that the doors are somewhat worn and difficult to finish, select a flush or a

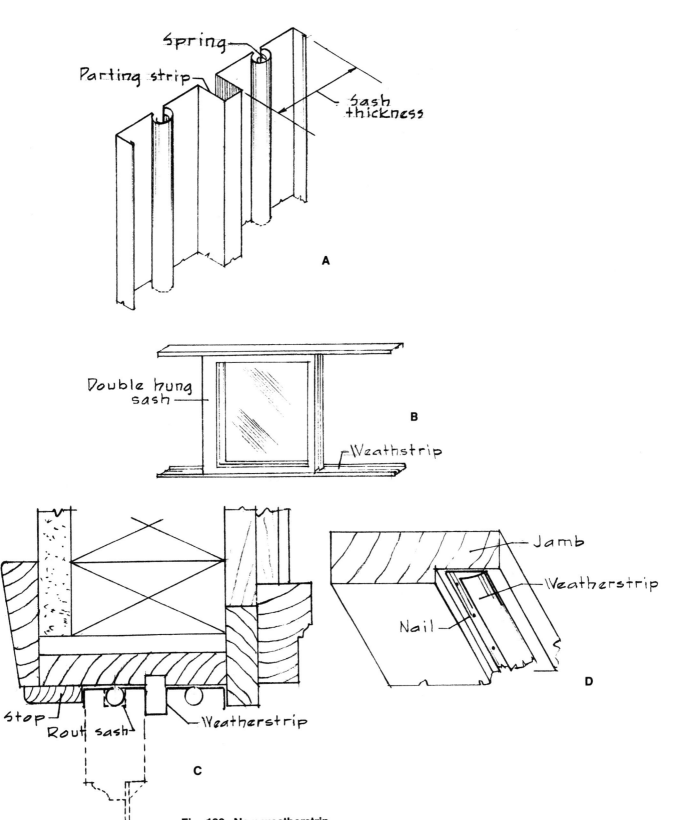

Fig. 139. New weatherstrip.

A. Jamb-width weatherstrip.
B. Sash-in weatherstrip assembly.
C. Plan section thru window.
D. Weatherstrip for exterior door.

panel door. Remove the hardware, door, and casing from the opening and hang the new door with new hinges and locksets. New casing will then complete this renovation. Depending on the species of the doors and casings, a stain followed by a varnish finish will produce a new look. It is not necessary to replace door jambs or stops. Just repaint if you wish.

IMPROVE YOUR BATH OR LAVATORY

It is possible, with not too much effort, to transform your old bath or lavatory into a room you can be proud of. If the lavatory is old and not pleasing in appearance and the water closet is satisfactory, just replace the lavatory with a vanity. A new vanity with new fittings, a ceramic tiled area around the vanity, new vinyl tile or carpeting on the floor, the walls above a wainscot covered with wallpaper, and new paint on ceiling and woodwork will transform the appearance at minimal cost and with little effort. A pair of small louvered cabinet or "cafe" doors might be mounted on the window, eliminating the need for drapes or curtains. A new cabinet or mirror will also add to the appearance of this room.

Complete vanities are available in a size that takes no more space than about 20 inches in width and 18 inches or less in depth in your lavatory if space is a factor. A minimum interior size for a lavatory (or half-bath) is about 4 feet 0 inch by 4 feet 4 inches, Fig. 140. In such a lavatory, a 2-foot-0-inch-wide door is normally used and hung to swing in. A 20-inch-wide vanity can be used in such a room when the water closet is placed correctly.

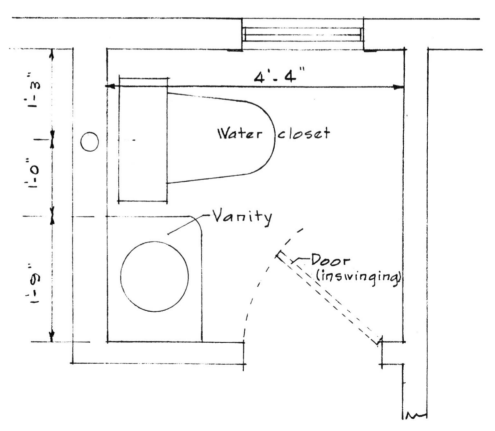

Fig. 140. Normal minimum size for lavatory.

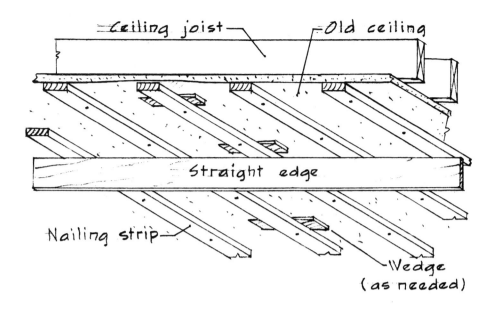

Fig. 141. Nailing strips for a new ceiling.

A NEW CEILING

Some of the older houses have ceilings which are cracked or uneven and covering them with wallpaper or repainting does little to improve their appearance. In such cases the remedy might consist of nailing wood strips to the ceiling and covering with gypsum board or tile or using a suspended ceiling with drop-in tile. The latter might be used in the older houses that have 9-foot or higher ceilings.

Nailing strips should consist of 1- by 2- or 1- by 3-inch wood strips nailed to and across the ceiling joists. Space then 12 inches on center when 12- by 12-inch ceiling tile is to be used for a covering material, Fig. 141. They should be spaced 16 inches on center when 4-foot-wide sheets of gypsum board are used as a covering material.

Use tenpenny ring shank nails at each ceiling joist crossing. First establish a level line by leveling the second nailing strip along each side of the room. Use a 1- by 6-inch straight edge and shim the strips where any dips occur along their length. Next, using the straight edge across the two leveled strips, level each partially nailed intermediate strip so that it is flush with the top edge of the straight edge, Fig. 141.

Use wood wedges such as shingles to level the strips. When all strips are level, finish driving in the nails. Two nails may be used at each joist when 1- by 3-inch strips are used.

Prefinished tile in 12- by 12-inch tile can be obtained in a number of surface textures. They are fastened to the wood strips with a staple gun. When the old ceiling is only slightly cracked but quite level, such tile can be applied directly to the ceiling with a tile adhesive.

Gypsum board in $\frac{1}{2}$-inch thickness can also be used as a ceiling finish. The nailing strips are usually spaced 16 inches on center rather than 12 inches. Its application has been covered in the Chapter "Interior Wall and Ceiling Finish."

A suspended ceiling system consists of metal wall angles fastened around the perimeter of the wall and suspended main and cross tees. Drop-in fiberboard panels in 2- by 4-foot size are used between the suspended framework. This system is also covered in more detail in the Chapter "Interior Wall and Ceiling Finish."

BETTER INSULATION AND VENTILATION

Attic

The easiest and perhaps the best areas for additional insulation is the attic space over inhabited rooms. Heating experts indicate that any additional attic insulation over an existing 6 inches is not practical. This is based on the possible savings in fuel versus the cost of adding the insulation. However, an important factor which has not generally been considered is the rapid increase in the cost of fuels which may be double or triple present prices. Another factor to be considered is the relative ease which the average homeowner can install the insulation, whether it is in the form of batts or is the fill-type insulation. Therefore, if you have only a 4- or 6-inch insulation batt or fill insulation, do not be satisfied until you have added another 6 inches.

With these considerations, the added insulation can not only mean lower heating costs but also a more comfortable house in winter and summer.

When adding insulation, it is good practice to provide better attic ventilation. Heat loss through the ceiling is reduced as the insulation is increased which means a colder attic. Thus any water vapor which escapes from the rooms below should be moved outside the house by good inlet and outlet ventilation to minimize condensation problems.

Insulation

Insulating companies do a good job of blowing in additional insulation. However, a great deal of money can be saved by adding it yourself when attic headroom is adequate. Several types of fill insulations are available, the less efficient being the vermiculite type. If you have insulation that is partly filling the space between the ceiling joists, two methods of adding more insulation might be considered. The first consists of adding 6 to 8 inches more of the same type of insulation over the old. A rough estimate for material cost is about 3¢ per square foot for each 1 inch of thickness. Thus if you add 6 inches, the cost per square foot for material is about 18¢ or $18 per 100 square feet. Such costs may increase in the future.

When using fill insulation, spread it evenly with a spreader consisting of a thin piece of plywood nailed across a long handle. For accurate thickness, small strips of wood can be nailed to the joists here and there with the tops designating the proper thickness. Blower units can be rented to reach those areas where insulation cannot be placed by hand.

Another method might be considered if the fill insulation is leveled to the top of the ceiling joists. Use 6-inch-thick batts laid across the joists. Unfaced insulation designed for such use can be obtained in rolls in 15- and 23-inch widths. When adding insulation near the eave line, be sure to leave an airway space for ventilation from the soffit, Fig. 142A.

Insulating Flat or Low-Pitched Roofs

Adding insulation to the ceiling of an already insulated flat roof is, perhaps, practical only by stripping the ceiling with $1\frac{5}{8}$- by 2-inch (full size) furring strips and gluing 2-inch-thick sheets of foam insulation to the ceiling between them, Fig. 142B. This would be the equivalent of about 3 to $3\frac{1}{2}$ inches of fill insulation. Gypsum board or ceiling tile can be used as a finish. Ring shank nails in twelvepenny or longer size might be required to fasten the strips to the ceiling-rafter members.

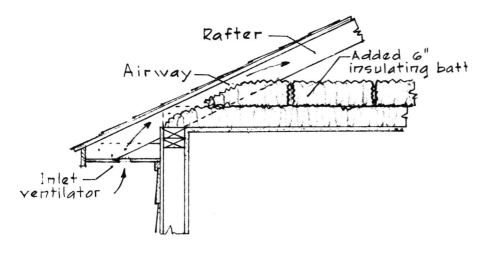

A

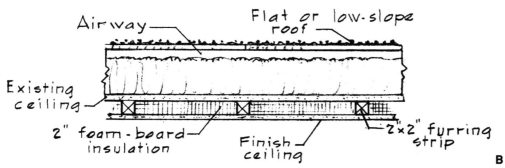

B

Fig. 142. Attic and ceiling insulation.
A. Attic spaces.
B. Ceiling of flat-deck house.

Adding Insulation to an Interior Wall

In many cases, such as a wall having a brick veneer finish or one having existing 1-inch blanket insulation between studs, it is difficult to add insulation from the exterior. Thus some means must be used to improve the wall on the interior face. One such system, not commonly used, consists of removing (then replacing) baseboard and window trim, adding sheets of 1-inch foam insulation board. This system can significantly reduce the heat loss of that wall depending on the amount of insulation present. For example, when there is 1-inch blanket insulation in the wall, this method will increase the insulating value more than 60 percent (from a total R resistance of about 9.5 to a total R of 15.5). If there is no insulation in the stud space, the insulating value of the wall is increased by more than 100 percent! Very important when fuel costs are so high.

The following sequence can be used in developing such a wall:

1. Remove baseboard, window (or door) casings, window stops, the stool, and the apron. Remove carefully because much can be reused.

2. Locate and mark studs, top and bottom.

3. Install full height sheets of 1-inch foam insulation board (usually in 4- by 8-ft sizes). Use a panel adhesive or one developed for use with foam insulation. The sheets can also be lightly nailed to plates and studs. Provide cutouts for the outlet and switch boxes. Also frame out for heat or return duct registers. Then nail 1- by 3-inch horizontal furring strips to the studs (and top and bottom plates). Space

them about 2 feet apart (at quarter points), Fig. 143A. Add furring strips around windows and doors. Reset outlet and switch boxes when required.

4. Apply new wall finish which can consist of: (a) $\frac{1}{2}$-inch gypsum board, (b) 1-inch wood paneling (tongued and grooved), (c) prefinished plywood paneling, or (d) other materials of your choice. Apply these materials vertically and nail to each furring strip. If $\frac{1}{2}$-inch gypsum board is used, it is good practice to use a joint tape that has an adhesive face.

Note: Gypsum board with aluminum foil backing adds to the insulating value of the wall.

5. Nail 1-inch-thick strips to the inner edges of the window side and head jambs and to the window sill. The edges should be flush with the face of the wall finish (gypsum board, etc.). These would be about $2\frac{1}{4}$ inches wide for the $\frac{1}{2}$-inch gypsum board finish.

6. Replace the baseboard. Add a new stool ($2\frac{1}{4}$ inches wider than the original if $\frac{1}{2}$-inch gypsum board is used). Replace the casing and add new wider window stops, Fig. 143B.

For slightly lower insulating value, the furring strips can be eliminated. Use appropriate adhesives for both the foam insulating board and (or nails for) the gypsum board. Long finish nails will be required for casing and baseboard.

After you have completed this project, you will not only have reduced heat loss substantially, but also reduced air infiltration for greater comfort. If desired, such a system can be used only on a north and west walls which are exposed to cold winter winds.

Improving Attic Ventilation

When adding insulation, always consider improving your existing ventilation. This should include adding inlet ventilators in the soffit and outlet ventilators at gable ends or roof ventilators along the ridge. If there are no soffit ventilators along the eave line, add small 4- by 16- or 6- by 16-inch "undereave" ventilators. Locate them between rafter ends, drill a hole at each corner, and cut out with a jigsaw, Fig. 144A. Space the ventilators about 8 feet apart for a gable roof and 12 feet apart for a hip-roofed house. The amount of ventilation to be used is outlined in the Chapter "Ventilation."

Outlet ventilators in gable ends when not present can be added at each end of the house. The rectangular types can be obtained in sizes from 8 by 8 inches to as large as 14 by 18 inches. Cut the opening so that the top rim fits under the butt edge of a siding course, Fig. 144B. Use a good calking material at all edges. A full wood frame with siding cut to fit between the casing can also be considered.

A hip roof house or gable house with a long ridge can use a standard roof ventilator. They should be located as close to the ridge as possible, Fig. 144C. Wind-driven turbine ventilators are very efficient when used to ventilate attic spaces. For a long hip roof house use four or five outlet ventilators.

Flat roof houses should have continuous ventilation along each side. An alternate would consist of a small screened opening between each joist-rafter extension. Because air movement in a flat roof relies on the wind, good ventilation should always be considered.

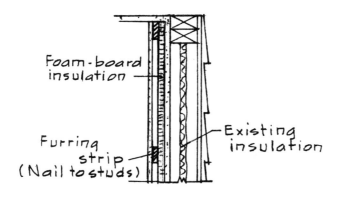

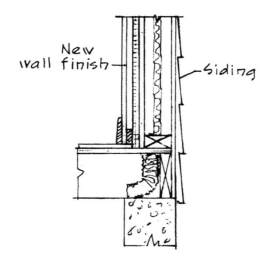

A

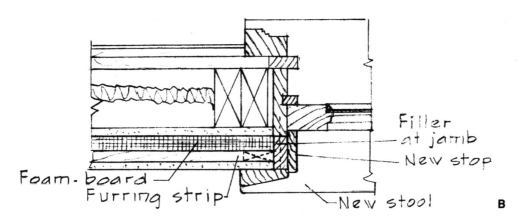

B

Fig. 143. Adding insulation to interior wall.
A. Section through wall.
B. Plan view at window.

SOUND INSULATION

Reducing airborne sound transfer from one room to another is not a simple task in an existing house. For the best results it might consist of the construction of a separate wall between a bath and the living room, for example. However, if sound from the bathroom is very objectionable and must be greatly reduced, the construction of a free-standing wall might follow these steps:

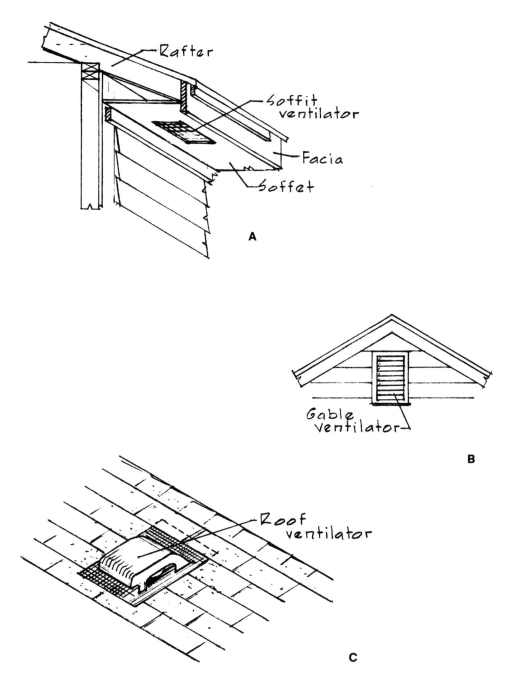

Fig. 144. Attic space ventilators.
A. Soffit inlet ventilator.
B. Gable-end outlet ventilator.
C. Roof outlet ventilator.

1. Use 2- by 2-inch top and bottom plates and studs for a separate wall located an inch or so from the existing wall in the bath, Fig. 145A.
2. Place 1½- or 2-inch blanket insulation between studs.
3. Use ½-inch gypsum board or other covering material over the studs and finish as desired.

Another system which can be used to reduce airborne sound transfer consists of the use of 1- and 2-inch furring strips with coverings of sound-deadening board and gypsum board. While this is not as effective as the free-standing wall of 2- by 2-inch members, it is a moderatley good solution.

Nail 1- by 2-inch furring strips to the studs, spacing them 16 inches on center, Fig. 145B. Nail ½-inch sound-deadening board to the strips followed by ⅜-inch gypsum board. Wallboard adhesive can be used to fasten the gypsum board to the deadening board, eliminating the need for most of the nails. Such a system can also be used on the ceiling, if so desired, to isolate sound from rooms above.

To absorb sound, acoustic tile might be used in the ceiling or above a wainscoat. A tight-fitting door with a threshold to close all openings would also aid in reducing the transfer of sound.

Another method which might provide some sound reduction consists of introducing pour-type insulation into the stud spaces of the wall between a bath and the living room. The 2-inch holes required for poured or blown insulation would be closed with patching plaster and the wall repainted or covered with wallpaper.

ADDING VAPOR BARRIERS

Adding a vapor barrier or soil cover over exposed soil in crawl spaces will greatly reduce the movement of ground moisture into the space. Excessive moisture in these areas could be detrimental if it condensed on the colder surfaces of wood members. Such protection has been described in the Section "Drier Basements."

Adding vapor barriers to exposed walls and ceilings of existing houses consists mainly of the addition of paint coatings. Such protection is not as efficient as a good separate vapor barrier or one on an insulating batt. However, when fill insulation is added to a wall, it is good practice in those rooms which produce excessive amounts of water to provide some protection. Use two coats of aluminum primer on the inside surfaces of all such exposed walls and finish with the decorative paint of your choice. The movement of water vapor into a wall during long periods of cold weather can result in peeling of paint on exterior finish.

SOLVING THOSE DOOR PROBLEMS

It is likely that some of the doors in older houses do not close properly or make contact with an edge or side when they are closed. This is likely to happen to a panel door with solid wood stiles (edge members) more often than to a flush door when humidities are high. In any door problem, first check for loose screws in the hinges that might have caused the problem. If screws are tight and any replacements do not help, the following suggestions may aid in having your door close like it should.

If the lock side is tight along the entire height of the door (or in spots), plane the edge so that it will close properly, Fig. 146A.

Remove the lock and latch before removing the excess wood. Remove the door and place on the hinge edge while planing. Taper edge on the lock side slightly (toward the door stop).

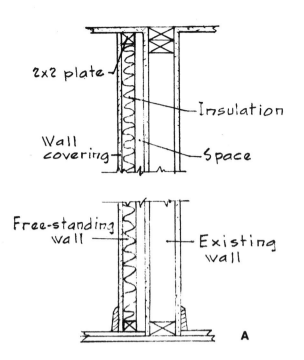

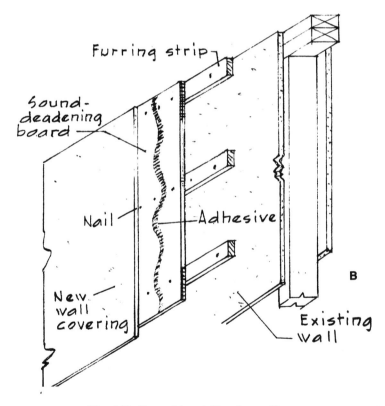

Fig. 145. Sound insulation for walls.
A. Free-standing wall.
B. Furred wall covering.

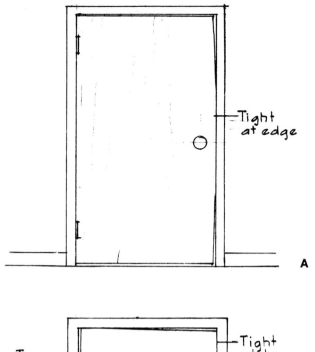

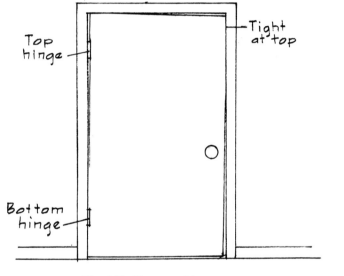

Fig. 146. Door problems.
A. Tight edge.
B. Tight top edge.

If the side edge of the door at the top drags on the side jamb, the following may solve the problem, Fig. 146B.

1. Tighten top hinge screws at the jamb or let in the hinge leaf slightly.

OR

2. Shim under the bottom hinge at the jamb or on the door edge.

If the lower edge drags on side jamb, Fig. 146C, try the following.

1. Tighten the lower hinge screws at the jamb side or let in the hinge leaf slightly.

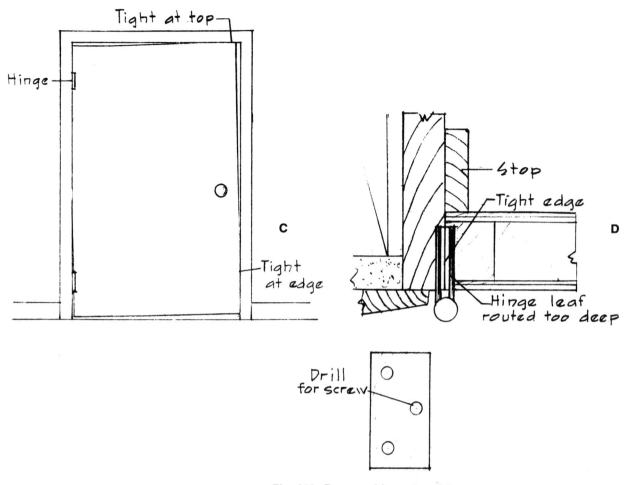

Fig. 146. Door problems (*cont'd*).
    C. Tight bottom edge.
    D. Tight hinge edge.
    E. Shim for hinge leaf slot.

OR

2. Shim under the top hinge at the jamb.

If the latch does not meet the strike plate properly, the plate should be raised or lowered slightly.

If the edge of the door on the hinge side is very tight and does not allow the door to close easily, it is likely that the hinge leaves are routed too deeply. This could be on the door edge, on the jamb, or even on both surfaces, Fig. 146D. The hinges should be shimmed out with rigid cardboard or a thin section of wood. Holes should be pre-drilled for the screws, Fig. 146E. The outer surface of the hinge face should normally be flush with the face of the jamb and the edge of the door. After such an adjustment, the edge of the door on the lock side might require some adjusting for a proper fit.

The door stops may also cause some closing problem. Check them to see if they require moving out slightly.

Doors and door hardware are designed to work properly together. If the previous adjustments are made on those that do have problems for various reasons, your doors should now be more than acceptable.

References

American Institute of Timber Construction

1972. Standard for heavy timber roof decking. AITC 112, Englewood, Colo.

American Plywood Association

1974. Plywood residential construction guide. APA6, 32 p., illus.

1964. Plywood truss designs, APA 64-650. 11 p., illus.

Forest Products Laboratory, Forest Service, U.S. Department of Agriculture

1974. Wood handbook: Wood as an engineering material. U.S. Dep. Agric., Agric. Handb. 72, 432 p., illus.

1968. Thermal insulation from wood for buildings. Effects of moisture and its control. U.S.D.A. Forest Serv. Res. Pap. FPL 86, Forest Prod. Lab., Madison, Wis.

Selection and use of wood products for home and farm building. U.S. Dep. Agric., Agric. Inf. Bull. 311, 41 p., illus.

Construction Guides for Exposed Wood Decks. U.S. Dep. Agric. Handbook 432. 78 p., illus.

Wood Frame House Construction U.S. Dep. Agric. Handbook No. 73. 223 p., illus.

National Forest Products Association

1971. Span tables for joists and rafters. 36 p., Washington, D.C.

Southern Forest Products Assn. New Orleans, La. 70152

So. Pine Technical Bulletin—Maximum Spans for joists and rafters

Glossary of Housing Terms

Air-dried lumber. Lumber that has been piled in yards or sheds for any length of time. For the United States as a whole, the minimum moisture content of thoroughly air-dried lumber is 12 to 15 percent and the average is somewhat higher. In the South, air-dried lumber may be no lower than 19 percent.

Airway. A space between roof insulation and roof boards for movement of air.

Anchor bolts. Bolts to secure a wooden sill plate to concrete or masonry floor or wall.

Apron. The flat member of the inside trim of a window placed against the wall immediately beneath the stool.

Areaway. An open subsurface space adjacent to a building used to admit light or air or as a means of access to a basement.

Attic ventilators. In houses, screened openings provided to ventilate an attic space. They are located in the soffit area as inlet ventilators and in the gable end or along the ridge as outlet ventilators. They can also consist of power-driven fans used as an exhaust system. (See also **Louver.**)

Backfill. The replacement of excavated earth into a trench around and against a basement foundation.

Balusters. Usually small vertical members in a railing used between a top rail and the stair treads or a bottom rail.

Balustrade. A railing made up of balusters, top rail, and sometimes bottom rail, used on the edge of stairs, balconies, and porches.

Barge board. A decorative board covering the projecting rafter (fly rafter) of the gable end. At the cornice, this member is a facia board.

Base or baseboard. A board placed against the wall around a room next to the floor to finish properly between floor and plaster.

Base molding. Molding used to trim the upper edge of interior baseboard.

Base shoe. Molding used next to the floor on interior baseboard. Sometimes called a carpet strip.

Batten. Narrow strips of wood used to cover joints or as decorative vertical members over plywood or wide boards.

Batter board. One of a pair of horizontal boards nailed to posts set at the corners of an excavation, used to indicate the desired level, also as a fastening for stretched strings to indicate outlines of foundation walls.

Bay window. Any window space projecting outward from the walls of a building, either square or polygonal in plan.

Beam. A structural member transversely supporting a load.

Bearing partition. A partition that supports any vertical load in addition to its own weight.

Bearing wall. A wall that supports any vertical load in addition to its own weight.

Bed molding. A molding in an angle, as between the overhanging cornice, or eaves, of a building and the sidewalls.

Blind-nailing. Nailing in such a way that the nailheads are not visible on the face of the work—usually at the tongue of matched boards.

Blind stop. A rectangular molding, usually $\frac{3}{4}$ by $1\text{-}\frac{3}{8}$ inches or more in width, used in the assembly of a window frame. Serves as a stop for storm and screen or combination windows and to resist air filtration.

Boiled linseed oil. Linseed oil in which enough lead, manganese, or cobalt salts have been incorporated to make the oil harden more rapidly when spread in thin coatings.

Bolster. A short horizontal timber or steel beam on top of a column to support and decrease the span of beams or girders.

Boston ridge. A method of applying asphalt or wood shingles at the ridge or at the hips of a roof as a finish.

Brace. An inclined piece of framing lumber appled to wall or floor to stiffen the structure. Ofen used on walls as temporary bracing until framing has been completed.

Brick veneer. A facing of brick laid against and fastened to sheathing of a frame wall or tile wall construction.

Bridging. Small wood or metal members that are inserted in a diagonal position between the floor joists at midspan to act both as tension and compression members for the purpose of bracing the joists and spreading the action of loads.

Buck. Often used in reference to rough frame opening members. Door bucks used in reference to metal door frame.

Built-up roof. A roofing composed of three to five layers of asphalt felt laminated with coal tar, pitch, or asphalt. The top is finished with crushed slag or gravel. Generally used on flat or low-pitched roofs.

Butt joint. The junction where the ends of two timbers or other members meet in a square-cut joint.

Cant strip. A triangular-shaped piece of lumber used at the junction of a flat deck and a wall to prevent cracking of the roofing which is applied over it.

Cap. The upper member of a column, pilaster, door cornice, molding, and the like.

Casement frames and sash. Frames of wood or metal enclosing part or all of the sash, which may be opened by means of hinges affixed to the vertical edges.

Casing. Molding of various widths and thicknesses used to trim door and window openings at the jambs.

Checking. Fissures that appear with age in many exterior plant coatings, at first superficial, but which in time may penetrate entirely through the coating.

Checkrails. Meeting rails sufficiently thicker than a window to fill the opening between the top and bottom sash made by the parting stop in the frame of double-hung windows. They are usually beveled.

Collar beam. Nominal 1- or 2-inch-thick members connecting opposite roof rafters. They serve to stiffen the roof structure.

Column. In architecture: A perpendicular supporting member, circular or rectangular in section, usually consisting of a base, shaft, and capital. In engineering: A vertical structural compression member which supports loads acting in the direction of its longitudinal axis.

Combination doors or windows. Combination doors or windows used over regular openings. They provide winter insulation and summer protection and often have self-storing or removable glass and screen inserts. This eliminates the need for handling a different unit each season.

Condensation. In a building: Beads or drops of water (and frequently frost in extremely cold weather) that accumulate on the inside of the exterior covering of a building when warm, moisture-laden air from the interior reaches a point where the temperature no longer permits the air to sustain the moisture it holds. Use of louvers or attic ventilators will reduce moisture condensation in attics. A vapor barrier under the gypsum lath or dry wall on exposed walls will reduce condensation in them.

Construction dry-wall. A type of construction in which the interior wall finish is applied in a dry condition, generally in the form of sheet materials or wood paneling, as contrasted to plaster.

Construction, frame. A type of construction in which the structural parts are wood or depend upon a wood frame for support. In codes, if masonry veneer is applied to the exterior walls, the classification of this type of construction is usually unchanged.

Coped joint. See **Scribing.**

Corbel out. To build out one or more courses of brick or stone from the face of a wall, to form a support for timbers.

Corner bead. A strip of formed sheet metal, sometimes combined with a strip of metal lath, placed on corners before plastering to reinforce them. Also, a strip of wood finish three-quarters-round or angular placed over a plastered corner for protection.

Corner boards. Used as trim for the external corners of a house or other frame structure against which the ends of the siding are finished.

Corner braces. Diagonal braces at the corners of frame structure to stiffen and strengthen the wall.

Let-in brace. Nominal 1-inch-thick boards applied into notched studs diagonally.

Cut-in brace. Nominal 2-inch-thick members, usually 2 by 4's, cut in between each stud diagonally.

Cornice. Overhang of a pitched roof at the eave line, usually consisting of a facia board, a soffit for a closed cornice, and appropriate moldings.

Counterflashing. A flashing usually used on chimneys at the roofline to cover shingle flashing and to prevent moisture entry.

Cove molding. A molding with a concave face used as trim or to finish interior corners.

Crawl space. A shallow space below the living quarters of a basementless house, normally enclosed by the foundation wall.

Cricket. A small drainage-diverting roof structure of single or double slope placed at the junction of larger surfaces that meet at an angle, such as above a chimney.

Cross-bridging. Diagonal bracing between adjacent floor joists, placed near the center of the joist span to prevent joists from twisting.

Crown molding. A molding used on cornice or wherever an interior angle is to be covered.

d. See **Penny.**

Dado. A rectangular groove across the width of a board or plank. In interior decoration, a special type of wall treatment.

Decay. Disintegration of wood or other substance through the action of fungi.

Deck paint. An enamel with a high degree of resistance to mechanical wear, designed for use on such surfaces as porch floors.

Density. The mass of substance in a unit volume. When expressed in the metric system, it is numerically equal to the specific gravity of the same substance.

Dewpoint. Temperature at which a vapor begins to deposit as a liquid. Applied especially to water in the atmosphere.

Dimension. See **Lumber dimension.**

Direct nailing. To nail perpendicular to the initial surface or to the junction of the pieced joined. Also termed **face nailing.**

Doorjamb, interior. The surrounding case into which and out of which a door closes and opens. It consists of two upright pieces, called side jambs, and a horizontal head jamb.

Dormer. An opening in a sloping roof, the framing of which projects out to form a vertical wall suitable for windows or other openings.

Downspout. A pipe, usually of metal, for carrying rainwater from roof gutters.

Dressed and matched (tongued and grooved). Boards or planks machined in such a manner that there is a groove on one edge and a corresponding tongue on the other.

Drier paint. Usually oil-soluble soaps of such metals as lead, manganese, or cobalt, which, in small proportions, hasten the oxidation and hardening (drying) of the drying oils in paints.

Drip. (a) A member of a cornice or other horizontal exterior-finish course that has a projection beyond the other parts for throwing off water. (b) A groove in the underside of a sill or drip cap to cause water to drop off on the outer edge instead of drawing back and running down the face of the building.

Drip cap. A molding placed on the exterior top side of a door or window frame to cause water to drip beyond the outside of the frame.

Dry-wall. Interior covering material, such as gypsum board or plywood, which is applied in large sheets or panels.

Ducts. In a house, usually round or rectangular metal pipes for distributing warm air from the heating plant to rooms, or air from a conditioning device or as cold air returns. Ducts are also made of asbestos and composition materials.

Eaves. The margin or lower part of a roof projecting over the wall.

Expansion joint. A bituminous fiber strip used to separate block or units of concrete to prevent cracking due to expansion as a result of temperature changes. Also used on concrete slabs.

Facia or fascia. A flat board, band, or face, used sometimes by itself but usually in combination with moldings, often located at the outer face of the cornice.

Filler (wood). A heavily pigmented preparation used for filling and leveling off the pores in open-pored woods.

Fire-resistive. In the absence of a specific ruling by the authority having jurisdiction, applies to materials for construction not combustible in the temperatures of ordinary fires and that will withstand such fires without serious impairment of their usefulness for at least 1 hour.

Fire-retardant chemical. A chemical or preparation of chemicals used to reduce flammability or to retard spread of flame.

Fire stop. A solid, tight closure of a concealed space, placed to prevent the spread of fire and smoke through such a space. In a frame wall, this will usually consist of 2 by 4 cross blocking between studs.

Fishplate. A wood or plywood piece used to fasten the ends of two members together at a butt joint with nails or bolts. Sometimes used at the junction of opposite rafters near the ridge line.

Flagstone (flagging or flags). Flat stones, from 1 to 4 inches thick, used for rustic walks, steps, floors, and the like.

Flashing. Sheet metal or other material used in roof and wall construction to protect a building from water seepage.

Flat paint. An interior paint that contains a high proportion of pigment and dries to a flat or lusterless finish.

Flue. The space or passage in a chimney through which smoke, gas, or fumes ascend. Each passage is called a flue, which together with any others and the surrounding masonry make up the chimney.

Flue lining. Fire clay or terra-cotta pipe, round or square, usually made in all ordinary flue sizes and in 2-foot lengths, used for the inner lining of chimneys with the brick or masonry work around the outside. Flue lining in chimneys runs from about a foot below the flue connection to the top of the chimney.

Fly rafters. End rafters of the gable overhang supported by roof sheathing and lookouts.

Footing. A masonry section, usually concrete, in a rectangular form wider than the bottom of the foundation wall or pier it supports.

Foundation. The supporting portion of a structure below the first-floor construction, or below grade, including the footings.

Framing, balloon. A system of framing a building in which all vertical structural elements of the bearing walls and partitions consist of single pieces extending from the top of the foundation sill plate to the roofplate and to which all floor joists are fastened.

Framing, platform. A system of framing a building in which floor joists of each story rest on the top plates of the story below or on the foundation sill for the first story, and the bearing walls and partitions rest on the subfloor of each story.

Frieze. In house construction, a horizontal member connecting the top of the siding with the soffit of the cornice.

Frostline. The depth of the frost penetration in soil. This depth varies in different parts of the country. Footings should be placed below this depth to prevent movement.

Fungi, wood. Microscopic plants that live in damp wood and cause mold, stain, and decay.

Fungicide. A chemical that is poisonous to fungi.

Furring. Strips of wood or metal applied to a wall or other surface to even it and normally to serve as a fastening base for finish material.

Gable. In house construction, the portion of the roof above the eave line of a double-sloped roof.

Gable end. An end wall having a gable.

Gloss enamel. A finishing material made of varnish and sufficient pigments to provide opacity and color, but little or no pigment of low opacity. Such an enamel forms a hard coating with maximum smoothness of surface and a high degree of gloss.

Gloss (paint or enamel). A paint or enamel that contains a relatively low proportion of pigment and dries to a sheen or luster.

Girder. A large or principal beam of wood or steel used to support concentrated loads at isolated points along its length.

Grain. The direction, size, arrangement, appearance, or quality of the fibers in wood.

Grain, edge (vertical). Edge-grain lumber has been sawed parallel to the pith of the log and approximately at right angles to the growth rings; i.e., the rings form an angle of $45°$ or more with the surface of the piece.

Grain, flat. Flat-grain lumber has been sawed parallel to the pith of the log and approximately tangent to the growth rings, i.e., the rings form an angle of less than $45°$ with the surface of the piece.

Grain, quartersawn. Another term for edge-grain.

Grounds. Guides used around openings and at the floorline to strike off plaster. They can consist of narrow strips of wood or of wide subjambs at interior doorways. They provide a level plaster line for installation of casing and other trim.

Grout. Mortar made of such consistency (by adding water) that it will just flow into the joints and cavities of the masonry work and fill them solid.

Gusset. A flat wood, plywood, or similar type member used to provide a connection at intersection of wood members. Most commonly used at joints of wood trusses. They are fastened by nails, screws, bolts, or adhesives.

Gutter or eave trough. A shallow channel or conduit of metal or wood set below and along the eaves of a house to catch and carry off rainwater from the roof.

Gypsum plaster. Gypsum formulated to be used with the addition of sand and water for base-coat plaster.

Header. (a) A beam placed perpendicular to joists and to which joists are nailed in framing for chimney, stairway, or other opening. (b) A wood lintel.

Hearth. The inner or outer floor of a fireplace, usually made of brick, tile, or stone.

Heartwood. The wood extending from the pith to the sapwood, the cells of which no longer participate in the life processes of the tree.

Hip. The external angle formed by the meeting of two sloping sides of a roof.

Hip roof. A roof that rises by inclined planes from all four sides of a building.

Humidifier. A device designed to increase the humidity within a room or a house by means of the discharge of water vapor. They may consist of individual room-size units or larger units attached to the heating plant to condition the entire house.

I-beam. A steel beam with a cross section resembling the letter *I*. It is used for long spans as basement beams or over wide wall openings, such as a double garage door, when wall and roof loads are imposed on the opening.

Insulation board, rigid. A structural building board made of coarse wood or cane fiber in $\frac{1}{2}$- and $\frac{25}{32}$-inch thicknesses. It can be obtained in various size sheets, in various densities, and with several treatments.

Insulation, thermal. Any material high in resistance to heat transmission that, when placed in the wall, ceiling, or floors of a structure, will reduce the rate of heat flow.

Interior finish. Material used to cover the interior framed areas, or materials of walls and ceilings.

Jack rafter. A rafter that spans the distance from the wall plate to a hip, or from a valley to a ridge.

Jamb. The side and head lining of a doorway, window, or other opening.

Joint. The space between the adjacent surfaces of two members or components joined and held together by nails, glue, cement, mortar, or other means.

Joint cement. A powder that is usually mixed with water and used for joint treatment in gypsum-wallboard finish. Often called "spackle."

Joist. One of a series of parallel beams, usually 2 inches in thickness, used to support floor and ceiling loads, and supported in turn by larger beams, girders, or bearing walls.

Kiln dried lumber. Lumber that has been kiln dried often to a moisture content of 6 to 12 percent. Common varieties of softwood lumber, such as framing lumber are dried to a somewhat higher moisture content.

Knot. In lumber, the portion of a branch or limb of a tree that appears on the edge or face of the piece.

Landing. A platform between flights of stairs or at the termination of a flight of stairs.

Lath. A building material of wood, metal, gypsum, or insulating board that is fastened to the frame of a building to act as a plaster base.

Lattice. A framework of crossed wood or metal strips.

Leader. See **Downspout.**

Ledger strip. A strip of lumber nailed along the bottom of the side of a girder on which joists rest.

Light. Space in a window sash for a single pane of glass. Also, a pane of glass.

Lintel. A horizontal structural member that supports the load over an opening such as a door or window.

Lookout. A short wood bracket or cantilever to support an overhang portion of a roof or the like, usually concealed from view.

Louver. An opening with a series of horizontal slats so arranged as to permit ventilation but to exclude rain, sunlight, or vision. See also **Attic ventilators.**

Lumber. Lumber is the product of the sawmill and planing mill not further manufactured other than by sawing, resawing, and passing lengthwise through a standard planing machine, crosscutting to length, and matching.

Lumber, boards. Yard lumber less than 2 inches thick and 2 or more inches wide.

Lumber, dimension. Yard lumber from 2 inches to, but not including, 5 inches thick and 2 or more inches wide. Includes joists, rafters, studs, plank, and small timbers.

Lumber, dressed size. The dimension of lumber after shrinking from green dimension and after maching to size or pattern.

Lumber, matched. Lumber that is dressed and shaped on one edge in a grooved pattern and on the other in a tongued pattern.

Lumber, shiplap. Lumber that is edge-dressed to make a close rabbeted or lapped joint.

Lumber, timbers. Yard lumber 5 or more inches in least dimension. Includes beams, stringers, posts, caps, sills, girders, and purlins.

Lumber, yard. Lumber of those grades, sizes, and patterns which are generally intended for ordinary construction, such as framework and rough coverage of houses.

Mantel. The shelf above a fireplace. Also used in referring to the decorative trim around a fireplace opening.

Masonry. Stone, brick, concrete, hollow-tile, concrete-block, gypsum-block, or other similar building units or materials or a combination of the same, bonded together with mortar to form a wall, pier, buttress, or similar mass.

Mastic. A pasty material used as a cement (as for setting tile) or a protective coating (as for thermal insulation or waterproofing).

Metal lath. Sheets of metal that are slit and drawn out to form openings. Used as a plaster base for walls and ceilings and as reinforcing over other forms of plaster base.

Millwork. Generally all building materials made of finished wood and manufactured in millwork plants and planing mills are included under the term "millwork." It includes such items as inside and outside doors, window and doorframes, blinds, porchwork, mantels, panelwork, stairways, moldings, and interior trim. It normally does not include flooring, ceiling, or siding.

Miter joint. The joint of two pieces at an angle that bisects the joining angle. For example, the miter joint at the side and head casing at a door opening is made at a 45° angle.

Moisture content of wood. Weight of the water contained in the wood, usually expressed as percentage of the weight of the ovendry wood.

Molding. A wood strip having a curved or projecting surface used for decorative purposes.

Mortise. A slot cut into a board, plank, or timber, usually edgewise, to receive tenon of another board, plank, or timber to form a joint.

Mullion. A vertical bar or divider in the frame between windows, doors, or other openings.

Muntin. A small member which divides the glass or openings of sash or doors.

Natural finish. A transparent finish which does not seriously alter the original color or grain of the natural wood. Natural finishes are usually provided by sealers, oils, varnishes, water-repellent preservatives, and other similar materials.

Newel. A post to which the end of a stair railing or balustrade is fastened. Also, *any* post to which a railing or balustrade is fastened.

Nonbearing wall. A wall supporting no load other than its own weight.

Nosing. The projecting edge of a molding or drip. Usually applied to the projecting molding on the edge of a stair tread.

Notch. A crosswise rabbet at the end of a board.

O. C., on center. The measurement of spacing for studs, rafters, joists, and the like in a building from the center of one member to the center of the next.

O. G., or ogee. A molding with a profile in the form of a letter *S*; having the outline of a reversed curve.

Outrigger. An extension of a rafter beyond the wall line. Usually a smaller member nailed to a larger rafter to form a cornice or roof overhang.

Paint. A combination of pigments with suitable thinners or oils to provide decorative and protective coatings.

Panel. In house construction, a thin flat piece of wood, plywood, or similar material, framed by stiles and rails as in a door or fitted into grooves of thicker material with molded edges for decorative wall treatment.

Paper, building. A general term for papers, felts, and similar sheet materials used in buildings without reference to their properties or uses.

Paper, sheathing. A building material, generally paper or felt, used in wall and roof construction as a protection against the passage of air and sometimes moisture.

Parting stop or strip. A small wood piece used in the side and head jambs of double-hung windows to separate upper and lower sash.

Partition. A wall that subdivides spaces within any story of a building.

Penny. As applied to nails, it originally indicated the price per hundred. The term now serves as a measure of nail length and is abbreviated by the letter *d*.

Perm. A measure of water vapor movement through a material (grains per square foot per hour per inch of mercury difference in vapor pressure).

Pier. A column of masonry, usually rectangular in horizontal cross section, used to support other structural members.

Pigment. A powdered solid in suitable degree of subdivision for use in paint or enamel.

Pitch. The incline slope of a roof or the ratio of the total rise to the total width of a house, i.e., an 8-foot rise and 24-foot width is a one-third pitch roof. Roof slope is expressed in the inches of rise per foot of run.

Pitch pocket. An opening extending parallel to the annual rings of growth, that usually contains, or has contained, either solid or liquid pitch.

Pith. The small, soft core at the original center of a tree around which wood formation takes place.

Plaster grounds. Strip of wood used as guides or strike-off edges around window and door openings and at base of walls.

Plate. Sill plate: a horizontal member anchored

to a masonry wall. Sole plate: bottom horizontal member of a frame wall. Top plate: top horizontal member of a frame wall supporting ceiling joists, rafters, or other members.

Plough. To cut a lengthwise groove in a board or plank.

Plumb. Exactly perpendicular; vertical.

Ply. A term to denote the number of thicknesses or layers of roofing felt, veneer in plywood, or layers in built-up materials, in any finished piece of such material.

Plywood. A piece of wood made of three or more layers of veneer joined with glue, and usually laid with the grain of adjoining plies at right angles. Almost always an odd number of plies are used to provide balanced construction.

Preservative. Any substance that, for a reasonable length of time, will prevent the action of wood-destroying fungi, borers of various kinds, and similar destructive agents when the wood has been properly coated or impregnated with it.

Primer. The first coat of paint in a paint job that consists of two or more coats; also the paint used for such a first coat.

Putty. A type of cement usually made of whiting and boiled linseed oil, beaten or kneaded to the consistency of dough, and used in sealing glass in sash, filling small holes and crevices in wood, and for similar purposes.

Quarter round. A small molding that has the cross section of a quarter circle.

Rabbet. A rectangular longitudinal groove cut in the corner edge of a board or plank.

Radiant heating. A method of heating, usually consisting of a forced hot water system with pipes placed in the floor, wall, or ceiling; or with electrically heated panels.

Rafter. One of a series of structural members of a roof designed to support roof loads. The rafters of a flat roof are sometimes called roof joists.

Rafter, hip. A rafter that forms the intersection of an external roof angle.

Rafter, valley. A rafter that forms the intersection of an internal roof angle. The valley rafter is normally made of doubled 2-inch-thick members.

Rail. Cross members of panel doors or of a sash. Also the upper and lower members of a balustrade or staircase extending from one vertical support, such as a post, to another.

Rake. Trim members that run parallel to the roof slope and form the finish between the wall and a gable roof extension.

Raw linseed oil. The crude product processed from flaxseed and usually without much subsequent treatment.

Reflective insulation. Sheet material with one or both surfaces of comparatively low heat emissivity, such as aluminum foil. When used in building construction the surfaces face air spaces, reducing the radiation across the air space.

Reinforcing. Steel rods or metal fabric placed in concrete slabs, beams, or columns to increase their strength.

Relative humidity. The amount of water vapor in the atmosphere, expressed as a percentage of the maximum quantity that could be present at a given temperature. (The actual amount of water vapor that can be held in space increases with the temperature.)

Resorcinol glue. A glue that is high in both wet and dry strength and resistant to high temperatures. It is used for gluing lumber or assembly joints that must withstand severe service conditions.

Ribbon (Girt). Normally a 1- by 4-inch board let into the studs horizontally to support ceiling or second-floor joists.

Ridge. The horizontal line at the junction of the top edges of two sloping roof surfaces.

Ridge board. The board placed on edge at the ridge of the roof into which the upper ends of the rafters are fastened.

Rise. In stairs, the vertical height of a step or flight of stairs.

Riser. Each of the vertical boards closing the spaces between the treads of stairways.

Roll roofing. Roofing material, composed of fiber and saturated with asphalt, that is supplied in 36-inch wide rolls with 108 square feet of material. Weights are generally 45 to 90 pounds per roll.

Roof sheathing. The boards or sheet material fastened to the roof rafters on which the shingle or other roof covering is laid.

Run. In stairs, the net width of a step or the horizontal distance covered by a flight of stairs.

Saddle. Two sloping surfaces meeting in a horizontal ridge, used between the back side of a chimney, or other vertical surface, and a sloping roof.

Sapwood. The outer zone of wood, next to the bark. In the living tree it contains some living cells (the heartwood contains none), as well as dead and dying cells. In most species, it is lighter colored than the heartwood. In all species, it is lacking in decay resistance.

Sash. A single light frame containing one or more lights of glass.

Sash balance. A device, usually operated by a spring or tensioned weatherstripping designed to counterbalance double-hung window sash.

Saturated felt. A felt which is impregnated with tar or asphalt.

Scribing. Fitting woodwork to an irregular surface. In moldings, cutting the end of one piece to fit the molded face of the other at an interior angle to replace a miter joint.

Sealer. A finishing material, either clear or pigmented, that is usually applied directly over uncoated wood for the purpose of sealing the surface.

Seasoning. Removing moisture from green wood in order to improve its serviceability.

Semigloss paint or enamel. A paint or enamel made with a slight insufficiency of nonvolatile vehicle so that its coating, when dry, has some luster but is not very glossy.

Shake. A thick handsplit shingle, resawed to form two shakes; usually edge-grained.

Sheathing. The structural covering, usually wood boards or plywood, used over studs or rafters of a structure. Structural building board is normally used only as wall sheathing.

Sheathing paper. See **Paper, sheathing.**

Sheet metal work. All components of a house employing sheet metal, such as flashing, gutters, and downspouts.

Shellac. A transparent coating made by dissolving lac, a resinous secretion of the lac bug (a scale insect that thrives on tropical countries, especially India), in alcohol.

Shingles. Roof covering of asphalt, asbestos, wood, tile, slate, or other material cut to stock lengths, widths, and thicknesses.

Shingles, siding. Various kinds of shingles, such as wood shingles or shakes and non-wood shingles, that are used over sheathing for exterior sidewall covering of a structure.

Shiplap. See **Lumber, shiplap.**

Shutter. Usually lightweight louvered or flush wood or nonwood frames in the form of doors located at each side of a window. Some are made to close over the window for protection; others are fastened to the wall as a decorative device.

Siding. The finish covering of the outside wall of a frame building, whether made of horizontal weatherboards, vertical boards with battens, shingles, or other material.

Siding, bevel (lap siding). Wedge-shaped boards used as horizontal siding in a lapped pattern. This siding varies in butt thickness from $\frac{1}{2}$ to $\frac{3}{4}$ inch and in widths up to 12 inches. Normally used over some type of sheathing.

Siding, Dolly Varden. Beveled wood siding which is rabbeted on the bottom edge.

Siding, drop. Usually $\frac{3}{4}$ inch thick and 6 and 8 inches wide with tongued-and-grooved or shiplap edges. Often used as siding without sheathing in secondary buildings.

Sill. The lowest member of the frame of a structure, resting on the foundation and supporting the floor joists or the uprights of the wall. The member forming the lower side of an opening, as a door sill, window sill, etc.

Sleeper. Usually, a wood member embedded in concrete, as in a floor, that serves to support and to fasten subfloor or flooring.

Soffit. Usually the underside of an overhanging cornice.

Soil cover (ground cover). A light covering of plastic film, roll roofing, or similar material used over the soil in crawl spaces of buildings to minimize moisture permeation of the area.

Soil stack. A general term for the vertical main of a system of soil, waste, or vent piping.

Sole or sole plate. See **Plate.**

Solid bridging. A solid member placed between adjacent floor joists near the center of the span to prevent joists from twisting.

Span. The distance between structural supports such as walls, columns, piers, beams, girders, and trusses.

Splash block. A small masonry block laid with the top close to the ground surface to receive roof drainage from downspouts and to carry it away from the building.

Square. A unit of measure—100 square feet—usually applied to roofing material. Sidewall coverings are sometimes packed to cover 100 square feet and are sold on that basis.

Stain, shingle. A form of oil paint, very thin in consistency, intended for coloring wood with rough surfaces, such as shingles, without forming a coating of significant thickness or gloss.

Stair carriage. Supporting member for stair treads. Usually a 2-inch plank notched to receive the treads; sometimes called a "rough horse."

Stair landing. See **Landing**.

Stair rise. See **Rise**.

STC. (Sound Transmission Class). A measure of sound stopping of ordinary noise.

Stile. An upright framing member in a panel door.

Stool. A flat molding fitted over the window sill between jambs and contacting the bottom rail of the lower sash.

Storm sash or storm window. An extra window usually placed on the outside of an existing one as additional protection against cold weather.

Story. That part of a building between any floor and the floor or roof next above.

Strip flooring. Wood flooring consisting of narrow, matched strips.

String, stringer. A timber or other support for cross members in floors or ceilings. In stairs, the support on which the stair treads rest; also stringboard.

Stucco. Most commonly refers to an outside plaster made with Portland cement as its base.

Stud. One of a series of slender wood or metal vertical structural members placed as supporting elements in walls and partitions. (Plural: studs or studding).

Subfloor. Boards or plywood laid on joists over which a finish floor is to be laid.

Suspended ceiling. A ceiling system supported by hanging it from the overhead structural framing.

Tail beam. A relatively short beam or joist supported in a wall on one end and by a header at the other.

Termites. Insects that superficially resemble ants in size, general appearance, and habit of living in colonies; hence, they are frequently called "white ants." Subterranean termites establish themselves in buildings not by being carried in with lumber, but by entering from ground nests **after** the building has been constructed. If unmolested, they eat out the woodwork, leaving a shell of sound wood to conceal their activities, and damage may proceed so far as to cause collapse of parts of a structure before discovery. There are about 56 species of termites known in the United States; but the two major ones, classified by manner in which they attack wood, are ground-inhabiting or subterranean termites (the most common) and dry-wood termites, which are found almost exclusively along the extreme south-ern border and the Gulf of Mexico in the United States.

Termite shield. A shield, usually of noncorrodible metal, placed in or on a foundation wall or other mass of masonry or around pipes to prevent passage of termites.

Terneplate. Sheet iron or steel coated with an alloy of lead and tin.

Threshold. A strip of wood or metal with beveled edges used over the finish floor and the sill of exterior doors.

Toenailing. To drive a nail at a slant with the initial surface in order to permit it to penetrate into a second member.

Tongued and grooved. See **Dressed and matched**.

Tread. The horizontal board in a stairway on which the foot is placed.

Trim. The finish materials in a building, such as moldings, applied around openings (window trim, door trim) or at the floor and ceiling of rooms (baseboard, cornice, and other moldings).

Trimmer. A beam or joist to which a header is nailed in framing for a chimney, stairway, or other opening.

Truss. A frame or jointed structure designed to act as a beam of long span, while each member is usually subjected to longitudinal stress only, either tension or compression.

Turpentine. A volatile oil used as a thinner in paints and as a solvent in varnishes. Chemically, it is a mixture of terpenes.

Undercoat. A coating applied prior to the finishing or top coats of a paint job. It may be the first of two or the second of three coats. In some usage of the word it may become synonymous with priming coat.

Under layment. A material placed under finish coverings, such as flooring, or shingles, to provide a smooth, even surface for applying the finish.

Valley. The internal angle formed by the junction of two sloping sides of a roof.

Vapor barrier. Material used to retard the movement of water vapor into walls and prevent condensation in them. Usually considered as having a perm value of less than 1.0. Applied separately over the warm side of exposed walls or as a part of batt or blanket insulation.

Varnish. A thickened preparation of drying oil or drying oil and resin suitable for spreading on surfaces to form continuous, transparent coatings, or for mixing with pigments to make enamels.

Vehicle. The liquid portion of a finishing material; it consists of the binder (nonvolatile) and volatile thinners.

Veneer. Thin sheets of wood made by rotary cutting or slicing of a log.

Vent. A pipe or duct which allows flow of air as an inlet or outlet.

Vermiculite. A mineral closely related to mica, with the faculty of expanding on heating to form lightweight material with insulation quality. Used as bulk insulation and also as aggregate in insulating and acoustical plaster and in insulating concrete floors.

Volatile thinner. A liquid that evaporates readily and is used to thin or reduce the consistency of finishes without altering the relative volumes of pigments and nonvolatile vehicles.

Wane. Bark, or lack of wood from any cause, on edge or corner of a piece of wood.

Water-repellent preservative. A liquid designed to penetrate into wood and impart water repellency and a moderate preservative protection. It is used for millwork, such as sash and frames, and is usually applied by dipping.

Weatherstrip. Narrow or jamb-width sections of thin metal or other material to prevent infiltration of air and moisture around windows and doors. Compression weather stripping prevents air infiltration, provides tension, and acts as a counter balance.

Index